THE ODIOUS WORLD OF THE UK'S OUTSOURCED CONTACT CENTRES

FLYPAPER FOR FREAKS

MAX FRANCES

Published by
Wordissimo
YOUR WORDS, ELEVATED.

WORDISSIMO.CO.UK

©2019 Max Frances

ISBN: 9781097587742

Author's Note

In a wider context, the term 'BPO' (Business Process Outsourcing/Outsourcer) does not always imply a relationship with contact centre-related activity.

In this text, however, all references to BPOs should be taken to imply 'BPO contact centres'. Therefore, in order to maintain the flow of the text, I refer to 'outsourced contact centre organisations' as 'BPOs'.

Where there are references to 'contact centres', these should be taken to refer to outsourced contact centres unless specifically stated otherwise.

§

The objective of this book is to shine a light on the culturally specific, epochal nature of outsourced contact centres and not on any innate characteristics of specific people who have worked in them or have been associated with them.

My concern with factual accuracy sits with what happened, not with who did what.

I have tried to recreate events, locales, and conversations from my memories of them and from information provided by sources and contributors. I have changed details relating to circumstances of individuals and places, identifying characteristics of physical properties and occupations, and have made extensive use of composite characters. In several instances, accounts are based on my own actions, and I have at times recounted the actions of others as my own.

All these steps were taken in order to protect the personal identity of inspirations, contributors, and sources.

Therefore, any resemblance to actual persons, living or dead, or actual events is purely coincidental. No identification with actual persons (living or deceased), places, buildings, and products is intended or should be inferred.

§

I should take a moment to say a few words about writing.

My goal is to provide you with an informative and entertaining account of the matters at hand. Writers sometimes remain rigidly formal to the point that they sacrifice their personality or stifle their creativity in order to adhere to formal grammatical rules. Others are informal to the extreme and to the point that their work is but a collection of fragments. Sometimes both styles work to great effect but neither approach would work for me, nor I think for you, with these kinds of subjects.

The style I have nurtured is therefore largely conventional but with some exceptions. I use contractions, which some purists would no doubt hate. I also make up words if the circumstances require it. And while I am an aficionado of punctuation, I sometimes slip in some additional commas for effect. It will annoy those who want to analyse what I've written, but my aim is to cater for those who want to read and enjoy it. I hope you will find it worthwhile.

If you do spot anything particularly egregious though, please do let me know via www.maxfrances.com – I am always ready to amend and update in the name of progress and improvement.

§

But now on to some acknowledgements. I would like to thank all those who contributed material to this work and for sharing their experiences of what is a uniquely culturally located enterprise.

For many of us, the outsourced contact centre world has represented a journey even an odyssey.

For me, it has been a rite of passage. A transition which ends with this book.

This will be my closure, and I hope that my analysis may help others to find closure too. For others, I hope that it helps you to understand the jungle a little better – and good luck with your continuing careers.

Whether you agree with the points I make or not, I believe that this book takes us a little closer to filling the large gap that exists in investigations on this topic.

In the words of Michel Foucault (1926-1984), philosopher, historian of ideas, social theorist, and literary critic:

> *'I don't* write *a* book *so that it will be the final word;* I write *a* book *so that other* books *are possible, not necessarily* written *by me'.*

I am no Foucault, but on this subject at least, I share this motivation. I sincerely hope that others will indeed continue to explore what has become an endlessly fascinating field of investigation.

Finally, I extend my eternal gratitude to colleagues past and present, some of whom still hold senior positions within the UK's outsourced contact centre arena.

Thank you for your candour and corroboration even if, during our discussions, we were not always entirely in agreement.

While your assistance may be seen by some as the revelation of secrets, we can all be reassured that there is no such thing in life as secrets.

Only hidden truths.

MF

'The strategic adversary is fascism (...) the fascism in us all, in our heads and in our everyday behaviour, the fascism that causes us to love power, to desire the very thing that dominates and exploits us.' ii

Michel Foucault (1926-1984)

Contents

1 – Please Allow Me to Introduce Myself 9
2 – Reverse Alchemy 14
3 – 'Service, Please...' 23
4 – Corporate Veil Use 35
5 – The Way to San José 47
6 – If You Can't Fight, Wear a Big Hat 66
7 – Absolute Cults 76
8 – Something for Everyone 95
9 – Snake Oil and Holy Water 113
10 – Holograms and Mirages 128
11 – Organ Grinders and Monkeys 141
12 – Client Surfacing 155
13 – Checkback Planning 164
14 – Guitar George and Sexy Sadie 168
15 – The Echo Chamber 179
16 – Selling Close to the Wind 184
17 – Hey, Charming... 191
18 – Hire and Hire 199
19 – Training at the Leash 211
20 – Shhhh...IT Happens 216
21 – Lame Duck PMs 221
22 – Dodgy Figures for Dodgy Figures 229
23 – The Carousel and Other Rides 235
24 – Means Bugger All 242

25 – (I Can't Get No) ESATisfaction 249
26 – The Empire Strikes Back 257
27 – Michael Fishing for Compliments 292
28 – Office Whoring 296
29 – Deign to Protect? 304
30 – Blowing the Gaffes 318
Endnote 336

1 – Please Allow Me to Introduce Myself

I first thought of the idea for this book in the late 1990s after having witnessed so many examples of poor management, crazy decision-making, and at times almost abject senselessness.

Some of the examples of things that I had spotted, I used to recount in social settings much to the amusement of others present who themselves had their equally amusing and despairing stories to tell. Indeed, at the time, many people had commented that perhaps we should write a book about what we had seen and experienced on a day-to-day basis.

Of course, since then, we have experienced the award-winning comedy *The Office* which was justifiably a phenomenal success and almost created an unsurpassable benchmark in relation to the production of an office-related work of comedy.

So, in effect, I had a collection of amusing anecdotes and situations, which I would only be able to string together without any meaningful or interesting theme to connect them. As a result, the idea went onto the backburner.

I also had to work, which as ever is a most intolerable distraction from living real life. At least it is for me as I am a job/career/interests/passion compartmentalist. I see work as one thing and personal stimulation as another. It means that while I am not ruthlessly striving to become the *CEO* of every telephone box I walk into, I have also not become borderline psychotic.

Nevertheless, one does have to play the game to an extent, just to keep ahead of the curve. So, a semblance of a career it had to be.

However, as I progressed, I started to reflect more and more on the situations that I had experienced and analysed them more in-depth in order to make sense of the wider context. I also became increasingly aware of a disconnect between the creation of the mirage of an 'industry' in outsourced contact centres and the reality of what they were actually like.

Now, a lot of people have commented in detail about what life is like in contact centres, understandably from the perspective of those who work in them at the coalface. The picture has been painted of the dark satanic mills of the twentieth and twenty-first centuries, the modern-day sweatshops etc.

I am neither criticising nor attacking that perspective in any way, but to me we needed some insight that was not simply from one single perspective in these organisations. We needed something that looked at all the individual components of how a BPO works and was written from multiple points of view.

Not just that of people who have worked at the coal face but also those who have worked as first-line and second-line managers even up to those at a more strategic level e.g. at site and operational board director level.

In essence, I wanted to achieve something that examined some of these essential concepts and tried to deconstruct them so that we could see what they really were, and what the constituent parts were. I also wanted to gain real angles rather than the selected ones that are pushed out as the 'public face'. I wanted to look into, not just what was going on, but if possible how it happened and why.

And that is the starting point of the journey.

One of the challenges with this type of investigation is that there were many fascinating characters that I encountered along the way whom I would love to have sketched out so that it could be seen how wonderfully complex – often inappropriately so – that the actors and actresses in a BPO actually are.

On the one hand, this would have served to illustrate my points with almost artistic precision.

However, it would have detracted from the analysis that I wanted to undertake that effectively would underscore the conclusions that I feel are in many of my examples indisputably self-evident.

It would also serve to create characters who might be identifiable and subject to ridicule.

It is of course certainly the case that I have encountered some incompetent people, some immoral people, and some frankly downright appalling people in the course of my journey. In some cases, the more notable individuals possessed all these characteristics and were incompetent, immoral, *and* appalling.

However, it remains a central premise of this investigation that BPOs – owing to their central purpose – will always attract a disparate (and often desperate) motley crew who at specific moments of time in their lives and careers need to work in those circumstances and in such places.

It is the mismatch between those individuals and the context that is created and the mechanisms of control that are applied that throw up, for want of a better expression, the apparent insanity of the situation and of decision-making.

At the heart of this situation are great people whose brilliance shines through regardless and who go on to bigger and better things. On rare occasions, those people even stay and perform brilliantly as solitary beacons of light.

The vast majority, however, are a mixture of bad people who occasionally do good things and good people who very often do bad things.

Indeed, many of the worst managers I have encountered in my time in BPOs have essentially been good people who were simply caught up in the madness of manipulation and immorality as they became more and more tied into their circumstances by wider life-related commitments.

As a result, I have steered away from creating characters and instead have cited individual examples of behaviours but avoided the temptation of replicating the perpetrators within the text.

This has always been about the behaviours and what happens rather than who does it. For me, it is often the case that the perpetrators of what is wrong are victims themselves of the situational context.

In writing this book, it is therefore not the intention to embarrass anyone. Indeed, I am not writing this from the perspective of an all-seeing and all-knowing author who is highlighting the failings of the world around him.

In fact, some of the examples cited in the text of poor decisions and bad management were down to me. I myself have lived through this and been party to some of the very worst things that took place. This is not an exercise in blaming, nor is it one of self-exculpation.

The reaction to this book from those who have seen advance excerpts and who are aware of the subject matter I am tackling has been mixed.

Some have been entirely positive, acknowledging that 80-90% of the situational content therein was immediately relatable to their own experiences in the various BPOs with which they are or were acquainted.

Others were dismayed that I would decide to release the genie from the bottle. Not only had I in effect bitten the hand that had fed us all for so long, but I had potentially damaged prospects for those who remained within the BPO environment.

Some in fact disputed my analysis and said that my interpretation of facts and events was off the mark.

All may have a point.

But what I have done is try to be fair in terms of what I have seen and what I have witnessed. As ever, we all have the choice to reflect and to make decisions on what we wish to believe.

As a social inquirer of sorts, I would love to have written a more ethnographically based study with high levels of quantitative and qualitative evidence and some strongly evidenced scientific outcomes.

However, this would have meant a highly specific study that would not have touched upon the whole range of constituent parts of a truly varied picture.

It would also have made the style of this rather dry and uninspiring to an audience that I hope simply seeks insight and a wider perspective on an industry that to many remained under the radar for a long period of time. Although it has now edged closer to the spotlight, it remains largely unexamined, save for high-level headlines and soundbites.

I have focused on BPOs, owing to the unique circumstances and context involved. This will become more apparent as we read on and examine some specific and particular perspectives. That is not to say, however, that some of the observations and findings would not be relevant and of interest to those concerned with contact centres in general or even non-contact centre-related organisations.

If that is the case, then so be it, and perhaps there will be a wider value to the work.

I hope you will find this book interesting, informative, and even in places, entertaining.

Well, we all have to remain positive, do we not?

2 – Reverse Alchemy

Call them what you will, but nobody can dispute the way in which call or contact centres have changed the way in which we interact with commercial suppliers or for a great many of us, the way in which we lead our lives.

A number of sources suggest that the activities of the UK-based Birmingham Press and Mail in the 1960s were the true origins of the contact centre industry in the UK, which used Private Automated Business Exchanges (PABX) for what would have been the first customer service agents to handle multiple customer enquiries.

In the 1970s, several industries started to use this centralised method of handling customer contacts and the term 'call centre' was incorporated into the Oxford English Dictionary in the mid-1980s.

As the importance of information in the delivery of services increased and long-distance calling became deregulated, the use of call centre facilities grew markedly.

Organisations generally either run in-house operations or outsource the contact centre-supported services they provide to external suppliers. In the early 1990s, there was a prevalence of outsourced bureau contact centres, which operated on a pay-as-you-go basis for clients, charging them for transactions that were handled.

These were very cost-effective ways for clients to outsource relatively low-volume services or services with uneven call distribution, as outsourcers with a combined client base had sufficient volume to run viable operations throughout the working week.

Such organisations ran multi-client operations or shared services for various clients, sometimes on shared operational floors. By the end of the 1990s and moving into the twenty-first century, there was a greater consolidation of bureau-type services into larger contact centre operations that were either taken in-house or outsourced on a larger scale where clients were willing to support larger teams of dedicated agents.

These dedicated teams are now much more than simple call handlers and use advanced technology and multiple channels of communication in order to provide integrated customer service. Such services may be in-house or outsourced. However, there is a marked difference between not only the service that these operations would provide but also their very basis for existence.

It would be a mistake to assume that the concept of service delivery that would be provided by a professional blue-chip organisation should be or is, intended to be replicated once the decision has been taken to outsource the service.

But don't let that get in the way of any BPO sales pitch.

It is in effect not a service that is being outsourced but a capability to manage units of work. This is not synonymous with service. The essence of this book is to unpack some of the different components of operation within an outsourced contact centre operation and to explore in some depth what happens and what does not happen. It is a world where face value perceptions frequently fall short of reality.

I have frequently viewed the relationship between the two as a form of *reverse alchemy*. This is where an existing golden ideal, which may be in existence to one extent or another, is transformed into matter that does not by any means glitter. Where great people enter the organisations and come out of them destroyed. The alchemical metaphor can also be useful when examining the approach to service on the part of the outsourcers themselves.

Everything they say and everything they do is geared towards the creation of something precious and of value, and yet the material that they begin with simply does not contain the required components to make anything other than a very ordinary product. Indeed, this is a product that simply does not possess within its DNA that which is required to fulfil the essential promises that it makes.

Were you to incorporate any sense of integrated operational capability into a standard definition, many centres would not come up to scratch. Certainly not the growing swell of outsourced agencies who through smoke and mirrors paint the picture of a slick and sophisticated customer contact machine that is so frequently a façade for a numbers game. This adds only to their balance sheets rather than to any semblance of customer satisfaction.

This theme is a favourite of mine, yet in this world of illusion and performance it is difficult to prioritise the numerous examples of intriguing double-speak that mask the innumerable activities of your average band of outsourcing charlatans.

The notion of double-speak permeates throughout the contact centre world. Orwell may have *slightly* misjudged how 1984 would turn out which in hindsight actually saw the world at that time progressing into a rather harmless flirtation with androgyny and electronic synthesisers against a backdrop of rigid Thatcherism.

But to call or contact centres, the spirit of the faux label is alive and very much kicking well into the twenty-first century.

Best of all these, the notion of the 'contact centre industry' stands out as the most shameless example of delusion and desire to conjure up something of substance where there is only a desire for recognition.

When you think about it, what are the people who promote this term actually trying to say? I mean, I absolutely see the legitimacy of certain industries such as the legal profession, dentistry, or professional football for example. Terms used to describe groups of practising individuals who are concerned with core or key activities.

But speaking to people on the telephone or responding to them by email hardly constitutes a 'core activity'. The core activity is the essence of what these people do, not how they do it, nor how they appear, nor organise themselves.

What would people think if all the police officers, firemen and paramedics joined together to form a 'uniform-wearing industry'? They could even invite supermarket workers, traffic wardens, and members of the armed forces to join them. How about forming an industry of those people who use printed messages on paper to communicate with their customers? When you take a step back, it really is quite absurd.

But to the contact centre glitterati, anybody who is engaged in any customer contact work with external customers forms part of their 'industry'. It is a staggering self-denial of any sort of inner substance – but do not be surprised to see immense swathes of people on the pages of LinkedIn or other self-promoting and self-congratulatory social media sites who describe themselves as 'contact centre professionals', or worse still, 'contact centre experts'.

In his novel, The Cat's Cradle[iii], the author Kurt Vonnegut wrote about a *granfalloon*, in the fictional religion of *Bokononism* which was stated to be a f*alse karass*. In effect, a collection of people who affect a shared identity or purpose but whose mutual association is meaningless.

Talk about life imitating art.

In fact, the *granfalloon technique* is used to describe a way of persuading people to identify with a particular group with a view to securing the individual's loyalty and commitment by taking on the rituals and beliefs associated with that particular group.

Now, when you are visited by a representative of one of these industry groups, you will start to see matters through a wholly differently tinted lens (hopefully not *rose-tinted*).

Some of these groups even organise 'awards ceremonies' so that certificates and trophies can be handed out to the organisation who, for example, delivered the 'best customer service' or was even the 'best newcomer' (to what?).

Notwithstanding the fact that the awards themselves are simply based on the quality of the story that has been told on the entry form (because clearly the awards panels otherwise have very little or perhaps no knowledge at all about the organisation concerned until they have read a submission), the baubles are distributed as a means of retaining the interest of the said organisations in the ongoing enterprise of perpetuating the 'contact centre industry'. And of course, the payment of membership and entry fees all help to, ahem, stimulate the economy.

I have no argument with trophies being awarded as the result of sustained achievement, for example, an FA Premier League trophy or a Rugby Six Nations trophy, but the whole contact centre industry trophy-giving reminds you of your time at junior school when the teacher would ensure that gold stars were equally distributed in order to promote inclusion rather than as the result of excellent performance. Perhaps the schooldays analogy seems somewhat facetious; however, anybody who has attended one of these awards ceremonies will probably find it depressingly evocative.

Those who work in contact centres should however not be so surprised that the so-called industry has progressed to the position where they are holding annual awards events. It has been a long-standing feature of contact centre life to have 'employee of the month' awards where individuals are provided with small prizes for the particularly great things they are purported to have done. Now often this is simply the job that they are paid to do, but it serves to gather everybody around and experience what they have now lamentably started to refer to as the 'feelgood factor'.

I suppose if you need to run specific events to generate such an effect within your organisation, there is probably an implied recognition that there is otherwise not very much feelgood factor on a daily basis at all. Nevertheless, these award ceremonies do take place and allow the bosses to give one lucky recipient a small prize, while all of the remaining employees who have been slogging their guts out can then feel thoroughly demotivated that they themselves were not recognised or indeed incredulous that somebody can be given a £20 voucher for simply doing what they were paid to do.

The bosses remain blissfully unaware that these events are welcomed only if they represent paid time off the phones which is always snapped up like a fish at a seals' convention.

These award bashes are not dissimilar to other activities that take place during the working week such as 'spot prizes' or leadership boards etc. and emanate from the same type of situation that parents are in when they are suddenly charged with looking after a small group of kids and simply do not know what to do with them in order to keep them entertained.

This is the same kind of challenge that your average contact centre manager has or at least feels that they have, in that they have a large group of people to whom they cannot relate through their interpersonal skills, so they need to generate some sort of false jollity in order to stop any sense of depression from permanently setting in.

I prefer to call it *forced* jollity. It just sounds so, well, unreal.

At least most employees can console themselves that they will sooner or later receive the employee of the month award if they stay there long enough. This is because, as with the gold stars and the industry awards, they are more about the illusion of inclusion than any particularly outstanding performance. Like when some schools award an 'Effort Cup' at the end of the year. You know the kind of thing – the prize that goes to the kid that did sod all for the best part of the year but had to make a small effort after his parents had been summoned and a suspension was imminent. The school then award the cup to see if they can build on the momentum by appealing to the human sense of ambition and achievement.

Staggeringly, there are some contact centre industry bodies who are now toying with the idea of dishing out lifetime achievement awards. No, let's just take a moment to repeat that to ourselves:

Lifetime achievement awards.

Even in the world of performance arts, it is an embarrassing moment when a lifetime achievement award is handed out to somebody. The recipients are usually cringing if they are there in person, which more often than not they are not. The savvy ones will be unable to attend and may record a short film and then engage somebody else to pick up the award on their behalf. It is simply another way to boost the credibility of the award ceremony itself, through the implication that the organisation has the status within the community or the authority to determine exactly what reflects a lifetime of achievement.

It also implies that there is such a thing as a lifetime of achievement in that field. In the case of contact centres, it stretches to the limit the general understanding of the term 'achievement' for any such awards to be made.

Of course, if after reading this magnum opus, the *World Contact Centre Conglomerate* or whatever thought-policing body currently governs what we should be saying about contact centres, decides to offer me an award, I would accept. Let's hope they put the perforations in the right place with no sharp edges.

But seriously. I would not wipe my lower colon with a lifetime achievement award even if it were printed on aloe vera double-quilted *Andrex*.

§

But I digress. Let's get back to this question of an 'industry'.

So how do people come to deny who they really are and come to position themselves firmly within the bracket of a contact centre professional? There may be several explanations for this.

Firstly, the economic backdrop to the explosion of contact centre activity in the 1990s was one of high unemployment and recession. Put simply, there was a considerable pressure on businesses to centralise and rationalise their operations and a considerable number of people who were unemployed and seeking work. This then presented the ideal conditions for growth – a demand for cost-effective and centralised infrastructure. Single operational centres over expensive localised overheads and a large number of (apparently) well-educated personnel.

Of course, during any such period of rationalisation, other workers are displaced. This takes place most frequently when the smarter businesses realise that if they are to streamline operations, it is a sensible option to remove those who are less competent, less willing, or a combination of the two. So, opportunities started to arise in abundance and there became many openings in call centre operations for the young, the inexperienced, and the cut-adrift.

And this is where the BPOs entered the market – businesses that specialised in providing services at the point of contact, which had premises, infrastructure, and access to people. Some of these came into being as parts or divisions of marketing services businesses with senior managers who did not understand the new world, and this represented one of the key growth challenges for some BPOs.

At particular risk were those who had been subject to a management buy-out.

These were more likely to continue to be managed into the new world by marketing experts – ideas and concepts people – who had little idea about what it took to land concrete deliverables and who had even less technical or contact centre-specific knowledge. They consequently hovered at the peripherals of delivery, dumbfounded at the inability of their organisations to achieve and equally powerless to effect any change. Many of these cashed in and jumped, passing over the reins to others who felt more comfortable in working in the new domain.

The BPOs do however sit at the centre of this so-called 'industry'. They are the location where the most intensive exposure to all aspects of contact-based work will be gained – and only where experiences will be felt at their extremity.

While they are characterised by borderline insanity, and sometimes full-blown irrationality, the BPOs are where you truly feel the force.

3 – 'Service, Please…'

So, once the reverse alchemists have set up their melting pot, they need to add people to their equipped location and start to produce something that the market will want.

This is some form of service which from the organisation's perspective will of course be 24-carat gold. Well, let's keep our judgements on that to one side for a moment and look at how 'service', for want of a better expression, is produced.

Of course, these people need to be managed which occasions the need for some form of supervision and organisational hierarchy. As the first line of management, you would tend to have *Team Leaders* or *Team Managers*. Both of these roles are lamentably misnomers because rarely would such people demonstrate any tangible leadership or management capability. Furthermore, the personnel under their supervision would not really operate in line with any commonly understood sense of what a team *actually is*.

And thereby begins a journey of double-speak and false descriptors. We had better get used to them. But let's move on.

Team Leaders in my experience would often be poles apart – either glorified operators doing essentially the same job as their teams with some additional administrative tasks or wannabee 'managers' who were so far removed from their direct reports and so far up the backsides of the 2nd line management team that you would wonder why they were actually there or allowed to remain there. I certainly could not work out how they were appointed in the first place during the early days of my initiation into the world of BPOs.

Before the advent of HR (in those days it was all about *Personnel*, but that's another story) and the now ubiquitous assessment centres, these first-line managers were generally appointed on the basis of how good they were at their operator roles. Now even for the moderately cerebrally challenged, it would be difficult to see how being great at answering customer service queries or in our case following scripts, would make you automatically capable of organising operational excellence or motivating diverse groups of people towards common goals. It is a lesson that was not fully taken on board by those at a senior level for some time, but in many senses I never really thought that it mattered.

Outsourcing was not and never has been about operational excellence. It's about volume, revenues, margin, and the presentation of service. Note the subtle turn of phrase here. And even if there is a high turnover of staff or high levels of internal dissatisfaction, why should it matter? If the job itself is basic or if the cost of re-training of recruitment can be nicely and proportionately absorbed into high revenues with the result that margins are strong, then take it from me, there is no problem. In this respect, BPOs are no different from any other business transaction. If you go into a shop and buy a sausage roll for £1 and it tastes great, you'll be a satisfied customer. As long as it is well seasoned to make it taste good, the fact that it's made from all the crap, sinew, and offal that was mechanically steamed off a carcass does not even enter your head.

In the same way that some of these meat product food manufacturers thrive in the UK, so do BPOs. As long as service appears good, nobody will scratch too hard below the surface to enquire how the 'great service' being offered at the cut-price rates can possibly be achieved. In some ways, it's similar to the concept behind a successful negotiation. If something of perceived high value but low cost can be delivered, then it's going to be a mutually acceptable outcome.

What will be cited as the overriding benchmark of service, is the service level measurement that is derived from the ACD (the *Automatic Call Distributor* or to the uninitiated, the *phone system*). Ubiquitously known as *The Service Level* or *SLA*, the measurement is derived from the percentage of calls answered within a certain number of seconds. Effectively it reflects the speed to answer when customers call in. You will often hear cited the *80/20* which means that the centre must deliver, either daily or weekly, monthly results that show that 80% of all calls offered are answered within 20 seconds. The 20% that fail will include all calls answered at 20+ seconds, plus any that abandon (where the caller decides to hang up).

The 80/20 is often noted to be the industry standard though rarely does anybody understand what 'industry' means in this context or why this would be either a standard, acceptable, or desirable. You would not believe how many clients of outsourcers lose all sense of propriety or self-control when faced with statistics that show that only 79% of their calls were answered within 20 seconds. Yet the same clients emit a glow of silent delight when their provider reports 81%.

Without delving too deeply into the mathematical implications, on 1,000 calls offered, the difference between the basis of outrage and satisfaction is fantastically meagre. In this case, it would be a tick in the box if 190 customers waited for more than 20 seconds, but it would be an unmitigated disaster, were that number 210. With daily measurements where call volumes may be as low as a couple of hundred, the difference between success or failure could be a couple of customers over a 10-hour period.

Of course, if the speed of answer were so critical to service quality, it seems nonsensical that it could ever be acceptable for 190 enquiries from 1,000 to fall outside of the service parameter. But so many clients who use outsourcers just do not get it. And outsourcers are in no hurry to engage with them in order to examine exactly what measures would truly identify performance levels that would enhance brand perceptions. After all, this number is so easily manipulated for the target to be hit.

On many occasions, particularly on lower volume lines, a Team Leader might enquire to trusted operators whether 'the lines are working ok'. This is outsourcer code for 'put in some calls to our own line which we can answer within the 20 seconds and which will push up our overall percentage'.

Alternatively, the ACD administrator can flex the service parameter so that the percentage measures calls offered within say 45 seconds though this is presented to the client as a performance against 80/20. The benefit here is that fewer costs are required to answer enquiries and margins are higher.

The truly inspired managers route calls through different applications or lines before the call reaches the operator. This means that during certain heavy volume periods, the calls are picked up and routed onto an internal or holding line. They are then routed into a secondary line where the required measurements are taken and recorded, and service is 'delivered'. The only way for clients to work out that they are being hoodwinked is to test-call and reconcile call lengths – practically impossible on high-volume lines. It was sometimes possible for a keen ear to pick out slight breaks in the ringing tone sequences; however, in the modern world of complex interactive voice response (IVR) routing loops and levels, this is now a common feature of legitimate if questionable experiential routing strategy.

Other ploys include the fabled *call receptioning* – taking calls out of the queue within the twenty-second limit and then calling the customer back during quieter periods – which reflects a good service level but a poor *customer experience*.

The out-and-out miscreants just go route one – they report performance data that is entirely fictitious via Excel sheets (NB. *never* raw data from the ACD itself). My personal experience of seeing this done saw some very clever exponents of this art. Rarely was extensive perfect performance reported – it would be typically a mixture of good, odd average, and high proportions of near-miss service reported that would not appear too out-of-kilter with the anecdotal reports of busy activity that may have filtered back to clients either from customers or via their own test-calling.

And when all fails with respect to the doctoring of reports, a commonly practised approach is to go (an alternative) Route 1 and adulterate the basis for the billings themselves. This can be done by adding in billed hours for agents who haven't worked or perhaps who do not even exist. Or more deftly, judicious use of the 'part thereof' clause in a per-minute billing commercial agreement may be exercised so that, for example, an average call length of three minutes and 50 seconds, becomes four minutes and three seconds which in turn pushes up the billable amounts by 20%. More on that later.

§

In the meantime, I can recount a practical example of how an obsession with numbers and the fabled *SLA* will drive some equally obsessive and wide-of-the-mark behaviour, to the point that it becomes delusional.

A BPO, running a blended shared service with inbound and outbound calls and emails, has an 80/20 inbound *SLA*. They are missing this because operators are picking up calls but cannot answer them as they are not trained on those campaigns. As they have outbound appointments scheduled in their diaries, they know that picking them up in the first instance will mean that they have to record a long explanatory note to pass on via email to the right team and they will then miss their outbound call (for which they will be penalised).

Being a Hicksville BPO, there is no Intranet support for the teams. They take the view that it is best all around if they allow the calls to queue – and they are savvy enough to have arranged with IT to have 'auto-in' removed from their logins, so the inbound calls are not forced(!). The management team are so detached from all realities that they have not realised this – even to the point that when staff leave, they are recycling the adulterated profiles to new starters.

The BPO sees this as a cultural issue with the teams and begins a good old-fashioned command-and-control screamfest that after a few weeks sees the *SLA* hit.

They trumpet this as 'evidence that we've achieved cultural change'.

Hmmm. In fact, not only a sweeping statement on one solitary dimension that fails to grasp what culture actually means and the breadth of its components but misses that:

- the statistics may have hidden gaming.

- the statistics do not reflect the quality of the interactions.

- on what planet does hitting 80/20 reflect anything other than hitting 80/20?

- the way it was achieved by control and coercion destroyed what was any positive cultural aspects in its wake etc. ad nauseam.

And you thought that this kind of nonsense had been left behind in the 90s? Think again.

Of course, there are always the lazy and the disengaged. However, issues with motivation in integrated centres largely stem from a reluctance to spend valuable time on tasks that take disproportionate time and include high wastage that prevents the completion of valuable tasks or from work that if not completed might cause the agent to be performance-managed. Avoiding the nonsense work, if they can get away with it, is therefore the preferred option.

The brute force, blunt object management push where hostile techniques are employed to scream staff into submission and scramble to pick up within 20 seconds is, when it works in the short-term, seen as a triumph of an improved cultural practice where motivated staff are keener to pick up work.

It couldn't be further from the truth. Staff become more demotivated and keeping the ostensibly positive figures over time is superlatively labour-intensive.
Working smart, a savvy manager knows that this is a challenge where the best solution lies neither in motivation nor culture. And while centres always need sufficient resources, failing to hit *SLAs* is most likely not even a resource issue.

It is more likely to be one of *information flow.*

Ensuring that staff have the right knowledge at their fingertips and the authority to promptly process enquiries and orders so that can work efficiently and effectively without encountering frustration or sanction. No surprise to learn that this BPO did not invest in a usable Intranet for years and then subsequently scrapped it altogether.

The same genre of manager will be screaming to get all hands on deck from all levels of management and support in order to clear backlogs and then lead the backslapping, internal PR puff of congratulatory mutual masturbation. While at the same time forgetting or simply not realizing that, through poor planning, the cost of delivery (plus opportunity cost) was many times what it needed to be. But framed as 'great teamwork', and the mugs will buy it forevermore.

§

In terms of 'service', there has been increased momentum behind the value of *Customer Experience* or *CX*. More about that in a later chapter, but do not build up your hopes too high that this has brought forth a service revolution. It has instead become another bandwagon onto which BPOs have jumped, in an attempt to make themselves look viable as *CX* becomes more fashionable with clients.

Unfortunately, when it comes to service delivery, BPOs fail to understand the true nature of what they are delivering – that service is borne out of the work and dedication of one person for another. They do of course try to put measures in place that give the *impression* that they are doing the right thing by their staff.

They use concepts like *CX* as they do *Pride* or *Mental Health Awareness*. Just another example of *virtue signalling* so that they fall in line with stakeholder commitments to being morally sound and cutting-edge. Some of them even have calendars of events planned for these kinds of activities in order to build the façade. It is a wonder of cynicism. Quite incredible really. How can BPOs promote positive mental health, and anybody keep a straight face?

It would be scandalous if it were not already, er well, likely the most scandalous gig most will ever encounter in their professional lives.

It is of course all about *seeming*, which in the world of BPOs trumps everything. Even *doing*.

And if you thought that *virtue signalling* was a twenty-first-century social media phenomenon where barriers to revealing sentiments are removed, think again. BPOs have been purveyors par excellence of this form of communication since the year dot – or at least dot in terms of their existence. Perfectly logical when you think about it because the appropriation of a moral or professional stance or commitment to one has to by definition be an empty act for BPOs, as these organisations simply do not have the collateral to support any substance.

What you can be sure of is that there is a direct relationship between the degree of activity you witness in these areas and the advanced level of moral decay in the organizations concerned. You should look at your own company and see how they fare. It is very enlightening.

Now, before any accusations are levelled at me suggesting that the concept of service delivery has come a long way since the glory days of the all-important *SLA*, let me tell you that actually they have not. Yes, of course, the BPOs are banging on to their little hearts' content about *CX*, running Webinars and producing endless content regarding *Customer Experience*. But in practice, what are they actually telling us?

Think about it – a blue-chip outsources some services to the BPO, so the BPO will be performing tasks that cover *x* percentage of all the touchpoints with the customer. Yet the rhetoric from the BPO will tell you about how they are enhancing and developing the *CX* for the client's business. How? They are not developing the strategy or managing end-to-end interactions. They are not involved in activities encompassing every aspect of a company's offering. Ease-of-use, reliability, product quality, packaging etc.? No, they'll be looking at email communications and the quality thereof. The speed of response to the customer.

And in terms of 'Experience', on how many levels do they impact on customer involvement – rational, emotional, physical, to name just a few? Well, they don't. Like everything else in BPO-Ville, it is another hot topic, so it's all aboard the bandwagon.

Like *SLAs* in the 1980s and 1990s, if the prevailing discourses state that a certain measure equals a measure of a big idea, then hitting the number will be taken to hitting success. And no matter how ludicrously irrational it might be, everyone will be singing the mantra. It is like a religion.

In real terms, *CX* is measured via 'How do you feel' surveys or – and this is the Big Daddy of all *CX* fanaticism – the *NPS* measurement.

NPS – or *Net Promoter Score®* is a management tool devised by what I like to think of as a group of management tools from Harvard who claimed it as a measure of customer loyalty. This, naturally, is held to correlate with a client's growth.

The idea is that customers are asked a simple question along the lines of:

'Based on your interaction with us today, can you please tell us how likely you are to recommend us to a friend/colleague/associate?

The respondent is then presented with a scale of 0-10 with 9-10s being *Promoters*, 7-8 *Passives* and 0-6 *Detractors*.

The NPS score is calculated by subtracting the percentage of customers who are Detractors from the percentage who are Promoters. The goal is for companies to demonstrate that they have a score greater than 0, i.e. more *Promoters*.

The essence of this makes sense. However, you can probably see the bandwagon already. If BPOs can provide a positive NPS score in relation to the work they are undertaking, they can establish a direct link between the outsourcing activity and client growth.

Now that is the chunkiest, beefiest tick in the box that can be achieved by a service provider. And don't they know it? BPOs are the flies around the NPS turd.

It is however a turd only in relation to the context in which it is used. It is of course limited as it asks just one question on loyalty (though the solicitation of additional comments is also recommended). It is also inconclusive whether likelihood to recommend would constitute a better predictor for growth than other measures, like overall satisfaction with the product or service. Furthermore, it would not be as revealing as, for example, a more developed suite of questions. You get the picture. It is a tool that was introduced as *a measure of one factor of customer experience* yet has grown arms and legs for the BPOs as a macro example of experience in its entirety. In some organisations, the NPS score IS the experience of the customer.

And of course, it would not be a BPO staple unless the outputs were manipulated in some way. So, when advisors are speaking to customers they will typically say — if the call has not been an obvious disaster for the caller — something along the lines of:

'After this call, you will be asked to respond to a survey — if you select a 9 or 10, I will get a lovely bonus'.

Badda-boom. Yes, please — 10.

As an aside though, it is not just BPOs who are obsessed with NPS. I know of somebody recovering from an appendectomy who was offered an NPS survey.

Absolutely bonkers — talk about looking down the wrong end of the telescope.

But the obsession with using these tools to conflate the measurements with the idea of your choosing is nothing new. Look how positive *Glassdoor* reviews are chased and chased by BPOs, and people are even incentivised to leave them. And when that fails, the HR team steps in with some of their own. One email account with endless aliases — it works every time.

Crazy times. I mean, over and above all of that, nobody has even questioned the issue regarding British culture and the fact that in the UK, the recommendation of a service may not necessarily be the follow-on next step after experiencing satisfaction at all. Are we a nation of ready recommenders? Arguably not.

So, you see, like the *SLA* before it, *CX* has become the next gravy train of the BPOs – and with good reason. But does it stand up to scrutiny? Along with just about everything else, no it does not.

§

The madness does however not end with measurements alone. Many are working frighteningly diligently to build their organisational contexts and collateral in order to present a professional backdrop to the service that they present.

I know of one BPO that put in place a company communications policy – the guidelines for how employees all needed to communicate with each other. Could there be anything more insanely batshit? Taking the most natural interpersonal human activity and over-engineering it in order to control and coerce. It's a one-stop shop for disengagement. But frighteningly on-brand.

Another company set up a whole project designed to bring people, who work for the same BPO but on different floors, together. Whatever happened to skilled managers with teambuilding skills? Classic examples of lazy or likely incompetent managers who rather than manage just fall back on a policy or document. You see it all the time with disciplinary procedures. Ticking off transgressions and progressing with formal reviews rather than engaging with people and working with them. Yes, it's more challenging, difficult, and sometimes painful, but that's why you get paid what you get paid, you tossmongers.

Many BPOs also run monthly 'Excellence' Awards where there is no standard or definition of excellence and which just become a share-out over time to make sure everybody wins a prize. Another favourite fish to throw to the seals. Like being back at school. I have even seen long-service awards where the longstanding servants themselves were not rewarded at all, and the prizes went to the Facebook friends or to Managers who had engineered awards, nominations, and results that bigged themselves up. Absolutely BPO-tastic!

However, operations are largely plagued by the prevalence of *Microsoft management*. Where activities are geared towards the production of *Word* and *Excel* documents and *PowerPoint* presentations that keep on-message and make the creators look good or like they are actually delivering something of value. Meanwhile, the business just drifts, as there is an inevitable leadership vacuum. Ironically, results may be fine which of course the management team take as evidence that they are great at their jobs. The rest of us, knowing that their repetitive rituals have had no bearing on performance, take it as evidence that a) these people are surplus to requirements and b) that the reporting period under question was a lost opportunity to have really made a difference.

You see, with service delivery, the powers-that-be – being immeasurably dim – paint a picture of what good looks like. This is invariably a low bar which, when it is hit, they then attribute everything they did as the driver for success.

They forget that the teams just get on with their work anyway, so whatever results are achieved are mostly achieved in spite of them, not because of them.

But that won't stop the promotions, bonuses and laughably, the presentation of certificates and glass globes to the senior teams which serve as a cue for everything to start anew in the same mould the following year.

And that signifies that the lunatics truly have taken control of the asylum.

4 – Corporate Veil Use

Anybody who has taken a brief tour around a contact centre in recent years will undoubtedly have seen high-profile displays of company values.

BPOs cannot get enough of them, and they are displayed, high-profile either utilizing 'out there' creative or often meme-style with a close-up of a model who would not be out of place at the Givenchy showroom, with a suitable value referenced below.

More often than not, there will be a selection of models from different ethnic backgrounds displayed in this style around the centre whose ethnicity will barely or not at all, be represented by the staff population.

But let's not get too carried away by the implied suggestion that values such as equality are in name only. Well, not just yet anyway.

'Values' are 'principles or standards of behaviour'; 'one's judgement of what is important in life'. In the corporate world, they are the operating principles or philosophies that serve as a guide for internal behaviours as well as for the way in which relationships with customers, partners, and shareholders are conducted.

These are often beefed up by means of a suitable creative theme that makes them bright, colourful, vibrant, energising and generally appealing:

    '*We respect our staff and customers*'.

    '*We are open and honest*'.

    '*We work as a team*'.

Etc., ad nauseam.

These are further supported by commitments to equal opportunity for all and to diversity.

These are all the constituent parts of what the company claims its culture to have. They are presented as the be-all-and-end-all. The fundamental components and characteristics of who they actually are. The essence and the ethos.

Now, I for one would not doubt that in an ideal world these values would represent what any company would want to be. They typically lay claim to integrity, honesty, and customer focus, to name but a few. All of the things that employees would aspire to be part of, and potential clients would want to buy.

The way the values work in practice is that they should underpin performance management processes so that when individuals do something good, their line managers can review their actions within the context of the values.

For example:

> 'Well done, Johnny, you did this very well and this was a fantastic example of teamwork'.

Or equally speaking, they can work with employees in areas that require improvements, again by illustrating these within the context of the values:

> 'Well Jackie, if you had done that in a slightly different way, you would have more effectively demonstrated a focus on the customer'.

Theoretically, this is a sound approach to performance management and the creation and enhancement of a positive culture within the workplace. However, as you might by now start to suspect, things are never what they seem in the world of the BPO.

In fact, you will doubtless start to see that the true values of such BPOs will in fact include *deception*, *dishonesty*, and *fraud*, again to name but a few. Nevertheless, let us put this to one side, as these companies are clearly not going to be acknowledging their scam credentials for all to see. On the other hand, if they are so disingenuous, how do they get away with operating in the way they do? That is the part that I would like to unpick here.

In the first instance, these values are not absolute – they are contingent on situation and circumstance.

Be very clear that in the event of a significant error that may have a marked adverse impact on the bottom line or on the relationship with clients, the BPO concerned will not be effortlessly gliding towards an unburdened confession and the unbridled promotion of openness and honesty, a value that will appear in most corporate value statements in the BPO world in some shape or form. It is after all, what BPOs identify as a core element of relationships and therefore an essential element of what needs to be seen to be delivered. Note that I choose my words carefully here.

Now *openness* and *honesty*-related values are among my favourites as they are the ones that are so supremely twisted in order to meet organisational needs when it suits them. If this is ever challenged, the guardians of the values will very skilfully demonstrate that in fact no values can be absolute otherwise there would consequently be some quite ludicrous scenarios unfolding.

For example, imagine a society where nobody tempers the absolute truth with judgement and often what we might call white lies in order to soften the harsh blows of absolute truth. Now nobody is going to deny that that is a reasonable proposition, and therefore in everybody's minds we are creating the possibility that one can still be open and honest while at the same time being – to a degree – misleading if there is an overarching rationale that equates to common sense.

The openness and honesty example is therefore probably a more straightforward one to grasp, but this manipulation of the values will happen irrespective of which one comes to the fore. For example, having a customer focus may not mean acting in the best interests of a customer but may be acting in a way in which we believe the interests of the customer are best served over a period of time within a certain set of circumstances. This of course opens up infinite possibilities – all of which might be to a greater or lesser extent self-serving for the relevant BPO.

The outsourced contact centre is the epitome of moral manoeuvrability when it comes to published values. The next time you are in one, take a look at what is emblazoned across the walls and just take a step back. Then consider whether adherence to said values happens – *or is even actually possible* – given the way that the BPO operates and has to operate in order to survive.

Remember to differentiate between what they present as truth and what they deliver.

Can they really put the customers front and centre, given the low cost of their services and their investment in technology that they make? (most of these companies will be using PCs that are 10 years of age plus, equipment that is even older if you are looking at ACDs and CRM platforms). Are their communications with you truly transparent – and do you really expect them to be?

Are their employees clearly going the extra mile for you on their minimum wage salaries which of course are never acknowledged in your presence? It is all misdirection. Like any conjurer, they make you look at one hand while the other performs the trick.

Of course, there are going to be occasions where ignorance of the values is simply kept under the radar or will simply be dismissed on the grounds that a *business decision* needs to be taken. This will more likely come to the fore for example in situations where somebody has been promoted to a position without there having been a fair and open competition for the job. Never underestimate the readiness of all these BPOs to fall back on the *business decision* justification for practically anything.

Naturally, the irony of this is that such decisions are frequently not very effective business decisions because they are unsubstantiated by any logical thought process or evidence.

§

The domain of internal promotions has always been a murky one, in relation to the preparedness of managers to take knee-jerk subjective decisions or ones that have been thought through but with more nefarious justification. These would be, for example, the promotion of managers without merit other than if they have demonstrated a willingness to support the unscrupulous game plans of the hiring managers.

People talk a lot nowadays about so-called *Facebook promotions* which are on the face of it bigger and better jobs handed out on the basis of somebody's social media connections rather than their skills and competencies. While these decisions seem incomprehensible to competent staff within the BPO, they are actually essential to some managers in order to strengthen their own positions.

In employing close personal allies, they can ensure there is a buffer between themselves and other members of staff with less likelihood that they will be called out for their own incompetence. In the event of the departmental performance falling, they can always highlight the opposition of other members of staff as a rationale for why service delivery has stumbled.

Facebook promotions can be comfortably observed in BPOs, in the first instance as the lucky recipients possess neither the skills, track record nor gravitas for the role concerned. Sir Richard Branson, when talking about the approach to the greasy pole, is often quoted that people should not focus on reasons why they cannot do a job – they should just get the job and then work out how to do it.[iv]

To the untrained eye, an awareness of this approach unintentionally provides *Facebook promotion*s with a veneer of acceptability. The positive characteristic ascribed to the otherwise hopeless incompetent is that they are 'ambitious' and 'hungry' or keen to 'go places' which in the BPO world are ranked considerably higher than competence and skill. Of course, Branson is describing how motivated people have the drive to learn on the job. Where the 'want-to' outweighs the 'can-do; and in many BPOs the driven, quick learners step up to the plate and carve out successful careers. And let's be clear – Richard Branson clearly knows what he is talking about in matters corporate.

However, in the BPO world, such hires are not made with a view to driving the business forward. The incumbents neither have the scope nor the opportunity to make changes or introduce innovation. Remember they have been hired, in order for the powers that be to tell them what to do. As a result, the newly promoted are frequently left stranded – without the essential knowledge and skills to provide themselves with any meaningful yocto of credibility and a brief to keep things exactly as they are.

It is observable when you take a moment to consider how they manage regular tasks and work that has been handed over by the previous job holder. In most situations, some of these processes will work well and can simply and seamlessly be picked up and continued. Same processes, same reports, same approach. However, there are always things that do not go to plan, have imperfections, or simply do not work at all. It is frightening how much these elements of the job are likewise simply just picked up and addressed in the same way that they always have been.

There is a real dearth of 'moving and shaking' in practice even though the prevailing discourse will suggest that the apparently unqualified and inappropriate candidate got the role for primarily those very reasons. And of course, do not forget that in the background the sound of the corporate values of openness, honesty, fairness etc. will have conveniently been turned down. Is it any wonder that staff lose heart?

§

This takes us to another favourite value that can be routinely twisted and which itself highlights another way in which the so-called values of a BPO are manipulated. The value in question is that of 'teamwork'. Now this is the holy grail of all contact centre operational cultures.

This is the value that gets quoted time and time again as being the most important feature of an organisation's performance and yet nobody truly understands what it actually means. I have seen signs posted on walls screaming 'Teamwork makes the dream work' and 'There's no 'I' in team', and yet nobody really takes the time to consider what a team actually is in a BPO. If this is simply shorthand for being cooperative and helpful, then I am sure even the most basic of organisations achieve this to a reasonably high standard.

However, in contact centres, it is in itself something of a unicorn. It is the one thing that people will beat you up about and which you will be hauled over the coals for and lambasted, yet no one can really describe in detail what it means in practice. So, if there is any opposition to the rather crass decision-making that unfolds with almost alarming regularity, you can bet your mortgage that your jobsworth manager will raise the question that your approach to teamwork is not what it should be. You may even be told that everybody is 'in the boat rowing one way and that you are rowing in the other'.

Ironically, you might deduce at this point that the manager themselves is perhaps not recognising your own openness and honesty, possibly not respecting you as a free thinker, particularly if 'respect' is another of the values (it most likely will be since they are frighteningly similar wherever you go). Alas, it is precisely this kind of logical thinking and clear rationale that will see you abruptly kennelled with the rest of the troublemakers in the proverbial doghouse.

Doubly ironic is that in doing so, the manager will have failed to spot that one of the most effective components of (ahem, real) teamwork is individuals flagging issues when they see them in the hope that what they say may be picked up on with the objective that the group does not take an ultimately unwelcome course of action. It is all about group collaboration while working together through options to a workable solution. You would hope.

On the subject of 'openness and honesty', there is a test that clients can apply when dealing with their outsourced suppliers. And it is a very simple one. Anybody who has ever been involved in any form of operational delivery knows that mistakes happen. It is inevitable that if you have people operating processes and procedures, things will not always work out as planned. In the course of any extended period of operation, there will be some mistakes that will have very little impact, but there will always be some that have a discernible impact on the quality of service to the customer which in all likelihood will also be experienced by the customer. That is inevitable and applies to any organisation, in any field.

Now think about the times when your contact centre outsourced partner has proactively flagged to you a problem resulting from a service error, about which you would not otherwise have known. I'm going to go out on a limb here and suggest that that has rarely, if ever, happened. I can never personally recall an incident in my career and can never recollect any such incident being encountered unless there was a high probability that the cat would in any event have been out of the bag through any other channel – for example, it being clear that a customer was preparing a complaint to a third-party regulator. That kind of transparency works only when relationships are strong to such an extent that they can survive a major setback.

But let's be frank. BPOs do not have relationships with clients. They have transactional arrangements that are subject to contracts and pricing schedules. They are as transactional as the purchase of petrol and have to be seen to be effective even if they are simply a front. That is the real world.

So, where were we? Ah yes. In terms of adhering to the principles of openness and honesty or customer focus perhaps, this means that such organisations without issues have achieved perfection in terms of their service delivery. But that is simply not possible. So how can the illusion of reality be delivered without having to make admissions to the extraordinarily incompetent faux pas that, internally at least, defines an outsourcer's capability?

The solution to this 'issuette' is to make occasional admissions and to ensure that some challenges and service delivery problems are indeed proactively and cleverly brought to the attention of their clients. I say *cleverly* because the matters that are disclosed without prompting are typically going to be the ones where there would be minimal, if any, actual adverse impact.

Thereby, these BPOs apparently meet the open and honest criteria but at the same time have not raised any matters that will damage your 'relationship' with them. It is an effective way of having one's cake and eating it.

What clients should do is not simply take note that a BPO is being seemingly open and honest with them, but they should also qualitatively measure the impact of what is being declared and ask themselves the question of *what is almost certainly not being declared*. They should also evaluate the degree of contrition displayed with their overall assessment of the likely impact of the issue.

If the remorse greatly exceeds the impact that would be obvious to even the most incompetent manager, then the chances are that the wool is being pulled over your trusting client eyes.

§

A similar ruse is applied internally, particularly when a senior manager or director has decided to take the matter of a complaint seriously and professionally. That is to say, that they have received a complaint and actually want to deal with it. This is not the way such matters usually roll out within a typical contact centre outsourced agency though these types of hiccups can arise if the outsourcer has recently hired an external manager who is not yet worldly-wise on how things actually work!

Complaints are, as you may have guessed, routinely ignored, or dismissed after a cursory review that ensures that the company's own position is covered. I have seen new managers who are customer-focused and keen to improve actual levels of service set up complaints procedures, whereby any expression of dissatisfaction is logged as a formal complaint and must be investigated. This is what I would call the essence of an effective complaints process.

How this is circumnavigated is that complaints are indeed logged; however, they are typically the innocuous events where procedures were not strictly followed, but where there was no detrimental effect for the customer or where there has indeed been dissatisfaction, but it was down to a mistake from the customer themselves. Therefore, internally the teams are recording complaints and demonstrating that they take complaints seriously; however, what they are recording does not lead to any further action or criticism of the operational teams themselves. It is a tried and tested way to demonstrate what is in effect masterly inactivity in relation to the delivery of progressive customer service.

In this way, a complaint can be seen to have been honestly logged and properly investigated. A great story for all internal stakeholders and everybody's backs are covered. And nobody goes to jail. Everyone's a winner. BPO complaint logs up and down the country are filled with these pages and pages of nonsensical non-compliant content. And they love it. It is part of the grease that makes the cogs turn. High in 'probity', low in pain. A winning combination.

The maintenance of these twisted values can often be facilitated by another flavour of staff advancement. That is the *punishment promotion*. The punitive part of all of this is the effect on those being managed. This is when a blatantly unsuitable or unqualified sycophant is put into a position of authority over a group within the organisation which serves to make life so uncomfortable for those within their team that it precipitates resignations. This allows the senior manager a way to oppress and frustrate those who do not toe the line without having to undertake any of the unpleasant, direct actions that may lead to scrutiny and the potential for a grievance or an employment tribunal.

We've all seen plenty of examples of these. The advisors promoted rapidly up through the ranks, following no discernible assessment process, so rigidly and unthinkingly enforcing process, irrespective of the context. These are the droids who box people into corners until resignation is the only option. In a *punishment scenario*, this is often done so that the new boss is managing their own former line managers. This of course precipitates the departures of those who are being targeted, at warp speed 10.

Now it may seem senseless to put managers in positions who are incompetent and do not know what they are doing, yet even when staff are so manifestly demotivated, there are still a number of effective professionals in the lower positions who have enough self-respect and sense of professionalism that they will carry the operation through irrespective of the incompetence of those who are tasked with overseeing it.

The so-called director-level bods are themselves so utterly self-absorbed that they are manifestly unaware of their own organisation's business to be in any position to form a rational view on the competence of anybody else. In their absolute self-delusion, they might routinely talk up mediocre results as positive and accordingly make little concerted push for improvement. They are so convinced that the businesses they head could not possibly be better. They do not challenge anything, and nobody challenges them. And in the event that one of their equally incompetent disciples drops a biggie, they defend them resolutely – after all, they can hardly admit their own incompetence, can they? The truth is however closer to the fact that they just do not recognize their own failings.

It is abject cluelessness at the highest level. The *Peter Principle* personified. Promoted to their level of incompetence.

While all this is going on, the middle managers at a more senior level do their utmost to manage upwards and convince the highest levels of management in the company that everybody is working very, very hard and that they are up against tremendous amounts of pressure but nevertheless are pulling through the vital numbers that sustain the company's all too fragile P&L.

You see, there are no values that underpin what goes on in these BPOs. It is just about the ends themselves. The 'values' are no more than the words on the posters adorning the walls. There is no respect or equality. Just disposable constructs and mechanisms that facilitate a journey from *A* to *B*. And when they burn out or fail, it does not actually matter as long as the shaking, creaking vehicle can stumble through to its destination.

Living the dream.

5 – The Way to San José

It was Nietzsche, in his 'Parable of the Madman' who asked the question:

"Where are we headed? Are we not endlessly plunging – backwards, sideways, forwards, in all directions?"

Now Nietzsche held the view that the exemplary human being carved out their own identity through self-realisation. In turn, this had to be done with reliance on anything that transcended the life that was being chiselled out. Essentially, God or a Soul or other such overarching deity or spirituality.

This brings us neatly to the subject of BPO contact centres. Places where aimless, directionless folk waddle in and establish a niche for themselves. Where they create (or re-create) themselves.

I suppose in many ways it was one of the defining features of contact centres in the 90s – that people ended up working in them who had no idea that such a role would be where their future lay. After all, there is a certain logical progression in the decision-making that young people make typically from the age of 14 when they in former parlance 'do their options' and they are already starting to think ahead to what they will read at University and perhaps what they might do in a later career.

At this stage, people might select Maths, Physics and Chemistry if, for example, they were looking for a career in Veterinary Science or Dentistry. I myself decided to focus my interests more on literature and the social sciences because I was very clear in my mind that I would be going to university to read an Arts-based subject with the intention of subsequently becoming a teacher. At this stage, in the 1980s, it is highly unlikely that people on the point of selecting their options and making their first significant career decisions would have envisaged a lengthy career working in an inner-city contact centre.

So, I guess one of the questions that first springs to mind is how people end up in contact centres – and why they end up in them. I suppose the principal reason, as would be applicable to most situations where those 'astronaut' dreams of childhood have not been fulfilled, comes down to money.

This probably stems back to that original decision that is made in the early teens in relation to 'options' because far from solely focusing on likely future careers, the decision is frequently tempered by an awareness of what the individual is actually good at. Now the two are not mutually exclusive because clearly people want to select a career in later life that is related to something they enjoy doing. After all, you would not want to devote the best part of 40 to 50 years undergoing tasks day in and day out that you really didn't enjoy.

Unfortunately, at the point that the decision is made, people tend to be slightly more focused on what they'd enjoy doing rather than on something that is actually realistic and achievable. This is why students end up doing Media Studies, Performance Arts, Archaeology, or Rocket Science, and as a result, they end up studying and investing in a subject for which a qualification will likely provide little return in the future. Which brings us neatly back to the subject of contact centres.

Contact centres are typically based in the inner city or in locations which are close to transport links and major telecommunications hubs. As most students live close to the centre of major cities in which their educational establishment is located, this will mean that any such jobs are readily available and slightly more viable because they do not involve significant amounts of transport on a daily basis and the costs associated with that. Students, particularly those who have attended university or higher education, have all the basic qualifications or you would hope they do, that the contact centres require. They are presumably well-versed in writing extensively and communicating effectively so therefore fully capable of having a conversation with a customer, updating a customer record, making an effective decision, or carrying out a simple task that will be one of a chain of actions required to satisfy a customer requirement.

So, in a nutshell, students are made for contact centres and contact centres are made for students. It should be a marriage made in heaven. Now while there is this strand or strands of commonality that run through the contact centre employee's profile, the variety of individuals who land on day one in their roles is significant. Of course, on arrival at the contact centre, everybody needs to have a story to explain why they're there. Why they have ended up as one of the hundreds, possibly the thousands, performing basic, repetitive, and mundane tasks for a minimum wage?

To anybody on the outside looking in, it is pretty obvious – precisely for the reasons which I have already stated. They are people who can read and write and can hold together a reasonable conversation. There are plenty of them in order to meet the volume requirements of the business performing the service, and they are prepared to work for low wages in order to survive.

It is a classic example of supply and demand in a capitalist society, which makes the world go around. Work is available in abundance and there are high numbers of staff available to perform that work.

But for the individual on arrival in the business, this presents a significant issue for self-esteem. After all, having studied for the best part of 10 years dedicated to one's specialist subjects and having racked up considerably large debts even in the 1980s and 1990s (infinitesimally higher now), it is a crushing blow to the old ego to have to acknowledge that you are surplus to requirements in your chosen field and that your life decisions which you have maintained and stuck to over the course of such an extended period of time, have hitherto been futile.

So, what do people normally do when faced with such a situation where the context and all available information and logic point to what can only be described as a giant cock-up of Gargantuan proportions when only the individual concerned can be blamed? When it is abundantly clear that the individuals have effectively backed the wrong horses, and consistently? It is a moment of gross exposure.

Well ladies and gentlemen, what people do and what people do in situations where their risk of exposure is even less and sometimes where the consequences are for want of a better expression inconsequential?

They make something up.

They create a past and take control of their own situation and when they create the past, they incorporate into it a storyline or a rationale that explains why, contrary to their best-laid plans of the last 10 or 15 years, they ultimately took the decision to enter into a job so far removed from everything that they have worked towards in their relatively short lives. You would think that this was potentially unlikely and that such a shift in career change is typically only witnessed when people are experiencing a significant life change, such as something more spiritual for example. Something which is so fundamental to the core of their inner being, that it transcends all logic and the sum total of evidence accrued over an extended period of time.

And so it is. That is why in my career in contact centres, I have encountered DJs with their own record labels. I have experienced real-life, professional sports stars on sabbaticals who are fed up with the meaningless excesses of the media spotlight, published authors who are seeking inspiration and one of my own favourite groups, the moguls who run their own businesses. I love these because they are rarely backward in coming forward about pointing out how badly the company is being run even if it is abundantly evident that they themselves are a personal car crash and on the edge of an abyss, struggling to hold down their own menial job. The Law is another area for the aspiring bullshitter. I remember one lady standing up at a conference and beginning with:

'As a trained lawyer...'

And yes, she had a Law and Pottery degree or something of that ilk from some backstreet polytechnic though her CV on LinkedIn read that she had gone straight from the end of her degree to, you've guessed it, a call centre role. No LPC, no BPTC, no training contract, no pupillage.

No trained lawyer.

And to top it all, at the same event, she mentioned in passing to one of the other delegates that she was shortly to be joining a new company that had been undergoing significant restructuring and that she was being drafted to 'give it all a polish'. The facts of her case were that she had been unceremoniously bombed out from her last job with the *MD* wearing her like a novelty slipper and after having blagged her way into her new place, then went on to oversee huge redundancies and a downward spiral of the chocolate fireguard variety. 'A bit of a polish', yes indeed. *Bride of Wildenstein* on acid.

And the chap who finished his Oxbridge law degree (1st Class hours as well) but decided to cast aside a career in Law to work in, yep, a call centre. Clearly, the career opportunities on the brochure request lines seemed infinitely more appealing than pleading a case before M'Lud in the High Court.

> *'Ladies and gentlemen, we have now arrived at Clown City Central, and we wish you a pleasant onward journey'.*

And these freaks have no shame in telling you that their current call centre position is their spiritual home. It is grade A1 Bonkersville. These guys completely lose sense of the context and do not give it a moment's reflection that the whole situation is preposterous.

§

The problem for a number of these people is that if you are fresh out of university you do not have a professional identity as such. So, when you go to work in a centre handling calls for HSBC or Orange, you can hardly say that you are in banking or telecommunications. You are effectively identity-free which is something of a social handicap in a society that thrives on the categorisation and labelling of everybody and everything. Together in these centres, you have the flotsam and jetsam of just about every other area of society who have flunked out and failed in their previous career choices and who, having demonstrated that they can at least speak conversational English, are welcomed into the call centre outsourcing arena.

Like the oddbods turning up wearing full military uniform on Poppy Day with their tales of failing to adjust to civvy life after 2 years' service and adapting to office life after their previous job involved sitting on the back of a lorry lobbing grenades into crowds of insurgents. It is so abnormal, it is normal.

For these people, the name of the game is reinvention. Start striking up a conversation with this motley crew of jokers and hobos in the break-out area or café of your local friendly outsourcer, and you will encounter all manner of people with their own businesses, company directors, actors, playwrights, and qualified lawyers. My own personal favourites are the DJs and record label owners, most of whom have probably never mixed music outside of their own bedrooms.

The more astute bullshitters opt for the loftier and less checkable background of the professional football triallist (it is always the trial that they reached but never beyond) and the best may even be able to describe the injury sustained that led them to quit. I have had the dubious honour of listening to many a far-fetched tissue of tosh and in many cases these stories are so far-fetched that it has been all I could do, not to blurt out at the extremity of the detail or the unlikeliness of the tale.

Often it begged for the straightforward challenge or even the innocuously indirect probing that may have addressed why a successful businessman was now working for £6 per hour in an organisation that was clearly not conducive to improved mental health but that would have spoiled part of the entertainment that made such a central contribution towards my own survival in among the lunacy.

And that is part of the self-perpetuating problem of outsourced contact centres. They are part-populated with a range of vulnerable, delusional, and often distressed people who feed off each other and contribute to a cross-fertilisation of institutional madness. While you might be able to recognise the situation if you are relatively well-balanced and in a good place, you have to adopt some clear coping strategies to avoid being sucked into their imaginary and delusional worlds. One of these is to remind yourself that what you see or hear is not real and is a form of leisure or a performance away from which you can walk when the curtain comes down every day.

At the end of the day, they are all there moving cars and pumping gas. They all end up back in San José.

§

I can remember one guy who was a qualified counsellor who was talking to members of his team one day when they were debating the rather pitiful hourly rate that they were currently earning. He expanded further to explain that he had recently been offered some additional work as a drugs and alcohol counsellor but that he was only going to accept that work if they could 'afford him'.

Naturally, this struck me as quite odd as *we* were quite simply able to afford him at half the rate that he claimed he would have been earning as a counsellor. What this example demonstrates is the inability of those on the inside to see the wider context that is so evident to everybody else.

And that wider context is evident to anybody who simply takes a step back in order to assess the facts. And the principal fact is that everybody who works in such an organisation is there because they have not got anything better to do. If they did, then they would be elsewhere doing exactly that. This is actually evident in relation to anybody who works within that or indeed any organisation at any given time. It is a piece of elementary logic or common sense to anybody with a firm anchor in the real world.

However, the fantasists and the vulnerable are long since detached. They are unable to take that step back and they therefore weave these extraordinary stories in order to build up their own individual persona and background as somebody who chooses to be here in preference to a more lucrative career or a position of greater standing. What they never can truly address though, is why they would take such a step to move from a position of higher status or greater earning power and decide to work in a contact centre on a minimum wage.

It is truly astounding that they believe that these personal biographies would be credible in any scenario, but you hear them day in and day out. Moreover, nobody seems to challenge them. It is almost accepted as valid and seems to serve to only encourage others to come forward with their equally implausible versions of how they came to be an employee in the organisation.

The classic is – and there are many of them – the former business owners. People who have been *Managing Directors, Chief Operating Officers, Chief Executives, Senior Vice Presidents* etc. etc. All successful businesspeople who have created these monsters of commerce which brought them tremendous success and kudos, and it is here they are working for £6 an hour in an inner city contact centre. Never challenged though, no one even asking the simple question: *so how come you're here then, you turd?*

While I always termed them as black belts in *bullshido*, the DJs and the record label owners are in a sense, from a certain perspective, slightly more credible than the more general and habitual pool of arch-fictionalists. Now my knowledge of modern music is somewhat sketchy, but I am aware of a vibrant underground music scene in a number of our major cities where styles of remixing such as 'Garage' and 'Grime' are *de rigeur*.

So, consequently, a lot of people mix music and perform it in clubs for paid engagements on the club scene. No one is disputing that. And with modern technology it is a lot more straightforward now to self-publish, in that software can be used to create digital tracks which can be uploaded to the Internet and purchased with the assistance of numerous off-the-shelf, ready-made Internet tools. It is then a pretty straightforward matter to create a company and give it a name which you can then loosely describe as a record label of which you are the *CEO*.

However, the way that this is communicated to anybody who will listen is that these individuals have some sort of status within the music industry on a par with that of Phil Spector (pre-breakdown and murder) or perhaps as a more modern example a fledgling Simon Cowell. In brief, they are earning £15-£20 a night plus a couple of free pints in front of audiences of 25 at the local pub with an extended licence.

Far from crowds of thousands of screaming teenagers, there are a handful of hobos and assorted misfits, dependent on prescription drugs, who rock back and forth in a seated position and lap up the mismatched beats that were cranked out over a twenty-minute period in the composer's bedroom. But to listen to them, you would think you were in the presence of Richard Branson. It would be tragic if it were not for the fact that tragedies need to have a flawed hero. These people are simply flawed from the top down.

In many respects, I feel quite appalled at myself for not having fronted out some of these people, for what were obvious deceptions. After all, in my academic career we had been encouraged to be very critical and to pick apart inconsistencies in what we heard and what we read, and, in many respects, this was the foundation of everything I had done myself. And yet here I was as a manager in a position of authority, and I was allowing these obvious examples of self-aggrandizement and fantasy to pass by without any comment or word to the contrary. I suppose in many respects that marked my own complicity in the creation of the bullshit culture that permeates the outsourced contact centre world. It is a world where everything is pretence.

From relationships within the BPO to relationships with clients and to the actual service delivered, nothing is as it seems. Of course, as a manager, it was in my best interest to keep the ship afloat and not make waves unless things were happening that may have directly threatened the operation of the business. So, it was not a question of contradicting everything I thought to be nonsense or insane, simply because I had the benefit of an exacting education which pushed me to the limits in terms of my critical abilities. As an employee and manager of the organisation, it was my responsibility to deliver a service that clients would pay for, and which would return sufficiently high returns for the shareholders and owners of that business. Therefore, it was necessary to play along with the fakers, the cheaters, and the liars as long as they were willing to turn up day in and day out for their £6 per hour and make their contributions to the wider effort.

I was tempted on some occasions to reinvent my own story, primarily for my own entertainment to see whether or not a similarly outrageous account of my own personal past would have been as readily accepted by some of the employees who were clearly fabricating their own stories to what were quite ridiculous extents.

To this end, I did make a number of Internet searches to see whether somebody of the same name as myself had done anything noteworthy which I could then try to pass off as my own. Aside from one famous person, I was unsuccessful in identifying anybody who would serve that purpose. There was a senior member of a big-time UK company who shared my name, but he was still working for them at the time and in spite of the extreme nature of the storytelling that was prevalent within the organisation, I felt that this would be too much for me to attempt to pass off. On reflection, it was hard to believe that I had even given this serious consideration.

Of course, in some instances, it was likely that people were reinventing themselves because they had a very good reason to do so. In the course of the early days at my first outsourced company, I was aware of some individuals who had committed some criminal offences which had led to a rather unfortunate earlier termination than planned on the part of their incumbent employer. While the Internet was in its fledgling days back in the mid-1990s, a number of contact centres were situated in close-knit hubs and inevitably everyone you met would have known somebody who would have known somebody else to whom you could have made an indirect connection.

It is via these routes that the grapevine and the chain of gossip kicks in and some elements of individuals' pasts become apparent. Usually, this amounted to a small amount of embezzlement with insurance companies where dormant pensions might be paid into employees' accounts or a little common or garden till theft in retail establishments. Naturally, these would be situations where people were understandably reluctant to even acknowledge that they had worked in particular industries. For them, this meant disavowing whole previous careers and substituting them for some form of self-employment which would be difficult to check or trace and which would throw any potential questions off track.

After all, in many towns if you work in any form of contact centre service delivery, once you divulge where you have previously worked, there will always be someone who will have worked there all will know somebody who has. Therefore, questions are likely to be inevitable.

Of course, this in itself did raise questions about background checks that were done on employees who entered the world of outsourced contact centres, and I have to say that these checks were generally rare or did not happen at all. In most cases, a question pertaining to the Rehabilitation of Offenders Act (1974) was not even asked and later on, once introduced, a CRB check was simply going to add potentially thousands of £25 cost units to the balance sheet. How many *FDs* were likely to sanction that?

However, when you consider that a lot of business we were involved in was providing information to customers of major high street banks or looking into customer records for online orders, there was a considerable amount of access to customer data that could have been used for the purposes of identity fraud and *phishing* expeditions. While *phishing* was not an established term at the time, it was absolutely happening on a wide scale before the turn of phrase entered the popular vernacular. Naturally, this is a much easier crime to undertake in modern Internet times – as the perpetrators have that additional layer of protection in that they do not need to make a person-to-person telephone call – it can all be done online.

The failure to carry out these checks did lead to a number of issues, some of which were exposed and some of which were tidily swept under the carpet. For one of the accounts that we supported – the customer services desk for an online shopping account with a major high street retailer – we were given the responsibility of processing EFT payments or simply 'customer not present' card refunds or more specifically, electronic fund transfers.

When I joined this account, the person with responsibility for processing these payments was another person who had a questionable story to tell about his previous life. While getting to know different people on the account, I did the rounds and walked the floors speaking to people, in the course of which you asked them everyday questions about what they had previously done before joining the company.

I remember that this guy came up with a fantastic story about working in the United States as a member of a supporting cast on a number of Hollywood productions and had appeared in West End musicals as a stage performer. And of course, now he was working for £6 per hour and processing EFTs. Not only did this story seem to be unlikely – although I would not necessarily have found that particular suspicious, given what I knew about the tendency of my colleagues to become rather creative when recounting their pasts – but his way of delivering his lines looked as if there was more that he might be shielding. He just was not as blasé as the others I had encountered. His body language and eye contact demonstrated to me that whilst he was prepared to offer up his ridiculous story, he did not wish to get too involved in providing the details of what he may have done. This made him slightly different from the others as they were quite shameless and almost quite oblivious to the terminological inexactitudes of their stories. At this stage, I parked this as I was already in the process of understanding the end-to-end operation. I then moved on to another area of the operation where it became clear to me that there was a tremendous amount of access to customer records that made the prospect of fraud a distinct possibility.

Knowing what I knew about the lack of background checks, I decided to run a report on the postcodes of all customers receiving deliveries in the preceding three months and compare that with the postcodes of employees from the HR database. Unsurprisingly I received an immediate hit, and quite sizeable deliveries had been ordered under a customer account whose address had been changed to correspond with that of one of our employees. After a cursory investigation, we suspended the employee concerned and this led to an internal investigation where we examined all aspects of customer transactions that related to payments and loyalty cards. Unsurprisingly the EFT process contained numerous payments made to a small number of cards, which in my opinion was prima facie evidence of fraud. This was all the more likely, given that the card payments did not match the names on the customer records when they were checked back into the main system.

It was clear that over a period of 9 months previously almost £15,000 worth of payments had gone out unwarrantedly. After uncovering these, shall we say questionable activities, it was decided that we should acknowledge the delivery fraud, but no further action should be taken in relation to the EFT misappropriations.

The employee with the grossly implausible Hollywood background, left the business while the investigation was taking place – he probably had something cooking with Steven Seagal or Adam Sandler – so no further action was ever taken against him internally. The delivery fraud lady resigned prior to her disciplinary hearing taking place, but I did learn an important lesson on how matters are presented to clients within an outsourced contact centre relationship. That is to say, when there is evidence of large-scale wrongdoing or errors, it is better not to deny everything but to make partial admissions which then have a greater tinge of reality than absolute denials. It is also always beneficial to demonstrate that your business has flaws and that you are being open about them as it will help to build trust with those relationships.

§

This was the beginning of when I felt deeply uncomfortable about the nature of the work that we were doing. I mean in the past, we had always 'double-bubbled' on charging for per-minute transactions when the costs of contact centre agents by the hour were already covered by other clients. This may seem like absolute and blatant fraud from the perspective of an outsider, but these were standard everyday practices. It sounds unacceptable and indeed it is. But the analogy I will use is one of the frog in water that is gradually being heated up. In this example, the frog doesn't jump out because it becomes so acclimatised to the ever-growing heat that it does not realise that it is boiling to death. Contrast this with the reaction of the frog dropping into hot water from an environment characterised by normality, and it will immediately jump out again because the heat of the water will shock it. In outsourced contact centres, we were simply boiling, and no one felt that deceptions or even criminality were something that would stop us from retaining an account with one of our clients. We were absolutely frogged out – up to our little green necks in spawn.

At a later date, I did hear of another classic BPO tale which was amusing and disappointing in equal measures. Yet again it involved an employee on whom nobody had done any background checks although I do believe they had asked the basic Rehabilitation of Offenders Act question in relation to unspent convictions. It all came to light when somebody had been on eBay and noticed that a person in our location was selling Plantronics headset equipment. This equipment was a standard and popular choice of kit for contact centres, though relatively expensive, and was starting to gain in popularity with Internet users who were using it in chat rooms, so they could listen and speak at the same time while they were typing. Not only was it expensive in itself, but similar equipment that you can buy for the same purpose was also very expensive and not as widely available as it is now with the advent of widespread Internet gaming.

They checked it out online, and it was clear that the seller in this case was one of their employees. This matter was subsequently reported, and I have to admit at that stage everyone was fully expecting it to be swept under the carpet. However, senior bods, who were relatively new in post, had a particular view about potential employee theft, namely that a clear message should be sent out to everybody that such actions would not be tolerated. They therefore arranged for the police to be called who subsequently apprehended him at his desk and marched him off to a meeting room. *Boom, bang, bosh.*

Interestingly at the point where they lifted him at his desk, he had a couple of parcels of the company's equipment nicely wrapped up and ready to be posted to buyers arranged on eBay or other Internet sites. He was clearly caught in the act and had very little defence and subsequently made full admissions to the police. This was a rare occasion when somebody in this environment was subsequently prosecuted, not only for theft but also for obtaining a pecuniary advantage by deception, as he had not admitted to those offences in his initial application to the company. While this was the right thing to do, there was a clear inconsistency in relation to so many other examples of theft and deception that had taken place on a tremendously wide scale during the preceding 10 years in that company.

Another incident that is worthy of mention was one which I have seen take place on numerous occasions throughout my career, namely the use of ghost employees on the payroll. The first time I did encounter this was in the mid-90s when a payroll manager, who in general did the job pretty well, got his pinkies unceremoniously wedged in the till. He was responsible for allocating hours from the resource plan and then processing overtime and the weekly payroll. The scam that did take place, involved the continued presence of leavers on the payroll after they had left. What used to happen is that when somebody left the business, naturally their employment would be terminated, and the relevant forms were filled out. What he did was change the employees' bank account details when they left but not terminate them formally with HR. This meant for all intents and purposes the company was under the impression that the employees continued to work for them, and they therefore carried on paying full salary. However, in reality, the spondoolies were going straight into the Payroll Manager's skyrocket.

This was only uncovered because the perpetrator had not fully thought through all the circumstantial evidence regarding an individual's employment. As any police officer will tell you, criminals who are adept at evading detection will ensure that they do not leave behind evidence at the scene. For example, burglars may wear gloves when breaking into a property so that they do not leave fingerprints behind.

However, the same cops will also readily attest to the fact that criminals cannot attend to all circumstantial evidence. Therefore, when they are questioned on wider matters concerning, for example, the context of their alibi, it is then that their stories will start to fall apart. An example of this may be the use of CCTV that disproves an alibi, and which is beyond the control of the offender. In relation to this situation, the circumstantial evidence of the crime related to paper payslips that were deposited by hand into pigeonholes within the office. On a weekly basis, the payroll bod used to collect these from the bundle before distribution so that they were not placed for collection and were simply disposed of. As such, nobody in the office was aware that paychecks were continuing to be generated for the employee concerned.

Unfortunately, after months and months of the scam taking place – and rather successfully – the payroll officer went on holiday at relatively short notice and forgot to make arrangements to collect and dispose of the payslip. His assistant, who was not complicit in the plan, dutifully distributed the slips into the pigeonholes, where they were spotted by former colleagues of the ghost employees, who questioned why they would still be receiving paperwork when they had not worked at the company for a number of months. The matter was reported to HR and the payroll officer left the field before he could be drop-kicked between the posts.

Interestingly, a ruse with some similarities was perpetrated on another occasion much later in my career, for altogether different reasons. On the subsequent occasion, my then company had employed a large number of temporary staff to work on a particular project for a major client but had experienced significant turnover which was affecting our service levels. The client was naturally querying why we were failing to hit service levels and was questioning how many agents we had working on the account. We were reluctant to confirm to them that we were understaffed, and we were equally concerned that we would be unable to bill the clients as per their hourly rate. We were billing them at a rate of around £14 per hour and when you multiply that by 162.5 which was the rate for the month, this was a considerable amount of non-billable time per head.

A plan was therefore hatched in order to ensure that we continued to roll in the Benjamins.

We therefore continued to bill for 8 people on a monthly basis for several months even though those individuals had failed to work for us for that period. This was something everybody was extremely reluctant to go along with, but the relevant director at the time was insistent that billings needed to be maintained at the said level, and – even more bizarrely – we needed to keep billings high in order that the senior management team would continue to be eligible for their bonus. This resulted in £18,000 per month being billed over a five-month period for work that was never completed. It was explained in the first instance by the impact of a number of challenging current service issues as a result of which we would review the ongoing capacity plan. The subsequent overcharging was then covered up by overstating the requirement for staff on the revised capacity plan after the initial service delivery issues had transpired. This was probably the most blatant example of fraud within the outsourcing service organisations I had encountered, in terms of out-and-out fraudulent (mis)representation of an act itself. Well, until I started working more closely with high street recruitment agencies, that is!

You wonder how somebody can be so brazen to order such actions and how they felt that this would not be challenged. How on earth do these people get to slip through pre-employment checks and get hired in the first instance?

Well, this was all perpetrated and driven by somebody who had joined the company at a senior level and had created a past on the basis of brief twelve to eighteen-month stints over ten years at organisations which had subsequently merged and been bought up by other companies making employment history difficult to check. This is a very common way of obscuring one's employment history. If you work for a company which is subsequently taken over, which may itself then be taken over by another, you can list just the final company and job title on your CV with service spanning the whole period. You position your CV in such a way that you name the company for your period of employment differently than how the company was named when you are actually an employee there in a specific job. You are not lying per se, but you create a history which is very difficult to check and disprove and you can, for example, change a few of the job titles along the way to alter your career path. This then helps to create a history of employment that has more breadth and substance than reality. Any number of permutations are possible that will help you to create a better fit for whatever new role comes along.

I am not sure what the most shocking point there is about all of this. Whether it is that people join BPOs on the basis of fraudulent representations or omissions and continue to perpetrate deceptive and often criminal activities once in employment or that people allow them to get away with it. Out of everything I have recounted here, only the eBay pirate was taken to task.

And while I have accentuated the extent of deception within my companies, it was clear from speaking to other managers in organisations throughout the industry that this was prevalent, and that the normal course of action would indeed be to sweep under the carpet. What was telling in this instance was that the person who was calling the shots on the Plantronics heist came from outside the outsourcing industry where values and adherence to the principles of criminal justice were clearly more keenly felt. In the outsourcing industry, nefarious activities are more likely to be swept under the carpet because so many employees know where the bodies are buried in relation to the company's own questionable tactics and behaviours. We are talking about mass graves rather than the odd corpse.

What is clear about this culture of reinvention is that the lies and deception seem to be accepted in the knowledge that *you have to allow deceptive people to flourish for their own good, in order for them to perpetrate even greater deceptions for the organisational good.* Yet the most striking hypocrisy is clear when you see the mission statements and the values that most of these BPOs are so keen to present to clients and to the wider public.

These will typically be concerned with openness, honesty, integrity and delivering excellent service though are some way off that in terms of what they actually deliver.

Supremely ironically though is that on entering BPOs, so many people take up the opportunity to create themselves with some gusto. Contrary to the Nietzschean view, there is an overarching force that transcends that identity — the BPO bullshit machine that sucks out individuality from its minions, faster than you can say *John Coffey.* By the time they have served a year or so, most are questioning whether they need time out in order to 'find themselves'.

That's quite a turnaround in terms of how much people end up embracing life after their stint in a BPO.

6 – If You Can't Fight, Wear a Big Hat

During the halcyon days of the 1990s, the cook-to-broth ratio in BPOs was one of the reasons why everything tasted great in the kitchen but not so well during service. Arguably one of the most confusing things when I first joined an outsourced agency was the sheer number of who was who and who did what. I remember one of the first encounters I had with a Client Services Department and being almost spellbound by the number of job titles and positions that people had. For example, we had *Account Executives, Account Managers, Key Account Managers, Account Directors, Group Account Directors, Client Principals,* and a *Client Services Director.* And I think they may even have been Board Account Directors and a *Managing Director* overseeing the whole shebang.

Now on the delivery side, we just had *Customer Service Representatives* and *Team Leaders,* and I think there was probably a manager overseeing the whole thing from an operational perspective. And of course, one *Operations Director* who looked after the whole site. Now if that was confusing for us, it must have been stupefying for our clients. During the many meetings and get-togethers that took place – because we needed to interact with the client directly – sometimes you may have had six or seven people from an organisation in a meeting with one single client.

As a result, people would sit in meetings for hours and hours at a time and not make any meaningful contribution. After all, they may over the course of several months of 'working on an account' not have done anything at all, other than process an invoice or some other general paperwork. When clients wanted to get in contact with us, they'd often have to make six or seven phone calls or different contacts before they were able to get somebody who was actually technically competent and able to answer the question. All of which was costing us huge amounts of money.

I was fortunate to go to a presentation with a major financial client when partly through the slides the client told the *Key Account Manager*, who was becoming more visibly shell-shocked at every sentence that came from the former's mouth, that if she had wanted to have attended a marketing lecture, she would have gone back to college. That was a turning point in the way that we structured our teams as that account was lost shortly afterwards and had left us with a considerable gap in our finances. But it did raise a question which has become prevalent at various times during my outsourcing career which relates to why we have so many people with so many titles and what in the hell they actually do. And the answer to that very, very straightforward question, is that most of them do very, very little.

They are there for show. Clients, by their very nature, are the ones who control the purse strings. Many of the vendor managers who deal with outsourcing agencies are repressed egomaniacs who love to be made to feel important. Therefore, if you introduce them to an Account Executive as their main point of contact, they are likely to feel that you are not recognising their position of importance within their own organisation. This is pretty much reflective of what happens in all areas of society – when dignitaries visit other countries – and the acknowledgement of rank is expected to be reciprocated with an appropriate person for them to meet. This is why for example, when Donald Trump visits the UK, he will expect to be met by the Queen as the corresponding Head of State. I am sure that if Prince Edward were wheeled out to meet Mr Trump, the Trumpster would be just slightly disgruntled that the appropriate courtesies had not been extended or that his position as the head of the world's greatest superpower had not been fully acknowledged in the choice of host.

So, one really important element in the make-up of organisations providing outsourced services is that there is the appropriate hierarchy in place as that client relationship unfolds. It has nothing to do with the technical expertise or efficiencies of the outsourcing organisation but more with the appropriate massaging of egos client-side. That is why there is usually an *Account Director* in place who will then be supported by a *Key Account Manager* while the *Account Managers* deal with the legwork and the Account

Executives are there to simply receive tasks to complete on behalf of the Account Managers who feel that they themselves are too important to deal with menial bumbling on the account.

Of course, this raises particular challenges for the outsourced client account teams themselves. After all, they have the prestige of their LinkedIn accounts to maintain in order to put on an acceptable front of prestige to the outside world, so they will often remodel their job titles accordingly.

In one company I worked at, a number of the *Account Directors* started to call themselves *Director, Account Management*. This of course gave the wholly erroneous impression that they were the sole director of an account management function. In fact, they were Account Managers of a slightly higher status who looked after a selection of accounts, who would attend regular monthly meetings, and who were mostly on a level par with second-line *Operations Managers* who in the contact centre itself would look after *Team Leaders*.

Unmistakably, this obsession with titles becomes more apparent when you start to involve yourselves with American corporations which have a potential for titling themselves as *Presidents* of various descriptions. Therefore, you might expect to encounter *Vice-Presidents* (or *VPs*), *Senior Vice-Presidents* (or *SVPs*), *Executive Vice-Presidents* (*EVPs*) and of course, *Presidents*.

Take a step back, have a think and you quickly take on board that it is bonkers. Stark raving nuts.

So as a result of this, it has become *de rigeur* in outsourcing companies with American connections, for an *Operations Director* to be known as *Vice-President, Operations*; *Divisional Directors* to become known as *Senior Vice-Presidents* and I am guessing that *Executive Vice-Presidents* are board-level directors in charge of particular functions although no one really seems to know the score. *President*, I am guessing, has the same kudos, if I might use that oft-regurgitated American expression of praise, as *Managing Director* of old though nowadays *Managing Director* can be used to describe the divisional head of a *clunge* (for that is or should be, the collective noun) of 'directors' who have 'director' titles but who are not real Directors in the true sense. Confused? You should be, and I am as well.

Of course, there is another range of titles used in commercial organisations which have been readily lapped up by the outsourced contact centre industry, namely the C-suite of titles (yes, what *pot de toss* was responsible for dreaming up those beauties? Probably some MBA Alumnus from one of our highly esteemed Business Schools – itself a travesty of the education system but I digress), so we also now have *Chief Operating Officer* (*COO*), *Chief Financial Officer* (*CFO*), *Chief Executive Officer* (*CEO*) etc.

Imagine who would be the head of old MacDonald's Farm – the 'CE-I-EI-O'? Why not – the whole shit show is essentially a childish game for who gets to ride the biggest bike in the kindergarten.

Some *CEOs* assume the joint position of *Chairman and CEO*, which sounds omnipotent but clearly misunderstands the roles of *Chairman* and *Chief Executive*, namely that the former should monitor the performance of the latter. This has been certainly recommended in the *UK Corporate Governance Code* since 2010, but what do I know?[vi]

The only worthwhile one that I can ascertain is that of *CIO* which I'm reliably informed stands for 'career is over'. Although you may also have heard that there are such folk as *Chief Information Officers* in some businesses, nobody is quite sure how such a formal position might have been carved out. Would such a person have enough to do in order to justify a role? That is purely rhetorical as none of us would surely have the time to think that one through.

The fundamental point being made here is that in the world of outsourced contact centres, the title of the *Director* or *President* is a key component of the illusion of professionalism and accomplishment which in reality will almost certainly be lacking in terms of the substance and the delivery of service. It serves the same purpose as the big hat that cowboys whereas they ride into town and from this you should infer that they mean business. In the same way that their subsequent barroom brawl with the local gunslinger is lapped up by the audience is demonstrative of heroic capabilities and feats, the discerning audience should spot the reality gaps that even the greatest choreographer cannot gloss over.

Some *Regional Directors* have even started to become known as *Country Heads*. Christ on a 3-speed, twist-grip Grifter. It is like they think they are heading up some sort of Banana Republic. It is a two-bit commercial enterprise man, not a nation-state. Get a grip. Has somebody been doing lines off the Space Bar again (you know who you are!)

I have seen *Personnel Managers* become *HR Managers* and *HR Directors* in turn become *Organisational Development Directors*. Now there is a body of academic writing and thought which would doubtless explain the difference between these roles and which could be substantiated by significant amounts of management models, case studies and in many cases I am sure, genuine lists of accomplishments. However, in the world of outsourcing services, the work actually accomplished by anyone with those three titles is likely to be shockingly similar. It will be in effect basic processes and procedures, hiring plans, redundancy scoring sheets and other assorted 'people activities' that are wheeled out, reused and re-presented time and time again.

Often – and I have seen this in practice on more than one occasion – the so-called experts gain credence in their new organisations, by bringing with them documents from previous organisations that they re-brand and pass off as their own work. In doing so, they facilitate their path from the status of mere manager to something that is on the face of it a little more special. But ultimately in terms of what they actually deliver, these title-obsessed storytellers are simply repeating and re-positioning the same old standard processes, procedures, and ideas.

§

I suppose in many respects we should not be too surprised that an 'industry' that has, in many respects, no basis should struggle to attract officers at the more senior level who have some substance that supports their appointment. Many of the so-called *Presidents*, *Chiefs* or *Directors* have no formal management qualifications, nor any real wide breadth of experience in the areas that you would need to have in order to manage such a multi-faceted organisation that an outsourced contact centre agency actually is.

For example, anybody at such a senior level should have a fundamental grasp of human resources, financial and commercial management, technology, marketing, project management, operational management, and a clear set of strategic and subject-related skills. What you tend to get are individuals with some knowledge of their own specific area who through various deceptions or subterfuge have managed to bluff their way through the ranks to a position of greater authority.

Unfortunately, this will inevitably mean that those in such senior positions will need to rely heavily on those subservient to them within the organisation but superior in terms of skill and technical knowledge in order to survive. However, if they do not recognise this or are placed in situations where they need to make quick decisions and do not have immediate records of the superior knowledge available to them, that is when significant errors can be made.

This is most apparent when dealing directly with clients where senior officers of outsourced agencies do not make effective decisions when immediacy and timing are of the essence. I can recall many instances where senior directors have failed to take the opportunity to provide services to clients or had dropped the ball dramatically because, at the point where those subjects came up in conversation, the directors were unaware that our organisations were able to perform those services and therefore were not able to take advantage of that situation.

One auto-eye-gouging example of this came during a senior client re-tender where the *Director of Operations*, UK, *Ireland, South Africa and acting APAC or* something depressingly similar but certainly just as futile talked for five minutes to the panel on how he would be able to deliver an appointment-setting function for the service, only to be told after he had finished that such a function had already been in place for the last 18 months. Whoops, contact centre capacity immediately freed up. When the guy finally left the business, he went on to become a consultant. Quelle surprise!

As another example, in one of my latter experiences in BPOs, a senior director was presenting a service review and referred to the *ACD* as the *Automatic Call Dialler* and became adamant that the reported abandoned rate was 8% when the statistics on his own *PowerPoint* slide showed that this was indeed 11%. On this occasion it was particularly crushing, as this individual's shortcomings were evident to all concerned which caused him a not insignificant degree of personal distress.

Up to that point I had not had much sympathy for that particular individual, but it made me realise that the circumstances and pressures of being forced to perform roles which people were clearly ill-equipped to do took a considerable toll on them personally. It was hard to believe in this example that this person could not perform elementary mathematics. It was my view that he was under so much pressure to present the totality of a slide deck which he did not truly understand that he had simply not checked his own numbers. It was equally likely that he had been provided with those numbers by somebody else and was not delivering his own content (guaranteed in any circumstances to problematise the smooth delivery of a presentation).

Either way, whether it was a simple lack of capability or a mental block in not being able to recognise at that point that those numbers were incorrect, it struck me that what I had previously deemed to be charlatans and crooks, were perhaps people who would get themselves into situations that they could not handle and were incapable of breaking away from. It was almost like watching people get onto a fairground ride which they subsequently immediately wanted to get off from but couldn't. In some ways it was heart-breaking.

Nevertheless, these examples are not unique in the world of BPO services which is heavily populated by senior-level managers who lack basic skills and understanding of the services they are purporting to deliver. In many respects, their skills are largely in the ability to remain undetected or unexposed for a sufficiently lengthy period for them to have identified their next opportunity. If you look at their CVs in detail, it is a common feature that many of them will be in multiple roles over a period of five or ten years where they have never been in a position for long enough to substantially achieve or build anything but just long enough to have acquired enough information to tell their next story that will facilitate their re-appointment at a different organisation.

In the same way that outsourced organisations will allow the deception and the lies of the San José residents, the leaders of those organisations are similarly allowed to pretend and to act as long as the performance is maintained for the benefit of clients, who continue to pay the bills.

For what other reason would a bog-standard *Account Director*, dealing with mainly UK services and perhaps the odd *offshore* overflow, be unashamedly styled a *Global Account Director* or the *Senior Vice-President of Global Account Management*? Even in the overhyped throwaway world of BPOs, this kind of hyperbole deserves a book or perhaps more appropriately a psychiatric study of its own. Maybe as a homeowner, I will have to start calling myself the *Global Director of Personal Real Estate*. It is desperately sad.

§

Within the context of the wearing of big hats, the senior managers with the titles are the ringmasters. They often have no tricks or skills of their own, but they have the title, they set the scene, and they close the performance. The problem with outsourcing is that the role they find themselves centre stage as the performance unfolds and many will have no tricks in their bag. Now that may not be a problem if there is a knife thrower or a sword swallower nearby. However, in practice, a number of them do make a move for the sharp implements which as we know can be hazardous.

The *bullshido* terminology is of course not restricted to personal titles. There was a time when call centres moved to contact centre terminology and recognition of channel diversification (from only calls, to also email and SMS at the time – much more now, of course). With the advent of social media, the big hat machine has gone full bullshit with the notion of 'Omnichannel' now prevailing. I suppose we could live with 'multichannel' at a push, for emphasis but didn't 'contact centre' neatly and concisely sum up that state of affairs? We will be told that 'omnichannel' uses one single interface for all channels, so it is different and new and exciting. But is it?

How could the originator of such a term have whipped themselves up into a sufficiently faux mindset that they could have straight-facedly proposed its use? The answer lies in every toss-centric marketing team in organisations the length and breadth of the country. It is what every slim-fit, narrow-tied, slope-haired sales-speaking spurter generates in order to dress up their drab and mundane products and services. Salt 'n' vinegar crisps have become 'handcrafted chips, freshened with Cornish sea-salt and Chardonnay white wine vinegar'. In the BPO world remember, the eagerness to latch on to such terminology becomes more than a sales technique and indeed a raison d'être. There isn't a tangible product or service on offer, so the adjective is no longer an enhancer but in their context a central plank. The service takes on a status of its own and elevates the proposition to a different level by adding dimensions.

Take a moment to think about what it actually means. Your contact centre becomes 'Omnichannel', simply by opening up contact options to your customers that are subsequently accessible from within one another. You don't have to deliver anything special, just respond to them in the same way as they contacted you and allow them to switch from one channel to another (this could even be a link in an email that takes them through to Chat). Of course, there are software packages in play that collect emails, texts, and social media comments. Just dressed-up versions of Outlook or other software clients that skim and copy the content to a different place and allow information to be fed back in the other direction. Like most IT solutions, they are all shiny, polished and beautifully wrapped.

But what do they actually create or transform? Over and above the word itself, what is revolutionary that is actually happening? I'm stumped. Maybe that means I can make my semi-detached house omnichannel, by adding a side gate and installing a landline and a mailbox at the foot of the front path. It's still the same house though, and you'll still get the same response, irrespective of how you enter my world, and you can switch from one to the other. I would probably feel somewhat embarrassed to ask the estate agent to advertise it for sale as an 'omnichannel domicile', as the descriptor, while factually accurate in accordance with the understood meaning of the words employed, is, to coin a phrase, *omniludicrous.*

Bonkers whichever way you look at it and in whatever order.

Unfortunately, the world of the BPO does not have time or space for measured self-reflection. All those in that world and the immediate galaxy will happily soak up such nonsense and merrily regurgitate it so that it becomes part of the prevalent *truth* of the so-called industry. In doing so, it builds a little more credibility for the story.

On the basis of absolutely nothing.

7 – Absolute Cults

So, having looked at service, values, and some of the volume players, it is now time to consider the question of formal structures and those who occupy elevated positions within them.

As an aside, I have always felt that BPOs had a small-town church feeling to them. You know, the ones that have a leadership team who play an active role in guiding the lives of their flock. After all, when any *MD* or *CEO* speaks, it is almost as if they are assuming the *'God told me to tell you'* authority for whatever crackpot, on-the-hop policy, or idea they have dreamt up.

But first, let us look at how these businesses line up.

Like any enterprise, BPOs need to be run effectively and therefore will inevitably have a hierarchical structure.

No news there then.

We cannot really go any further into a discussion about organisational structure without mentioning the age-old and familiar concept of the organisational chart or structure chart. And let me tell you that the structure chart has a very special position in the world of BPOs.

And I'm not talking about the upside-down triangle that your averagely demented *MD* will tell you about as he is blowing his beans while engaging you in some grand revelation that as the leader of the business, he supports the whole organisation rather than being at its pinnacle.

Yes, that old crock of cold turd still does the rounds with alarming regularity. Heard it myself recently while my inner self was shooting up a supermarket with a Kalashnikov.

But back to the (traditional) structure chart. In essence, such a chart should reflect who does what and who is accountable and responsible for what. Well, that is the theory. On such charts, people are allocated roles and responsibilities for their particular specialisms and the charts themselves through their thick lines reflect who reports to whom i.e. the authority relationships. There may of course be dotted lines which reflect closer working relationships without line management responsibility being involved. All sounds familiar, no doubt.

However, this is not the real purpose of the structure chart because as everybody knows, when you work in a BPO, there is no clear delineation between who does what on a number of fronts. For example, I have worked on projects before where there has been a project manager and a client services manager, and it is the project manager who will manage the client relationship, often because they have detailed knowledge of how the solution and service work as they have been involved in the set-up of the project and of course in partnership with the client right from the very start.

In that situation, the Account Manager did, to put it bluntly, very little. Nevertheless, to look at the structure chart that was in place at the time, it would have been evident that the Account Manager would have had responsibility for the client relationship for the whole of that project. What tends to happen in practice, is that in spite of the *de jure* responsibilities assigned to an individual, people undertake tasks and actions and a *de facto* role dependent on their own personal inclinations, skills, or motivations – or even as a result of value placed in them by the client concerned.

Now this may seem somewhat strange or even unacceptable to people who've worked in a professional services environment where there is a high degree of discipline with roles, responsibilities and accountability that carry up through the line. And such people with this view would of course be correct. As I have already indicated when discussing other areas of the make-up of outsourced contact centre operations, I have started to unpack the notion that organisational matters are somewhat dysfunctional, indeed that the whole aim and purpose of outsourced call centres is misaligned with the purpose and stated ambitions that purportedly underpin their existence. But it goes much further than this – it goes to the heart of how they actually operate internally.

As a result of individuals effectively making up their roles and responsibilities as they go even with the best will in the world, it would be a challenge for even the most competent line manager to hold those individuals to account for the role they do. This is because what they are charged with doing on a day-to-day basis, or what they need to do in order to react to the demands that are placed upon them, is completely different from the stated job description that they would have received on their first day on the job.

However, were you to listen to any HR Manager or HR Director in a BPO, they would be quick to point out that all employees are appraised on the basis of competencies and their adherence to the values of the business that they would need to demonstrate giving practical examples of when and how they have 'lived the dream'. Furthermore, not only would this be tested at an annual appraisal, but it would be the methodology employed during regular 121s that are mandatory for employees at all levels.

You might now be posing yourself a few questions.

Namely, if people are not actually doing what they should be doing and are not demonstrating the competencies through real-life examples so that their performance can be objectively measured, how does it work in practice in relation to the 121s and appraisals?

The answer is that BPO 121s in practice glide over specific competency-based delivery and end up being superficial chats about how people are feeling and how their families are. They are in effect, an opportunity to ensure that employees are generally comfortable with their position so that they are not going to be unsettled and contribute any further to the already spiralling levels of attrition BPOs need to address.

The documentation that is produced following these meetings for the record, is often, to put it bluntly, falsified. There will be standard performance notes that are written up in competency-based terms so that the records will show that the individuals have received an effective competency-based review of their performance. For example:

> *'Johnny dealt with a home delivery customer today and by demonstrating effective listening skills, correctly identified the customer's problem and provided a solution. The customer was satisfied with the response and Johnny followed up with the customer 48 hours later, to check that there were no further issues. The customer then contacted me to say how happy they were with the service'.*

Customer Focus, tick.

Except that there was no customer, and you would not be expecting your team to be spending (possibly unbillable) time on something that is not going to add to your bottom line. But you have a documented and auditable record that states that you have. Furthermore, you have an employee who is not going to rock the boat – Johnny will, after all, get a good appraisal and may even snare a pay increase. And you as the manager, will not have to waste time sitting down with somebody for an hour to go over the same old rubbish. Nice work if you can get it.

This is a widespread practice which although sounds complicated and difficult to achieve is a very quick process for an experienced line manager who has worked in BPOs for an extended period of time. This is also crucial for the line managers; in that they will need to demonstrate to their senior managers that best practice HR processes are followed and delivered in the management of the centre as a whole.

The real aficionados will take it a step further and with them, 121s do not take place at all. You would not have to trek too far through the BPO jungle to find line managers who have written up summaries of meetings that had never actually taken place. Of course, in the world of outsourced contact centres where measurement accreditations and statistics are key, it does not matter whether what is purported to be measured is actually true or not. It is simply enough to show documentary evidence or statistics that reflect something being measured which is what the external client or internal client needs to be satisfied is being measured.

§

In the same way, clients welcome a report which shows them that a service level has been met even if there is conflicting evidence that suggests that calls perhaps are not being answered within the agreed service level threshold. It is a question of taking on what they want to believe rather than undertaking a detailed critical analysis of the information that is presented before them.

So not only do we have a situation where people are routinely asked to fulfil roles that are not clearly defined and spelled out for them at the start of their employment but a whole exercise in creative re-positioning taking place by the line managers. Now that doesn't mean to say that some appraisals and 121s do not take place in accordance with the process that some assiduous HR manager has painstakingly drawn up, an attempt to accurately define how a role within an outsourced centre is structured. And when line managers do attempt to follow this process, that is when the real fun begins. The reason for this is that HR teams structure performance management processes in such a way that the most mundane and tedious roles might look exciting and vibrant.

After all, if your job is to sit on the phone and answer queries or tap out templated responses by email that bear very little relevance to the unique customer query that has been presented, it is actually quite challenging to throw up repeated examples of effective communication, teamwork organisation and planning etc. It is even more challenging as a line manager to react positively and to say something innovative and interesting, possibly even motivating, at the regular regurgitation of one-dimensional and quite tedious recollections of what is an essentially repetitive job.

In essence, in trying to structure a role in terms of a range of competencies with detailed descriptions and indicators that sit behind them, HR teams are attempting to perform alchemy or at least call upon their operational team managers and managers to provide a lively justification of attainment against those competencies where there is very little raw material to work with in the first instance. And this is one of the reasons why it is a lot more straightforward for managers, to take the appraisal process out of the real world and re-work it in the realms of creative writing and fantasy. As an aside, one of the interesting features of appraisal processes is that they are often linked by companies to annual pay reviews which can make these regular rounds of performance review quite testing for all concerned.

Notwithstanding the almost forensic detail into which employees then wish to argue every single point on every single facet of their performance, the best-laid plans often go to the dogs as a result of statistically inept scoring matrices that are advanced by people who are ill-prepared to quantify their frequently outrageously inaccurate competency models into a numbered scoring system.

A good example of this would be in a scoring system that relied on an average score over six competencies where a candidate would need to advance by one point on their overall score in order to achieve a pay rise. Now as any statistician would note, on a range of 1 to 5 for a competency score, the employee – if they achieved an increase by just 1 point on each of let's say, two of the six competencies, their overall score would only increase by a third of the points on average. The number of organisations where I've seen the same or similar scoring mechanisms is mind-blowing and the overall disgruntlement that emanates from such a process is never truly addressed because management teams are so wedded to processes that they will always accept what the process tells them even if the process itself is clearly incorrect.

Again, this may come as a surprise to people who are used to working in organisations where a high level of critical reasoning takes place and people are not afraid to challenge things that are clearly wrong. However, in the world of BPOs – and this is in part owing to the fact that people are not confident that they are filling the roles that they have been given on paper – such challenges are few and far between. This is because the individuals themselves know that if they raise their head to high above the parapet, it is likely to be shot off.

And the reason why it can be shot off is because they know that they are not fulfilling the role as detailed in their job descriptions.

Therefore, it would be very easy for a senior level manager with an axe to grind, or a vendetta, to take them to one side and be able to document clearly for the benefit of a third party that the individual concerned who was raising these issues and challenging the status quo, were not fulfilling their role obligations. This would facilitate a fast track through to a capability hearing which in turn is the fast track towards dismissal. Ladies and Gentlemen, we have now entered the less than salubrious world of *managing out*. Pulling the rug out from underneath somebody you do not like and assessing them on some documented de jure standards that have not been de facto for months or even years and which in practice are impossible to achieve. It is a structured path to the departure lounge for Johnny or Jackie and can be executed entirely within the published processes and regulations. Game, set, and match.

I've seen people ruthlessly pursued in the aftermath of management meetings when they were asked for an opinion which when given went against the prevailing policy. People who were bending over backwards, working all hours to deliver against all the odds and performing near-miracles and later presented with a piece of data showing something they were falling short on versus their official job description.

It's as brutal as it is warped, but that's how these BPOs roll.

So, on the face of things, and if you were looking into an outsourced contact centre from the outside, you might think that there were nicely neat and structured departments where everybody knew what they were doing, in accordance with detailed role descriptions and processes and procedures.

How wrong you would be.

§

This does therefore beg the question; how do these organisations actually function effectively? It is a good question and in brief, we can answer this by talking not of processes and procedures which is the way in which such organisations project themselves to the outside world but in terms of the sheer force of personality of senior figures who manage to install themselves at the top of such businesses or at senior positions at the head of the relevant functions.

It is all about the cult of personality. And my dear chums, they are cults of the highest order.

What you will often see, is a new big cheese appointed who will then ensure that his or her previous followers from former organisations are quickly installed into key roles within the business. This allows the relevant head honcho to ensure that the myth or the legend of their greatness is perpetuated at all levels within the organisation.

This is an attractive proposition for the new boss as they are effectively the patron for all of the key positions that are filled below them and therefore immediately cement themselves into an unassailable position within the organisation. It is, in effect a transactional arrangement with high salaries and terms and conditions being offered in exchange for a consolidated power base at the head of the organisation. And it never used to cease to amaze me how people would be prepared to sell out in this way, to accept an increased salary, purely to propagate the myth of brilliance of a leader who in effect was growing their own personal cult within an organisation.

Keep drinking the Kool-Aid. It is like all these mini *Jonestowns* have been popping up all over the UK.

And the followers cannot get enough of the drug. They are like junkies clucking for their next fix. I once worked in a centre close to the main prostitution/heroin/crack mosh pit and on a daily basis, I used to see worse addicts in the office than out on the street. But for them, power and influence were the fix. Being close to the centre of apparent decision-making. And obeying everything.

§

I remember attending a management away day where a biggish cheese of the organisation was presenting to the management group on the financials and the approach to motivating staff etc. Painful to endure but all the sorts of things that you would expect to hear at such a gathering. Content which, once you've heard it once, you've heard it all before.

After the sessions are finished, his sidekick at dinner was constantly propagating these anecdotes of how brilliant this *assez grand fromage* was, how he had a 'razor-trap mind', how he was a business genius, the future *CEO*, and a man much admired and respected throughout the organisation ad nauseam. At the time, it struck me that at no point was she ever qualifying this with real achievements or examples of how this individual had led the organisation to a greater degree of achievement.

It was simply PR and manifestly transparent, and this may be down to politeness as much as anything, but it was not openly challenged even if indirectly through any prompting for detail on what the gentleman had actually delivered. This whole puff continued throughout the evening, to the point at which, had you been otherwise ambivalent about the company, you would have been starting to think about knocking up a new CV.

On the second day of the meeting, the same cheese presented to the wider group on the essential fundamentals of client relationships, standing in front of us with a marker pen in his hand and lecturing merrily away, giving lots and lots of individual scenarios of how he had been successful in building relationships with his clients. In each instance, he was not providing the punchline, but what he was doing was providing multiple examples that would lead us to the same conclusion.

Being moderately intelligent, I had already ascertained that the punchline would be that he was building trust with all of these different clients in the different scenarios. But what captivated the audience more than his exhilarating style of delivery was that he seemed to be edging towards a screen where he was about to write up some key bullet points using his marker pen. Now the tension in the audience was palpable because our leader was about to commit a significant faux pas in the use of the marker pen on the screen. You could see people on the edge of their seats cringing to the point where they wanted to cover their eyes with their hands because this guy was about to make a serious error and potentially cause some serious damage to the conference facilities owned by our hosts on the day.

Sensing the apprehension among his audience, our leader pointed to the marker pen and deftly drew his presentation to a conclusion by pointing out that people in the audience clearly did not trust him as the marker pen was not an indelible marker but a dry-wipe marker. He then smiled self-assuredly and quickly drew up his bullet points on the screen behind him.

From his perspective, I am sure, cleverly delivered, and masterful theatre.

Unfortunately, the wincing and cringing demeanour of the audience had not been a result of us thinking that he was holding an indelible marker because as we knew, there would have been no use for indelible or permanent markers in a presentation suite. It was because the dry wipe screen for the use of marker pens was situated on the presenter's right and he had been directing his attention to the screen on his left which was a canvas screen for the overhead projector.

He then proceeded to write with the dry wipe marker on the canvas screen which as we knew and had anticipated would have the same effect as an indelible marker, in that it would not easily be wiped off.

Sure enough, later on at dinner on the second evening of the event, some sheepish-looking sycophants were mingling with the management population, to enquire how to remove dry wipe ink from a canvas screen. While nobody had previously been prepared to challenge the obvious hyperbolic PR being put out about this biggish cheese during the first night of the off-site, somebody did at least have the apparent wherewithal to suggest that red wine might remove the stain (Jesus, yes it was suggested, albeit poker-faced).

At this point, I almost choked on my lamb cutlet as the ridiculously obsequious middle manager took a bottle of wine from the table and disappeared in the direction of the presentation suite. Sure enough, the next morning when we went into the meeting room for day three of the off-site, there was a green and pink cloudy circle on the canvas screen, and the presenter on this day was now correctly using the dry-wipe screen to aid their presentation.

I guess that the conclusion drawn was one which I have drawn on many occasions in my career working with BPOs. That is at many junctures, it is felt appropriate for leaders within those organisations to address the wider management team and galvanise and motivate them towards the delivery of higher strategic goals. And it never ceases to amaze me how little preparation they take in order to facilitate the effective delivery of the message. They rely purely on their technical knowledge and their force of personality. They are so keen to present themselves and have themselves presented as all-knowing powerful individuals, that they would not even take the time to fully consider the detail of a given situation where the effective delivery would be the be-all-and-end-all for how they were perceived by effectively their most important audience. And I say this, notwithstanding the knowledge that clients who pay the bills should always be the most important audience, but these were the people who would be delivering his business and making the client billing possible in the real world.

Following this meeting and many others, the management team left with the suspicion that there was a certain disjoint between the senior team and those cranking out billable services on-site.

Steve Jobs once made the point that the purpose of recruiting good people into your business is not so that you can tell them what to do but so that they can tell you what to do[vii]. Richard Branson notes that your employees, not your clients are the most important people in your organisation[viii]. And while it may be strange to quote Mr Branson, as he is a man who is seen by many to have a very influential and forceful personality, that is not the way in which he has run his businesses. As an individual, he is actually quite low-profile and self-effacing, but he understands the value of his people and of hiring great people, knowledgeable people who are experts in their field and who will ensure that the wider team is the strongest possible.

This is not an approach I have ever seen in practice in the outsourced call centre world. In these organisations, it is about a cult of personality that develops to which all employees must be subservient to the detriment of critical reasoning and the full realisation of individual and collective talent within the business.

§

Another example of a now infamous office party reflects how the most charismatic leaders can fall foul of a resistant workforce pulling in the opposite direction.

Prior to the event taking place, a whole array of activities went underway, ranging from glossy banners with senior managers pictured mid-toast with champagne bottles, desk drops with personalised Aero bars and even a cake with the various faces emblazoned across it in the group photo. Yes, ladies and gentlemen, a cake.

The preparations for the party were considerable and to be fair, it was quite a generous outlay for staff. All that was arguably missing was a giant branded dragon meandering its way down through Chinatown with a full sycophantic crew presumably desperate to get into the backend of the said decorative and mythical beast.

It was nevertheless clearly an event that would be presented as a gesture from management to the people – otherwise, it would have carried an image other than that of the bespectacled former accountant who adorned the surface of the iced glaze.

As part of the efforts to get the party started (shamone!), it was decided that drinks tokens would be produced and passed to the management team in order for them to be allocated to everybody on the night. Now in my view, that was a really positive move to make which was well received by employees at all levels.

What was crucial to how the party went however was that the drinks tokens were handed out during the afternoon of the day the party was due to take place. As the tokens had been produced within the office itself, it was simply a question of tokens being printed onto paper which were then subsequently cut up, counted, and distributed to the relevant teams within the contact centre.

Given the animosity that existed from the shop floor towards the senior managers (who were starting to run the business in a way that the old guard was resisting) and of course, given the entrepreneurial spirit that exists in most businesses, particularly when there is the possibility of free drinks being on the horizon, it did not take a tremendous shift in strategic thinking to come to the conclusion that the advisors could and would print off these vouchers in the same way that the HR team had done so in preparation for the party.

Consequently, hundreds and hundreds of additional vouchers were printed off and taken by the various teams to the event in the evening. At the party itself, the senior management team were very much enjoying the party. On the following Monday, however, it became apparent on the receipt of the bar bill from the host company that more than £1000s of vouchers over and above what had been printed and allocated had been spent on the night. People walking around with bottles of *Moët* in each hand.

The overall cost of the party practically doubled and only the sound of lead balloons dropping could be heard after the last party popper had sounded.

It was a classic example of leaders, several of whom were without doubt very talented individuals who really wanted to make a positive cultural difference, not truly grasping the extent of the hostile underbelly and the nature of the business at that time. With so much emphasis on the senior managers featuring in the paraphernalia, the hoi polloi was absolutely and resolutely going to bring them down a peg or two.

This unbudgeted increase in festivities serves as an example of the way that others, more conversant with the temperature of the organisation, were sitting on their hands and not offering the perspectives that their positions demanded. Surely it was obvious that photocopied vouchers were likely to be counterfeited with ease? Surely the banners and the cake were going to antagonize an already peeved workforce. Why not just sanction a no-frills booze-up? When have they never gone down a storm?

It was all the more painful given that in dispersing some vouchers on the night in the course of some rather generous rounds, the directors were unaware that the rank-and-file employees had already assumed control over spending on the night, and in effect the drinks were on the people, not the bosses. Or rather, the discretion over the cost of the drinks was on them while the bill itself would come back to the bosses. Whatever way you looked at it, it was a generous step that backfired because none of the obsequious tongue-scrapers with their ears closer to the ground had stepped in to offer any advice to the senior management team that would surely have been readily available from anybody who had recently taken a temperature reading from the wider business.

The grassroots positions at that time were not occupied by Mother Theresa and her band of nuns. The rank-and-file were going to see the angles and exploit them.

In some ways, this example can serve as a metaphor for wider examples of how things actually work in practice when leaders can become removed from what is really going on, to such an extent that they believe they are still in control of what goes on in their businesses, yet the power has been to an extent wrested from them and the business runs its own course. In the BPO industry, this is often seen when the delivery of customer service is unrecognisable from that which is promised during the ITT and pitch stages of a new business proposal. It happens purely and simply because these organisations lead on the force of personality rather than structured processes and procedures that can be delivered in practice.

In essence, it should not matter who the leader of an organisation is as long as they can effectively show the way that the organisation should proceed in accordance with an established modus operandi. That way of operating needs to be clearly established and documented and be proven to work in a valid and reliable way. When I talk about validity and reliability, I mean that the process delivers what it purports to deliver and will do so time and time again, once repeated. This is in effect borrowing principles from scientific testing, which is not a bad point of departure if, as an organisation, you are hoping to provide consistency and high levels of quality in relation to your outputs.

From my experience in the contact centre industry, there are always big words, principles, and rhetoric. Yet in practice, the actual quality of the service provided by employees is often unregulated and decided by those who interact at the customer interface, based on what they think works or very often what they feel like doing at that point in time.

The example with drinks vouchers mirrored precisely what would happen day in, and day out with the provision of services to clients: a statement for a fact with no contextual planning or depth of thought into how things might play out in practice.

Now there was a huge uproar in the aftermath of that incident which was termed at the time as 'theft' or at the very least fraudulent activity and yet no one stopped to look at the root cause of the incident. Now I am not saying that those who took the dishonest approach to duplicating vouchers without authority should be excused. And yet such is the power of the personalities involved at the head of some of these organisations that no one sought to understand that this example was reflective of a fundamental and core issue at the heart of that business. In the same way that nobody wanted to flag up the risks before the party. The acolytes are so wedded to their positions within the inner circles that they would not date to upset the apple cart with a contrary suggestion or comment. They simply follow blindly and completely lose sight of the reality that even great individuals have knowledge gaps and miss things.

This is furthermore not to say that businesses do not survive with charismatic and enigmatic figures at the head of the organisation. This is clearly the case with many high-profile businesses in the UK. However, those still have fundamentally solid processes and procedures which would operate irrespective of who was at the helm. The point about BPOs is that they are smoke and mirrors from top to bottom. The rigour associated with processes is in document form only. In fact, in many cases, the documentation is neither referred to nor used in practice. It is all about marketing collateral – documentation that supports the notion that something meaningful exists without anybody living this in practice. And it is held together by the presence of strong individuals who can carry the business forward on the strength of their personalities and their charisma.

At the time I wondered how long that business would continue to function effectively. When I say effectively, I don't mean as one might expect a successful organisation to work, in terms of tangibly excellent results of a high standard. I am actually referring to effectiveness which simply means that the business would not crash and burn sooner rather than later. It didn't last too long.

Often it is the case that these BPOs are sold sooner or later, often because at the time they had managed to retain a sufficiently impressive client list that immediately provided credibility for any organisation taking it on. Typically, the new parent company will be an even bigger and growing contact centre outsourcer which will actually run on a petty similar basis.

And so, the story will continue albeit with different actors but approximately the same type of storyline. Once that business takeover is completed, it will be clear that the incoming board will have their own big personalities and invariably there will be a new *grand fromage* at the helm.

§

On occasions, the *CEO* might be somebody who had bought into the business, so while nowhere near as knowledgeable as others, they have by virtue of their ownership and their own band of glorifying sycophants, an even firmer grip of control on the organisation.

One example I remember would certainly not have indulged in the printing of drinks vouchers, because he was not one who was given to parties for his staff whatsoever. Some leaders are outgoing and gregarious, while others have a presence within the organisation which is practically non-existent. With this guy, it was a strange situation as it was almost as if the organisation wanted to create not a cult leader but a legend or a myth. Like a rather distant headmaster whose power and strength you could feel through the awe in which others spoke of him or when they referred to his legendary rantings when the P&L was £50 shorter than forecast.

In some ways, it seemed like his strategy was to create a God-like persona which would be worshipped from a distance by people who never truly got to know who he was and could not therefore examine exactly what he did or perhaps more appropriately what he did not do.

In many respects, I actually preferred other regimes where at least there was the semblance of leadership even if they were at times detached from any substantial rationales or connection to real-life delivery. With this regime, it was a void where we almost imagined that we had a strong leader without being able to substantiate that ourselves through any experience or evidence that anything was actually happening from a leadership perspective.

In fact, it was never known during anybody's tenure that the *CEO*, as he was then termed, addressed the management team in terms of any motivational or inspirational message. The only evidence that he really existed came through a handful of tersely scripted emails that highlighted deficiencies in the financial forecast, usually in the form of a rant at a specified individual with the rest of the company copied in. However, on two occasions he did attend client meetings where each time he told exactly the same story about a service he had set up for another client that was entirely irrelevant to the project we were delivering. At the second meeting during a comfort break, one of the senior clients asked one of the team:

'Who's that old guy again?'.

I suppose these meetings did strike everyone as telling as this was somebody who continued to dine out on previous successes but did not feel it necessary to break new ground and continue to be re-engaged and drive innovations within his business. In all my dealings with clients, I always got a strong impression that progress and breaking new ground was the unrelenting pressure that was driving senior people on and on. The implication of this was that if they fell behind the eight-ball, their own positions would be in jeopardy and moreover, that they would not themselves merit the leadership roles that they had. In this instance, the head honcho simply did not feel the pressure himself, because he had such an unassailable position. He part-owned the company, albeit with a minor shareholding approximating the usual management buy-out percentage, and he surrounded himself with others who allowed themselves to be downtrodden without riposte, in exchange for comfortable salaries.

It was hardly in the mould of Jobs who would hire good people to tell him what to do and therefore keep driving the company forward. This was somebody who saw the role of Chief Executive as a position of unquestioned authority to whom it would have been a serious affront to have been questioned, let alone challenged. I suppose that from a position where he could not be challenged, it made sense not to put himself on offer as his previous incumbent had done, so therefore the lowest possible profile buttressed his position as absolutely safe. And on a quarter of a mil per annum, who could blame him?

Essentially, BPO Directors live and breathe *what they understand to be* their work out of desperation to survive but don't understand what makes their people tick. They fail to appreciate that in a BPO there will be a diverse range of motivations. Not everybody gives the slightest shit about being the No1 provider of CRM solutions or the like. Pushing on relentlessly to get 'buy-in' from everybody is just pissing in the wind, in the same way that steamrollering people is where you expect everyone to be enthralled by your cult of personality or your naked aggression.

Real *engagement* derives from understanding and respect at the grassroots – individual contracts between staff and their managers where everybody benefits. The wholesale misguidedness shows how the power of the cult becomes all-consuming and how directors break the number one rule – *don't get high on your own supply.*

8 – Something for Everyone

'I think of myself as a journeyman actress. I will attempt almost anything that I think that I can bring off. It could be almost anything'.

(Angela Lansbury)

I sometimes have a quick look through LinkedIn profiles, just to see what people have done in their careers and how people's careers have developed. And sometimes there are some very impressive CVs that are outlined within those profiles. You see how people have moved up through the ranks from, for example, being an *Account Executive*, moving up to *Account Manager* then *Account Director*, and then finally the *Head of Client Services*.

You can see their career progression and you can understand that somebody, particularly if they've worked for one or maybe two organisations, has successfully built something that is long-lasting and is recognised by their employer or their employers as worthwhile. From that, you can understand that they've been entrusted with more senior roles and thus, their career has developed. It has a credibility about it. You can read it through and immediately understand that there is somebody who has achieved something.

And there are certainly people within the BPOs with which I am familiar who can demonstrate similar CVs. Often these will be people who started at the very bottom of the career ladder, possibly as *Customer Service Representatives* answering queries over the phone who then progress to *Team Leader*, then *Operations Manager* and sometimes even as far as *Site Director* or *Operations Director*. Others, of course, establish a nice niche position in the business, particularly in relation to those who work for example in technical support roles where upwardly linear promotion is not necessarily the most appropriate direction for career development. This is because they might be technical experts who actually develop by gaining broader knowledge at the same level rather than taking on higher management or administrative responsibilities. Both types of examples are probably fairly indicative of examples that you could pluck from any organisation, in any field.

However, what was exceedingly common in the BPO world were people who would move from company to company in the same roles, spending limited time in each position – often one year to 18 months – and then moving on to a different business. It would not be uncommon for an individual to have worked for five or six of the main competing outsourced organisations within a 7 to 8-year period, often fulfilling a broadly similar role in each one.

Sometimes they would move to marginally more senior roles as they went from organisation to organisation, and in doing so, would create a whole career path and effectively gain several promotions without actually ever having been in any one company for long enough to have achieved anything. It is one huge, networked game of musical chairs and there is a whole host of folks who are paranoid about the music coming to an end in their own organisation with the risk that they would be shortly out of the game. You get people flying about like hand grenades with the pin pulled. It is desperate stuff and when one of them is on the slide, you can watch their frantic degeneration.

The common roles where you would tend to see the practitioners of musical chairs were typically going to be in New Business Development, Client Services and Operations. Now with Operations, I can kind of understand that this would not present an individual with too many conflicts to resolve. After all, in operational delivery, your responsibility is to effectively deliver the solution that has been decided by your organisation with your respective client. It is about ensuring that *b* follows *a* and that *a* and *b* are delivered on time and to specification. With Client Services positions, clients change all the time so new relationships need to be nurtured and built so even if you do stay in the same role for the same company, the chances are that there is going to be a considerable amount of change in what you may do on a day-to-day basis.

But the New Business Development – and maybe this is where I am slightly naive – where you are promoting and selling something with a passion and belief that you are providing the client with the best in breed, I never could understand how people could go from one company to another and effortlessly switch from saying that one was the best and then the following month be suggesting that another organisation was the best for the same reasons. It seems like a form of hypocrisy that I do not believe I could carry through and yet that is the area where there is the most turnover and the shortest periods of service. While I look at new businesspeople in a later chapter, these were without doubt the individuals who had the lowest moral fibre of any within what I came to consider to be the least morally upstanding (so-called) industry imaginable.

I mentioned my naivety and, as I grew more familiar with the tactics, perspectives, and standpoints of salespeople, I realised that it is an area of operation where truth, integrity and transparency have no place.

Put simply, it is an environment where the greater propensity for creativity in description and promise garner the greatest currency and where the sizzle is truly seen to be more substantial than the steak itself. The other area where there is a fantastically high turnover is in the more senior levels of Operations and Client Services. This is where you are most likely, apart from the New Business Development teams, to see the greatest number of journeymen.

§

Now I quite like the term 'Journeyman' which is effectively a skilled worker who is considered competent in their role but has not attained the status of a master craftsman. In former times journeymen were paid on a daily basis, the term *journée* deriving from the French term for a whole or complete day. A journeyman would be entitled to charge for each full day's work and would be employed by another person, such as a master craftsman but crucially could not employ others.

In mediaeval Germany, a wandering journeyman (*Wandergeselle*) would move from one area to another in order to build on his experience and this was thought to be important training and development for one who wished to be considered a master craftsman of the future. In many respects, this is how the wandering employees of outsourced contact centre operations roll out their careers.

They spend short amounts of time at each organisation, gaining snippets of knowledge and back-story to facilitate their next move, and they move from company to company, leaving just before they are either found out or called into question for having delivered very little in their incumbent role. Unfortunately for the organisations concerned, the journeyman analogy does not remain true to history within this context. This is because in its historical application, the journeyman was held accountable for their work and guidelines were put in place to ensure that responsible tradesmen were in operation. It was an early form of quality control.

Sadly, in the BPO world, such quality controls are non-existent. The only saving grace for companies is to rely on informal networks of people within the industry or hope that the previous organisation in which an individual has worked provide a more detailed reference other than the standard references that the majority in fact do supply. There are of course legal ramifications around providing more detailed accounts of a person's previous employment which is why standard references are now the favoured approach. They provide absolute protection in the event of possible legal action which should be avoided on the basis that a civil court relies only on a balance of probabilities i.e. the likelihood that one story is more probable than another. Furthermore, significant costs are incurred, not just by those who necessarily lose cases but also by those who have to fight them in the first instance.

Interestingly the informal network is often quite effective in identifying these journeymen and then heading them off at the pass before they are successfully employed (or unsuccessfully as is often the case for the new company concerned). What you will find with some of the more senior roles is that once journeymen have exhausted some of their immediate opportunities within the UK, they may seek placement abroad in the offshoring sector, such as in India or South Africa where they will not be as well-known and where there is less chance that they will be exposed. This then gives them the opportunity to reinvent themselves and also to add the seemingly prestigious section to their CV which indicates that their expertise has been desired and required in one of the largest growth areas in Anglophone or former Commonwealth industries. This is particularly the case in India.

However, these opportunities abroad are often not readily available, so sometimes you may glance at a journeyman's CV on LinkedIn and see the tell-tale signs that they are struggling to get back into employment.

These are often evident through job entries that will say things like, *'I am currently enjoying a sabbatical and travelling'* (this can be read as, *'currently unemployed or unemployable'*), which are then later updated to state, *'I am now turning my thoughts towards my next challenge'* (this is shorthand for *'I'm currently running short of money, and I desperately need a new job'*).

Typically, after a period of a year possibly 18 months, the person concerned will return to the UK, having successfully used their *offshore* experience as collateral in securing a new job base closer to home.

What this all does amount to, however, is that whole careers are built on the basis of a continuing journey where the journey itself is the means and the end. It is hard to imagine another industry where this could actually be possible.

Of course, people do move from role to role, and some can point to CVs of successful individuals who perhaps in the course of a lifetime may have held twenty or twenty-five different positions. But it is the norm in those circumstances that individuals can at least point to along the way significant points of achievement things that they have created, things that they have developed or innovations they have put in place. But with outsourced contact centres, actual achievement is not required.

These whole journeys can be individual periods of money for old rope that are just repeated over and over and over again as the individual concerned hops from one company to another. And all that actual 'doing' is simply business as usual that involves very little engagement and very little input because the actual delivery work is being done by the same staff who have perhaps been there over a period of time.

When you think about it, it is hardly surprising that a tenure of 12 months in an organisation is actually insufficient to effect real change. Take for example the implementation of a new piece of technology. This would need to be conceptualised, investigated, supplier presentations evaluated, proposals drawn up and cost-benefit analysis reviewed internally and signed off with clients prior to any implementation. The solution would then need to be put in place and then be operational for a period of time before it could have been deemed to have been a success.

Consider that such an innovation is unlikely to be carried forward by any individual within the first 3 to 6 months of their tenure, and it is not difficult to see why such major changes that would lead to a significant service innovation are rarely undertaken by people with such brief times in situ. Now that's not to say that every innovation needs to be technological, nor that it would necessarily take as long as I have outlined here.

But for major changes of organisational development or operational delivery, you are talking many months, as opposed to a couple of weeks and therefore a quick fix. And you need to understand that senior operational staff are not put in place simply to come up with quick fixes. They are hired to make significant ground-breaking changes. The quick fixes are deemed to be business-as-usual operational matters that could be introduced and implemented effortlessly by existing staff at junior- and middle-management levels.

Of course, when these journeymen are appointed, it is the source of much concern among those occupying middle-management positions but not in the way that it is a case of despondency, but the overriding sense is one of 'here we go again'.

I used to wonder whether or not there was perhaps an introductory handbook for the journeyman as the opening gambit always seemed to be of a particular type. The blanket introductory email is usually one such approach that follows a period of a week or so of distant observation and usually coincides with a concern that has been raised by a more senior director, which the journeyman feels he must jump on very quickly in order to avoid any suspicions that he himself is not up to the job.

§

I remember being shown an email that came out beginning with the sentence:

> 'Dear team, and I use the term team because no one person is important enough or competent enough to be able to perform as an individual when in organisations only the team counts. Remember there is no 'I', in team...'

Yada, yada, yada, etc, ad nauseam.

And that I recall was in response to the fact that a forecast had not been updated in time and no doubt the new incumbent had received a not-so-insignificant flea in his shell-like.

Naturally, the impact of these such missives is entirely contrary to the intention on the part of the sender. In brief, in the opinion of the recipients, the new boss here had identified himself as someone with few leadership skills, no real understanding of the organisational network and how that functioned and somebody with a significant credibility gap.

Needless to say, this set the tone for his tenure, and he was largely mocked for his interventions when he was mentioned, the focus of conversation quickly shifting to his lack of contribution to the business and incredulity at his ability to evade dismissal.

However, one skill that he did possess that was largely underestimated, was his consummate and first-class skill set of sycophancy that allowed him to slither into the good books of those at the higher echelons and, almost inconceivably, further advancement. His ultimate undoing was the now familiar approach of such individuals who are focused on a desire to surround themselves with former colleagues who were trusted to propagate the myth of superiority that such individuals cannot establish through their own accomplishments. While he filled a number of positions with wholly ineffective personnel who simply sat in their respective offices surfing the Internet for ideas on how to do the essential elements of their newly found positions, he brought in a former colleague and ahem, close friend, to oversee a key, business-critical area. This was a fundamental error of judgement even for the most adept of Machiavellian manoeuvres as in doing so and creating a further level of incompetence, he lost a direct connection with those who actually knew how to do the job.

As some of the individuals who were capable of delivering at ground level had been outraged at being overlooked for promotion, they effectively withheld cooperation at those subtle but telling moments and allowed both the new hire and the consummate journeyman to fall into some deep holes. In this instance, both individuals were bombed out spectacularly after some glaring omissions threw the spotlight on their gross negligence and lack of supervision.

It was a clear example of how those who pretend and create the illusion of ability always need to offer a trade-off to those who have a close link with effective service delivery. The mistake made by this individual was that he effectively believed his own hype. In convincing the leadership team that he warranted a promotion, he should have promoted a competent member of staff into his current role to oversee such a key position so that he could at least be confident that a capable hand was on the steering wheel. In bringing an outsider who was manifestly incompetent into that position, he effectively lost control and left himself open to be attacked on the basis of service failure. He didn't last long.

He did however arrange a leaving do which one of his team joyfully requested he did via *Skype*.

One of the interesting things of course about these journeymen is that they have very little in terms of substantial career achievements and this is relatively easy to sniff out from the outset. When you encounter a competent senior manager, they usually will in the course of an introductory meeting in the early days talk about what you do on a day-to-day basis and how that might compare with some of the things that they've achieved in the course of their careers. This will be typically couched in terms of commercial or financial success, operational delivery, or relationship management. For a senior figure in operational management, any or all of these examples would be likely to feature during the initial meeting.

§

One journeyman I met in the course of my career was a striking example when none of those such examples were mentioned. This is because as a journeyman, he had not actually achieved anything in the course of his career or at least anything that was tangibly impressive that would have served as a positive role model CV during those initial conversations, during which the senior manager is attempting to break the ice but also to position themselves as somebody who can provide effective leadership. As I recall the opening statement, I think, concerned some of the famous people that he knew in Newcastle, and he then went on to explain how he was seen as a personal adviser to the Robson family and how he had been a pallbearer at Sir Bobby Robson's funeral.

Ok now, step back from the Absinthe...

Now of course you never know who people know and I am not saying that this was an evidently deliberate terminological inexactitude. The really bizarre point about this chap was that he was claiming that he was a personal adviser to the family. This kind of suggested that he had some particular talent like he was a qualified Solicitor or a financial adviser perhaps. But he made no attempt to explain in what capacity he was a personal adviser, just that he was one. However, freakish that that may be in itself, it really is difficult to understand why you would bring up such a subject when introducing yourself as a new senior manager. It just didn't make sense. I was almost expecting him in the next instance to talk about the time when he had perhaps met Madonna or maybe even the piano player from Sparks when he referred to a time that he had played Alex Higgins at Snooker. I think this may have been in response to an earlier question about my own hobbies and interests.

Consider that for a moment though and it may shed some light on the personality of this particular journeyman and the motivations for such a person when meeting a colleague for the first time. As somebody who should be setting a business-related example and setting out their credentials, there was very little if any work-related content at all in what he had been saying. Instead, he had made a number of comments which in my opinion were rather far-fetched about his involvement with a footballing icon and then, in response to a question about me where I had expressed an interest in snooker, he had steered the conversation to how he knew Alex Higgins and had played him at the very same game.

Unfortunately, this conversation followed on from the earlier exchange around football when he talked about the World Cup in France in 1998, I think which may have included him being present at the Final in Paris and a personal quest of Sir Bobby who apparently had guest lectured on one of his MBA modules at the University of Liverpool, or the like.

Fortunately, he did not make any claims to have played in the match himself which given the direction of the conversation would actually have not come as a surprise to me, had he done so.

He proceeded to outline how he had played Higgins in London several months after the World Cup when he had travelled to London to watch England versus Luxembourg in a World Cup Qualifier. At the time it seemed like there was this whole collection of facts and information compressed into one story that was all seemingly designed to impress me – and at that moment I had no concrete evidence with which to refute his story, nor did I have any real inclination to do so.

However, after that discussion, I did allow myself a little background reading, when I established that the match against Luxembourg in October 1998 or to be precise 14 October 1998 had actually taken place in Luxembourg and not in London. I further managed to ascertain that Alex Higgins, while alive and kicking at that point, had been diagnosed with throat cancer earlier that year and had undergone major throat surgery on – quelle surprise – 13 October 1998.

So, while my esteemed colleague quite clearly could not have attended an England international vs Luxembourg in London on that date, it was also very unlikely that Alex Higgins would have been present in London and up and about on the day following a major cancer operation. Moreover, knowing the reputation and persona of Mr Higgins, it is unlikely he would have been partaking in casual snooker matches with random individuals unless a considerable amount of money in the form of a side bet was on offer.

The jury is however still out on the Liverpool lecture.

I suppose on reflection, I felt sorry that somebody at this level of seniority felt that they had so little in the toolbox in order to stimulate a positive working relationship with somebody in a subordinate position who might have been motivated and excited at the prospect of working with a professional who had achieved so much in his career up to now.

In a sense I pitied him, and it was all I could do even before I had evidence that his story appeared to be a tissue of falsehoods, to keep a straight face as the situation he had described to me was such an unlikely combination of circumstances.

But on what planet would a person genuinely believe that such a story would be convincing or even necessary? For even if the story about Higgins and the England match were true and that this person had been a close confidant of the Robson family and been a pallbearer at his funeral, why would that impress me as an operational manager in a contact centre?

Why would I even find that relevant or worthy of respect or admiration?

Needless to say, similar interactions with other colleagues rather set the tone for ongoing relationships with him as people found they had very little if any respect for anything that the man said from that point onwards. It just seemed to me that the most important thing for him was that he was the star of the show and that he had to be loved on the basis that he was the star rather than on the basis of what he had actually delivered and what he would actually deliver. This fell markedly short of what I expected in terms of leadership but sadly was on a parallel with almost everything I had seen in the preceding decades in this so-called industry. Individuals in positions of authority were entrusted with leading large organisations, and the basis of everything was founded on smoke mirrors and a vacuum of tangible facts.

In many ways, the individual here epitomised the very industry in which we were involved. So perhaps any implied criticisms from me in relation to the way he approached our meeting and indeed his role within the organisation are harsh. Perhaps the irony is that I was simply an outsider with expectations at a particular level and yet all of the other actors in the performance are fully aware that the play is fictitious and that their own parts are part of the illusion. But the incredible point about this is that such individuals can, by hopping from position to position and from organisation to organisation carve out the semblance of a career that within this industry holds value.

If anything defines the validity of an organization or of an industry, it is the quality of the people who work within it. And a large number of these people – these journeymen – when you scratch just below the surface, have no credentials other than a chronology of appointments.

Having described the way in which such journeymen are able to create this series of opportunities where the means actually become the end, you may wonder why they are never truly exposed in all their nefarious glory. Firstly, for reasons that I have already explained, the basis of the existence of these businesses is predicated on a false promise to clients. Clients outsource business often because it is the detritus of their service or the unwanted effects of their core activities. It may also be a question of activities that are too expensive to run in-house or have intermittent peaks and troughs throughout the year so that they are no longer cost-effective to run with a certain baseline of in-house staff.

Therefore, you can outsource the services so that they can be turned on and off when required with the risk of redeploying staff held firmly by the outsourced agency. However, when putting this work out to tender, of course, the outsourcing clients will demand a response to that tender that pays sufficient focus on for example, quality, high standards, and service delivery excellence.

In reality, though, they know very well that the outsourced agencies will be cutting corners and will be doing just enough to keep the boat afloat. After all, the clients can see very clearly just by a quick search on the Internet for advertised jobs that the outsourced agencies are paying very often the minimum wage. Clearly, when you pay minimum wage, you are not going to be attracting the highest calibre of employees.

Accordingly, the services delivered by those employees are not going to be of the highest order. It does not take a genius to make these connections and to understand that there is a certain double standard in operation. It is almost as if people who make the decision to outsource their service are happy to be told that the service is great, so they can tick the box for their shareholders and hope that the inevitable issues will simply not surface.

I liken it to a magician's performance when you attend the show with the knowledge that you are about to be deceived.

You know that what you are seeing is not really magic, but you are happy to enjoy the performance as long as the illusion is sufficiently adept that you are unable to unravel it and truly know its secrets. Of course, it cannot be too slick – because then it will really look like real magic which of course we all know cannot be real.

It is a subtle technique, but BPOs carry it off masterfully.

Therefore, as far as the senior management team within the outsourced agencies is concerned, they are content to allow the illusion – often a little rough around the edges – to continue to be perpetuated. You are therefore judged on your ability to maintain the illusion rather than on your ability to deliver excellent service. This is exactly the same approach taken at all levels in the organisation which is why 121s and performance appraisals are not what they seem.

On the face of it, actual performance and excellence are measured, and all documentation will reflect this. However, in practice, the actual conversations are discussed, and the roles performed by individuals will almost certainly not reflect their formal job descriptions and their contracts of employment.

§

Which brings us back to the question of why these individuals are never exposed. The short answer is that nobody wants to expose them. As long as the illusion is being created and maintained, they are doing what is required of them. The real issues arise when less senior members of staff who naïvely believe that they should be delivering services of high quality for their clients start to query the effectiveness and the abilities of the journeymen who are purportedly leading service delivery.

And those individuals constitute a significant risk to the outsourced agency and its senior management team. One of the things that is very clear about the people who enter employment in contact centre agencies is that while they may be vulnerable, sometimes at difficult stages in their personal lives or sometimes even desperate for immediate funds and a job that pays any salary, they may also be people who have undertaken a university education who are well-versed in writing arguments and presenting cases on particular subjects. And it is those people who are likely to be able to put a case forward that could – if it went further – create significant amounts of noise client-side or at a potential employment tribunal.

Now while there may be things that the journeymen are not very capable of doing organisational politics is not one.

They are extremely adept at managing perceptions and surviving. After all, that is the essence of what they do – the raison d'être of the journeymen is to create an illusion that persists long enough to establish a justification for their existence. So as soon as they are aware of a whiff of challenge to their position, they will immediately set about ensuring that the threat is neutralised.

§

One of the approaches they will take is to embark on a process of *contexting*.

Now *contexting* is about sowing the seeds and creating a new back-story that sufficiently explains somebody's discontent if there is a risk of a strong performer leaving. It is the preparation of the story or the groundwork required to manage any wider implications of the fallout with an employee who has latched on to the truth behind the lack of capability of somebody in seniority.

If a good person quits, people ask questions. If they then start to question the journeyman's capability, that is the beginning of a shitstorm that will need to be avoided.

This is particularly important where the person who raises the concern is actually somebody who is well thought of by the leadership team in question or the most senior managers within an organisation. For the journeyman this provides them with a challenge to overcome as they cannot readily manage a high-performing employee out of the business in the usually favoured way – that is to say, their performance is picked apart, capability gaps are established and then under the threat of possible capability or disciplinary hearings, the person concerned is encouraged albeit indirectly to resign with the promise of a positive reference.

In the case of a high-performing employee, particularly one where the journeyman himself may not have sufficient technical knowledge in order to establish a gap in performance, it is important to establish the perception of their dissatisfaction with the company, perhaps with development opportunities so that when that employee does ultimately leave, the more senior members of the management team will not question this as a matter for further investigation. They will accept it as a naturally occurring consequence of somebody's career progression.

At the same time, the journeyman may have a conversation with the individual concerned that differs significantly from the content of what they report to the senior managers. This may be more direct, possibly testing the waters with some high-level question marks on capability, perhaps initially to probe the resolve of the individual concerned. An alternative method may perhaps centre on absenteeism or timekeeping as these may be factors that could be more objectively measured and established to a third party.

However, in the case of high-performing individuals, these are unlikely to be realistic levers to pull and, in any event, higher-performing managers in the operational sphere, for example, are more likely to have a clearer view of what will stand up and are likely to resist. At this point the tactics are likely to shift and focus on the less-than-productive relationship between the two and the possibility of a compromise agreement may be explored. If this compromise agreement is attractive, it is likely that the person raising concerns about the journeyman's performance may well cut their losses and leave with a substantial sum in their pocket.

This may be seen as a preferable alternative to continuing to work under circumstances that they find on many levels insupportable. The compromise agreement is a favoured tool of the journeyman because it will likely contain a clause that precludes any 'bad-mouthing' which guarantees the silence of the individual concerned. It is in brief a payoff for the individual who by then in any event is jaded and disillusioned by the dysfunctional nature of the outsourcing agency but a payoff that can be made by the journeyman under the journeyman's terms and at no cost to the journeyman himself.

In my long and varied career, I have lost count of the number of compromise agreements that have been made with individuals who have simply resigned from their positions – put into place by more senior line managers who are fearful of being exposed during an exit interview or in the course of a grievance that is raised after the individual has left the organisation. Until I had worked in outsourcing agencies, I had never experienced compromise agreements being made in response to simple and straightforward resignations. This is primarily because they would have no reason to be made or entered into in these circumstances.

One final point on *contexting* is how it is frequently paired with the concept of *inevitability*. Once the target leaves the business, it will be summarised as *inevitable*. No blame, no further investigation – it all gets put to bed there and then.

This tactic is also used by Account Managers when relationships start looking ropey owing to their inactivity or negligence. The context of pressure on costs is created and played back to the senior team. Or of a new director client-side who had always previously worked with a competitor.

Then the business is lost, and the conclusion is:

'The work was taken in-house for cost reasons'. Inevitable. Tick.

'X director wanted a change and brought in a team he'd worked with for many years'. Inevitable. Tick.

'White losses' as they are termed. Nobody gets shot. However, in BPOs, it is never just plain and simple black and white. White is sometimes Black.

I recall one piece of inevitably lost business (taken in-house, ahem) when the *Account Director* had not visited the client in 11 months. So never sat down with the client at all during their tenure. Inevitable, of course, because the cretin managing the account had contexted that the client had had 'budgetary challenges'.

Another was when the client talked about moving part of the service in-house, and a senior manager then went to discuss how we might support the transition rather than making the case for outsourcing. Again, inevitable as the context set out had been that the strategy for outsourcing was never going to be long-term. In fact, it was because the senior manager concerned was so detached from the work itself, he just could not be arsed to get his head around the main arguments.

Surely it is just easier for these journeymen to actually do the job and be successful? Stupefying is it not?

But we move on.

When you take into account the high level of salary paid to some of these journeymen in senior positions, plus the cost of paying off other members of staff who leave, plus the cost of replacing those leavers, surely somebody at board level in the BPOs would take a step back and ask themselves the question of whether this is really worth it? But perhaps that's the problem – maybe they do, and their conclusion is when looking at the bottom line that the numbers still continue to stack up.

Maybe they are fearful of joining the ranks of the elite organisations that thrive on quality, service delivery and customer excellence and perhaps they are afraid that they will be threatened by bringing in truly competent and exceptional professionals who will challenge them and who will aspire to take their own board level positions?

As we have seen at all levels in BPOs, it is not about what you deliver, is about how you protect your position whilst still creating the illusion and hopefully still delivering the financial bottom line that will prevent further questions asked and more in-depth investigations being made. It is a travesty that these businesses do just enough on their performances regarding what is expected rather than truly excelling and being the best that they can be.

Perhaps that is why the journeymen are the most viable, disposable assets for the job.

9 – Snake Oil and Holy Water

The BPO consultancy primary principle:

The volume of serious issues requiring a resolution within a BPO shall correspond directly to the availability of consultants and available budgets for consultancy.

It is observed almost religiously.

Well, having talked about journeymen and covered the obviously serpentine nature in which they slide from company to company and integrate themselves into the fabric of company structures, I felt like I was almost doing a disservice to contact centre consultants by not giving them pride of place in the hall of fame of outsourcing miscreants.

I have to say that in my lengthy and often undistinguished career, I have yet to meet a consultant worthy of a fraction of the fee they were charging. In fact, the justification for contact centre consultants is so absurd, it is difficult to know where to start with any discussion on them. I first encountered them in the mid-1990s when client organisations had very little understanding of the core skillsets and expertise required to run an effective contact centre operation.

So, at that time there was an opening in the markets for individuals who had previously worked their way up through the middle to senior management ranks in organisations that provided contact centre services – sometimes these were in-house operations and sometimes outsourcers themselves.

At that time most of these individuals had reached the end of the line in the development of their own careers and of course in order to gain credibility with an *Operations Director* or *Managing Director* of the client organisation who may seek to employ additional help, you are more likely to have the right level of credibility with them if you have operated at a similar level in your own career. So already it is probably a safe bet that those who have entered the world of contact centre consultancy have ordinarily gone as far as they can go.

As a brief aside, some work less as consulting consultants and more as vendor managers. These can be potentially tricky to handle, as, by definition, they are employed for their tacit knowledge of outsources that the client organisation does not ordinarily possess. They are also employed only when the client is already suspicious that they are being shafted.

Which of course, they are – by the BPO and the consultant. Think about it – the consultant is not going to expose the BPO because it will be cutting off the oxygen of their own billings. You therefore need to establish a common ground, identify the right kind of inoffensive crumbs that can be tossed the client's way so that they remain confident that the consultant is all over it, *big up* the consultant in front of the client – and carry on milking it. *If you can't beat 'em, join 'em* – and that cuts both ways.

But back to the ones who are actually claiming to 'consult'. In some cases, they have reached the end of the line as journeymen and are enticed by the prospect of self-employed status, tax benefits, and the feast-and-famine balance of high day rates versus free time. For BPOs, the benefits of bringing in comparatively expensive consultants are that you can extricate yourself from previous bad decisions and have a ready-made patsy to shoulder the blame and the inevitable fightback from disgruntled employees who will be markedly dissatisfied with the introduction of somebody who will do your dirty work for you.

Note that I do not criticise the use of professional services consultants, who are used extensively by prestigious blue-chip organisations as a means of injecting immediate and specialised expertise in order to support existing teams and ongoing operational delivery. What I am most concerned with are the consultants who seem to have created their own niche industry within the contact centre world. These are frequently people who are neither professionally qualified as consultants nor have an extensive range of the real issues involved in delivery within contact centre environments.

Of course, I don't make reference to specialised knowledge of the contact centre industry, because in my view that is the most ridiculous concept that seems to gain the most inordinate amount of airtime. The notion that there is a contact centre industry is preposterous in itself. Therefore, to believe that there is any credibility in somebody who positions themselves as an expert in such a non-industry is something that any credible professional or commentator would find too outrageous for words. It aggravates the most mellow among us to pre-spree anxiety levels.

However, in the contact centre circus that seems to have sprung up, there is no shortage of people who are willing to step into such a position and to promote themselves as *contact centre consultants*.

And just in case you thought that this murky sector could not sink to a more pitiful level, I am sorry to say that you ain't seen nothing yet.

§

As we now have entered the twenty-first century, many of these so-called 'experts' have not even achieved divisional director level in their initial careers but have been people who have previously attained Team Leader or Operations Manager level roles and who are employed on day rates of £500-£1000 a day in order to regurgitate often outdated management principles that they acquired through leading 25 FTE over a period of two years. Oh dear, yes. It beggars belief to the still sane among us, but we are arguably all now much more acclimatised to the shift from reality that the collective contact centre clownery has taken us.

It is difficult to comprehend how some of these BPOs can justify in their own minds paying such extortionate rates for people who frankly are no better than the mid- or lower-performing people within their own organisation. In most cases, they would be better off investing in training and development for staff members who are struggling to deliver to the often-stringent objectives that they are setting. As an observer though, I have always been faintly amused by the approach that contact centre consultants take when they are introduced into an organisation. It has become cliched to a degree, but you have to admire their bare-faced cheek in continuing to churn it out to the masses.

Almost inevitably the standard first step will be to perform a *'health check'* on the operation that they have been brought in to examine. And surprise, surprise, they will never come back and say that it is just a question of some easy fixes to implement, or heaven forfend, a clean bill of health.

Now, if you are in a situation where you do not have a consultant, any operational manager worth their salt will look at a difficult situation and be able to identify what the quick wins are.

Unsurprisingly, external consultants very rarely identify any meaningful 'low-hanging fruit'. They will flag up cosmetic matters that would likely have little impact on overall productivity or service delivery. Things like setting up a team meeting and raising the issue of communication and then throwing in a few handouts with (unattributed) references to *Shannon and Weaver (1949)*, for example, or any other management model that might have a ring of validity and which will serve as an indicator of their worldly expertise.

Nothing of course, that will not already have occurred to the staff or that cannot be discovered via a quick visit to Google. In fact, the lectures would be given to a team that is – aside from the odd falling out – pretty effective in communication and under the circumstances getting along with their jobs just fine. At this point it is worth considering the second rule of external consultancy – that is:

> *The number of problems that external consultants identify will directly relate to the number of months' worth of work that they need to bill you for.*

In brief, it's not about identifying problems to be solved but creating work to be done. With these shysters, the means is the end.

As an aside, they all seem to be on 'assignments', never 'contracts' – as they see themselves as secret agents parachuted in behind enemy lines. You cannot hear them say it without having to stifle a laugh. Clowns of the highest order.

Often though, the contact centre consultant is brought in for more nefarious reasons. Clearly, if the incumbent staff were deemed to be competent in their positions, there would be a need for outside help or support. I have sadly witnessed situations myself where leadership teams have brought in consultants over the head of the departmental management team in order to install the principal consultant as an interim boss. The primary objective here is to commence a war of attrition and subtle undermining and marginalization in order to make the position of the incumbent untenable and to facilitate his or her departure. I know of situations when this was coupled with the desire for a complete overhaul of operational delivery centres and led to some of the most outrageous situations I have ever heard about during my career. These included requests to tape colleagues so that their dissent to the change could be captured and used in disciplinary proceedings.

Here is a typical scenario. These consultants look to curry favour with some of the junior members of staff with the promise that they will receive promotions when the new order is established. In most organisations, in spite of attempts to keep such things under wraps, people inevitably talk. It is therefore not long before fragments of the consultants' plans are out in the open. This naturally leads to considerable amounts of friction within the existing management team and a split of loyalties. After a while, it becomes apparent that the consultants' plans are being stymied by resistance among the middle and senior management team. This leads to the inevitable meeting with the head honcho who clearly establishes that the lead consultant will now be the senior point of contact for all members of staff within the operational team. A clear indication to everyone that the position of their head of department is under direct threat. And from then it is downhill all the way.

It is difficult to imagine how anybody could believe that the department of hundreds of people which will have been sustained for a number of years on the basis of close cooperation, constructive relationships, and in many cases friendships, could be maintained by the almost insidious introduction of somebody who clearly lacks basic awareness of interpersonal human psychology and believes that the most appropriate way to effect change is in and establishing underhand and fundamentally unethical practices. But never in these places should you assume that common sense, science, or ethics might even feature strongly, let alone prevail.

It becomes a war of attrition with the view of the new Junta that resistance is being applied simply because people are 'afraid of change'. This is a common weapon that consultants use in such circumstances as a rationale for imposing whatever crazy and illogical batshit schemes they believe are central to the success of their project.

As anybody will tell you, when working in a BPO, *'resistance to change'* is one of the deadliest sins that can be imagined. It paints the picture that people are stuck in the past unwilling to progress and in effect are dead wood. People who are labelled 'adverse to change' are effectively checking into the departure lounge.

And so, it comes to pass. Whole operations are plunged headlong into a series of operational measures and project streams derived from the almost comical 'health checks' that these operational centres have to undertake. I liken it to visiting your GP with a sore throat and being booked in for open heart surgery, a double hip replacement, and a course of chemotherapy.

During one borderline bonkers consultofrenzy I witnessed, one of the highlights of the health check diagnosis was that the operational centre was struggling with efficiency (well, name me one where is this not an ongoing point of focus?). It was therefore decided to undertake a wholesale programme of cross-training. At the time, a number of core skills were cross-trained within the delivery centre which of course made sense in terms of increasing efficiency.

As any manager worth his salt would tell you, while cross-training is an effective tool, you should use it sparingly so that you have effective control over the individual sections of your operation. Cross-training everybody on everything means that you in effect open the floodgates in relation to your high-volume activities making this a counter-productive exercise. You also run the risk – unless all of your teams have regular exposure to every area of activity on which they are trained – that they will not be sufficiently well practised in all areas and will lose it if they do not use it. Consequently, you do not get the return on investment of your training as the staff will in a brief time need to be re-schooled.

Needless to say, they all embarked on a full programme of cross-training which took approximately 8 weeks. In terms of cost meant that 700 or so employees needed to undergo extensive training, and they also had to bear the opportunity cost of that training time when the agents concerned were unable to undertake billable activities.

At the end of the eight-week period, it became clear that people who were trained at the beginning of the program needed to be re-trained as they had had no practice on their newly acquired skills. And so, it went on with the constant re-training and re-training of people within the teams who were never going to use the skills in practice for any extended period of time.

So, you can imagine the synchronised coffee out-spit when one of the Executive PAs copied and surreptitiously floated out a progress report that had been submitted to the board outlining the service benefits that the change project was achieving. All very cleverly crafted but a scratch below the surface and none of it was anchored on reality. But presented to a desperate board who do not understand the operational nuts and bolts of their own business and you have a group of folks who will believe what they want to believe.

After all, these are the captains of industry who would have bought the original pitch and signed up for the Imelda Marcos day rates. Once it goes so far, the Board becomes inextricably complicit, and any reviews become about supporting the story that they can then sell to their investors rather than exercising critique and changing what does not work (sound familiar?).

But putting all of that abject failure of governance aside, how is it that these consultants do what they do and are comfortable with their own decisions to follow through with these bizarre and lamentable plans?

It all sounds difficult to comprehend and to take on board that such things actually happen. But this is common practice in outsourced contact centres when consultants are used. They come in with their hackneyed methodologies, create work, and disrupt the cultural fabric of an organisation, simply to guarantee their inflated paychecks. They thrive on continuing problems, so they actually set about creating them. Even when there are bonafide issues and helpful advice is given that will at least allow their often crazy and outrageous plans to progress without the catastrophic results that were experienced with the cross-training example, that advice is always going to be ignored.

They see themselves as Gods, so accepting help themselves detracts from their infallibility. It also shortens their shelf-life at the organisation in question. They are furthermore in a position where they are accountable to nobody – their positions are of course time-limited – and at the point where they have to go, the board of directors who approved their appointment all have a vested interest in supporting the view that it was all a resounding success.

Trebles all round chaps.

§

During a memorable consultant clusterfuck, I remember being in a meeting where we were talking about how we were going to effectively deliver change within the organisation that had a strong culture and way of doing things over an extended period of time. By then the lead consultant had been joined at the organisation by one of his egregious colleagues from the same agency. No surprises here, because consultants will always try to create further opportunities for those with whom they work in partnership. It is the theory of *land and expand.*

I remember the subject of conversation was very much on how we were going to gain buy-in from people within the business for what was a quite controversial change that involved effectively changing the terms and conditions of their contracts of employment. We therefore needed to avoid having to enter into open conflict with people on whom we still needed to rely heavily for the skills and expertise in the ongoing delivery of services for major client accounts. I remember in that meeting the new consultant expressing with some disdain his view that we were 'not a democracy'.

It struck me then, as it still tickles me now, that somebody who was charged with the task of realising a major cultural change was so oblivious to the idea that landing a major piece of change is so much easier when you can achieve cooperation from all parties rather than it being a question of mandatory enforcement. And this guy was being paid £1,000 a day, a fact which he implicitly communicated to the organisation later in the project when he turned up one morning the day after redundancies were announced in a brand-new metallic lime-green Maserati, still bearing the salesman's drool, and ceremoniously parked outside the main staff entrance.

Now I have no religious bent, and I am also neither an advocate of violence nor criminality, but at that time I did say a short prayer for retribution. It was sadly not overtly granted though it was arguable from that perspective that God in his majesty had already future-proofed vengeance via creation into such hateful and obnoxious cockwombles.

Astoundingly, in the aftermath of the tenure of one consultant whose incompetence had reached unparalleled heights (or lows if you prefer), the said placebo had received hearty recommendations on his LinkedIn profile, overtly suggesting that a number of senior employees within the organisation valued the contribution he had made and praised the success of the projects that he had delivered. Of course, when you consider this within the context of how all of those other individuals operated within the business, everybody is using different perspectives and measurements of what they constitute to be a success.

§

For most of us, success is about excellence in the delivery of a high-quality service and superlative levels of client satisfaction. But to those involved in this so-called industry, it's all about survival. The positive feedback for this individual was not that he was necessarily seen as a brilliant performer within the context of what any sane person would consider to constitute success, but he was somebody who had successfully survived as they were aiming to survive themselves. Nowhere is this more clearly seen than on LinkedIn where recommendations are sought and swapped, and reputations and careers faked and bolstered.

It is this concept of survival in business that is fascinating and probably worth a study in itself. This is not of course the survival of the organisations themselves but of the people within them as they keep their personal vessels afloat. And it is all about portrayal.

After all, to be popular in prison, you don't walk around lecturing people on the importance of virtue. You do what is necessary to survive by portraying yourself as the person they need to see and most pertinently as the person you need them to see.

Perhaps the prison analogy has a certain ironic tinge. It must be painful to have to keep on surviving and deceiving, just to get by each and every day. Not able to be yourself and actually strive to achieve. You know, for a moment there I actually felt sorry for the army of consultant locusts I have encountered in my career. But no. They will deserve every moment of self-reflection where they see themselves for what they truly are.

§

The one redeeming point of the whole consultancy story of the last 30 years was a ray of sunshine that one of my former colleagues allowed forth, namely that an arch-shyster of my past had found that some of his fees had ultimately been withheld and a member of the operating board had subsequently questioned his competence to fulfil the role. In one sense it was too little too late, but at least there had been a wider recognition and perhaps a glimmer of hope for the future that he had at least in part been rumbled. It does take a senior manager to have a black belt in balls to call them out, but when it happens you at least feel that the world has not completely lost its senses.

These consultants were however not unique in their approach nor in the extent to which their incompetence was evident. I have encountered many of them over the years, and all of them have broadly the same methodologies and the same jaded outputs. But the most incredible point about them is that they are clearly people who have not got a clue about people-based businesses, and they are employed as experts by heads of organisations who themselves are equally clueless. They charge exorbitant fees, paid by senior managers who cannot equate these fees with any tangible uplift in performance within their organisations.

Now you might think that is insupportable in any business that places a premium on return on investment. But you would be wrong because the return on investment is rarely evidenced by a shift at the bottom line and amounts to any discernible improvements. Often the business concerned does see improvements in performance, but these would have happened anyway. Managers get better at their jobs and as time passes, tacit knowledge and efficiencies are created organically. When boards press the red button and call for an outsider, it is often because they do not understand their own business to understand that ups and downs can be cyclical. They therefore just need to be more supportive of their teams, perhaps start to be more engaged and work collaboratively through the challenges.

In the cases where the consultants are engaged, the ROI is linked with the protection of status, and more precisely the status quo. It is about establishing a commentary that can be passed on to other interested parties as a form of justification. In bringing in these consultants, the management board demonstrates to investors and shareholders that they are doing something. As long as the outputs provide a convincing story to tell, it did not matter whether the activities of the consultants could be directly linked to a tangible improvement on the bottom line. More often than not, the seeds of improvement have already been sown and there are already enough capable people in situ to deliver them.

Now in many respects discussing consultants is a rather painful subject for anybody who actually values the concept of quality customer service or professionalism, but it does have its positive side. Clearly, we are talking about arch-bullshitters who have created an industry within a so-called industry, based solely on bullshit itself. Were there such a thing as a Russian doll carefully sculpted from bullshit, this scenario would be it.

And I suppose those of us who have become disenchanted and disillusioned with the whole circus of outsourced call centres can gain some, if not satisfaction then, faint amusement from the fact that the BPOs who go through the pretence of providing an excellent service to clients themselves pay through the nose for the regurgitated tosh from these customer service witch doctors. They are in fact paying extortionate rates for so-called solutions that fall way short of improvements that they could themselves generate from within their own organisations. And in doing so they might even surprise themselves by delivering exceptional services to their clients and at considerably higher margins.

They may even win more business that they retain over longer periods of time. Now that would be a novelty. As for the consultants themselves, well, it may seem that they make a killing by endlessly charging money for old rope, but when they look back on their careers I am sure they will realise that their undoubted talents – now I am an optimistic man so I see the good in everybody or at least the potential – might have been better employed and possibly just as lucratively in generating something that was meaningful and which they could look back on with some pride.

On the downside, they may well be laughing all the way to the bank, having established an easy touch with no comeback other than the faint hope held in the hearts of many that the taxman may one day come calling.

§

It would however seem incomplete to write about the predators and the chancers of the contact centre world without a few lines on GDPR. How I frothed with anticipation at how this would be latched onto by the unscrupulous alphabet maestros when it was clear that this legislation would be incorporated into UK Law. The whole subject of data protection merits its own section.

GDPR was of course destined to be the new Y2K — a Haley's Comet of the charlatan economy and what luck? They did not have to wait for a full 76 years for the next one to come along!

Oh dear, oh dear. What possessed companies to pay up to £1k a day to GDPR consultants who were not legally qualified and just people who may have read the statutes thoroughly, posted at a superficial level in layman's terms from their limited perspective in LinkedIn groups and allowed their equally dubious peers to positively reinforce their self-appointed status as data law experts. You know the people — they are the ones who posted examples of customer feedback flyers in restaurants and highlighted where they believed major data-related crimes were being missed. They so flippantly discussed the weaknesses of others in trivial contexts without taking on their own failures to address complex data issues that had competent lawyers of opposing sides winning and losing cases in equal measure. And they thought that the 3-hour seminar they attended, run by an equally ill-equipped shark, would put them on an equal footing with a top Barrister with 20 years PQE? Oh yes, they did.

Now you would think that in the BPO world, where shysters dominate, such pretenders would have been unmasked. You know, set a thief to catch a thief logic. Well, yes and no. You see the BPO managers know very well that this gang were blaggards of the highest order. But they were and are also paid cheerleaders who will continue to buttress the positions of the twatterati of the hiring organisations both internally and externally and long after they have left having trousered their stipends. It is all part of the ongoing construction of cumulative means that largely only in hindsight and on reflection rarely delivers the promised ends. More journeymen who keep the plates spinning long enough so that nobody works out that nothing meaningful was ever created.

In relation to GDPR organisations would have been better off paying higher unit fees to some good lawyers who would have provided bespoke advice and support that was regulated and whose quality was guaranteed. Ultimately if you buy cheap, you buy twice – and more.

The Y2K catastrophe was a concept of the highest ingenuity. Fear was created and whipped into a sublime frenzy that captured the imagination of anyone with money to burn or money to borrow to burn. One festering tosspot into which so many companies threw in their lot. And nobody can really remember what happened on 1 January 2000.

Mainly because nothing happened. Not only did toasters, razors, TVs, and cars continue to work. So did everything else.

The only things that broke down were the relationships between millions of *CFOs* and their IT Directors. Never was this more acutely felt in the BPO fraternity with almost overnight Infrastructure Managers starting to be propelled into newly formed Head of IT roles as the six-figure ITD positions were deftly shaved from the P&L.

And what happened on 25 May 2018?

Nothing.

Apart from thousands of *CFOs* realizing that for the second time in 20 years, they had been bent forth and furiously rogered *sans lube* by the arch-charlatans.

Expect more of the same reactions once the wider *CFO* population learn that lightning really does strike in the same place and it sinks in that even more money has been shelled out for the provision of advice that is even worse than what they can currently get internally on the *DPA*. And which they generally largely ignore anyway.

Ironically, some of the truly unprofessional BPOs – we are now talking about some of the hardened criminals of the BPO world who crash through legal and ethical barriers with self-bestowed immunity – will largely fare better from the whole GDPR debacle. Their approach will likely have been that they took little action on GDPR anyway and will continue to face broadly the same risks as they do now, disregarding its requirements in the same way they always did the *DPA*!

§

You would like to think that given enough old rope; these consultants would hang themselves. Regrettably, the bottom feeders of the BPO ocean are the final safety net for the dreckballs who operate at the higher levels. The disposable distractions serve to deflect enough attention away from institutionalised failure. Incompetence that allows the whole sorry ship to keep sailing.

It is excruciating to watch them enrich themselves, but there is some relief in the awareness that many must realise they are frauds.

Imagine how much money your average BPO could make if the leadership teams were competent, and consultants were not required.

They might even be tempted to go legit.

10 – Holograms and Mirages

As in most organisations, and particularly in those where there are relatively high numbers of younger people seeking to advance, the question of personal development is one of the most highly charged and hot topics that you will encounter within the outsourced contact centre domain.

Given what we have already ascertained, it is probably worth looking at what this involves from the different perspectives of the stakeholders in such a situation. This is because there are two very, very different perspectives.

For the employee, there is a greater sense of immediacy. The 'Millennial Generation' arguments that are thoughtlessly tossed into the mix in this context can equally be comfortably consigned to the shredder. People do not just think one way because of the age at which they grew up. Insupportable, lazy categorisations from a society that loves to label. There are specific pockets of attitude and belief in all areas of every part of the population.

Yet the whole world has changed as have the perspectives of its inhabitants have begun to shift. People of all generations and backgrounds are living more immediate lives. Not everybody but enough to affect a sea change in attitude. Corporations and organisations are pushing in new directions and trying to change approaches and thought processes that focus on the here and now. I mean, you can even cash out and free up pension cash at 55.

BPOs are of course heavily populated by the under-25 age group, so a higher proportion of people are keen to get onto the first rungs of the career ladder.

In many cases, some of these individuals are indeed very bright. You would of course think that an organisation that was able to attract so many intelligent individuals with so much to offer would seek to establish ways in which they could harness that talent and channel that into an area of their business that would help them to grow, innovate and of course ultimately bolster the bottom line.

However, that is not the way it works in BPOs. The relationship between employer and employees is almost exclusively transactional. It is about what you are able to do in units of time, in accordance with an agreed specification and whether or not that completed task can be billed to a client. There is certainly no question that everybody will have an equal opportunity to pursue a more advanced role that makes the best use of their individual talents.

As I have previously pointed out, the performance management processes that exist within BPOs are simply a sham – something that supports the facade that the organisations themselves are mainstream and hides the core of dysfunctionality that permeates every area of operation. But having said all that, that does not mean to say that there are no opportunities for progression. It is simply that progression that is encouraged and accepted is based, not on talent and ability but on the talent and ability to support the continuing promotion of the facade.

In brief, you are only likely to progress if you have the political skills and a kind of insidious motivation to want to perpetuate the true modus operandi of the organisation. This is why BPOs bear out the old adage that people are promoted to their level of incompetence. And that is plain to see in the rank and file who are constantly and never-endingly astounded at the promotions that are made and sometimes of the external appointments that are signed off. It is the exception rather than the norm that a competent manager is given a position in such an organisation. When I say competent, I refer to the skills and traits that are generally understood to be a prerequisite for high-quality managers and leaders.

Nobody who has extensive knowledge of working in a BPO environment would dispute the truism that people managers generally do not have people-friendly skills.

That commercial managers often have no firm grasp of real numbers.

That client service managers do not understand the true notion of relationship-building.

We could go on ad infinitum. But what they all possess is a degree of political nous and a key sense of survival. These are going to be individuals who will baulk at nothing, no matter how unethical if it means that the will of the senior management team is progressed – and that they themselves survive.

The dynamic between employee and employer is a very interesting one and is in itself tome-worthy, but put simply it is a dynamic that relies on the willingness of one party to perform tasks in accordance with a written agreement but also to go the extra mile and to perform those tasks enthusiastically in accordance with what is promised to follow in the future.

This gives you an indication of why the tenure of contact centre staff averages out at approximately four to six months as opposed to roles at a similar level in an in-house and reputable organisation where employees might be expected to stay for at least two years. Now that is not to say that attrition is not a concern in outsourced contact centres. However, it needs to be considerably less than six months before it will make a discernible impact on the commercials which in turn will always factor in an average of six months as a probability.

At this point is worth highlighting the discrepancy between the promise of the organisation and what is actually required for a member of staff to deliver the role to the correct specification. It is one thing stating that an organisation is people-centric and that people are their most valued asset; however, when you consider that the roles are frequently simply one-dimensional, can you be surprised that higher than standard levels of attrition are generally not an issue?

If it were true that people were the greatest assets of such organisations, then the essence of their roles would be considerably more involved than they are. Surely it would be more honest to make a commitment to staff that the CRM systems and the ACDs were the most important assets in such a business because, without those, there really would be an issue in terms of service delivery. If the people themselves leave, they can easily be replaced following a quick call to a local agency. After all, how long does the average training period take? I would be surprised if most roles it was more than one week. In fact, in most cases training lasts for 1 to 2 days – if that – and it is for all intents and purposes more like a briefing session. Essentially instructions on how to operate the mechanics and the equipment with which you need to be accomplished in order to speak to customers and to record data.

However, the organisations concerned are never going to be open about the true nature of their business or their true motivations. On arrival at the company for the first time or more than likely in the course of their application for the role, employees are told that they are the most important asset of the business, that there are many, many development opportunities, and that this is a great organisation in which to progress one's career.

Along the way, someone will undoubtedly produce an inspirational quote from Richard Branson that they have lifted from their LinkedIn feed. Now while that may well reflect the ethos of Virgin, the same cannot be said for Mr BPO Director down the road who is looking to turn over some swift transactional dollars.

It is all vacuous twaddle. The only way you are going to progress is if more senior levels of management quickly identify that you are comfortable in complying and executing the will of the management team who are progressing their own sub-agendas. I say sub-agenda only in the sense that it is the one that sits beneath the froth and bubble of the organisation's PR though in fact it is the primary agenda and the one that delivers the required numbers to the bottom line.

But the deceptions do not end there. I mentioned that some people do indeed progress and that they are the ones who are prepared to do the bidding of the senior management team rather than being effective role model managers themselves. But that doesn't afford those individuals the status of co-conspirator because they too are victims of a different kind of malfeasance. I remember watching *The Office* when it was first aired. In one of the episodes, Tim, the character who sees through all of the boorish and tragic behaviours of the office manager remarks to Gareth – who has been made 'assistant to the manager' – that he is simply being given a title as a way of facilitating his acceptance of extra work for no more money. Never was a truer word spoken, which was probably the essence of the success of that production. It was so true to life, albeit with certain elements accentuated for comedic effect.

I have lost count of the number of times people have been promoted or offered development opportunities simply as a way of providing them with more work to be delivered at either no extra or very little extra cost to the organisation. That is after all the essence of a good negotiation – giving something at a low cost to yourself but a high perceived value to the other party.

I remember seeing one person promoted to a position where they were responsible for a whole site, being paid only marginally what they were being paid as a managerial shit-kicker but seeing their workload practically double overnight. Now this person was hardly what you would call an accomplished manager in the first instance but was exactly what the senior management team in such an organisation would look for when driving numbers to the bottom line.

A command-and-control micro-manager who shouted and screamed their way through the working day with a focus purely on numbers in a spreadsheet. No consideration for the feelings, aspirations or hopes of their people and no regard or respect for the individuals working within their team. A brutal and ruthless conveyor belt of billing with an unrelentingly growing pile of collateral damage in its wake.

In any other organisation, such a person would not only never rise through the ranks but would arguably be removed via a formal process on the grounds of incompetence and conduct. However, in the world of BPOs, these individuals are seen as worthy of more senior positions. Of course, there is never a happy ending even for those tyrants. And that person I know was ultimately removed when they were deemed surplus to requirements.

You see, even promotions that look like opportunities are simply transactions. £5k for a role in which they will rinse you. And at the end of it, you are burned out and with a skillset that in no way translates into something similar externally.

Morally it is like your very own 30 pieces of silver. The people who lap it up certainly sell out in totality. It is not hyperbolic to suggest that you will see these promoted ones dumping mercilessly on the people and principles that they would previously have fought courageously to defend. All for a couple of grand and a job that half kills them.

I mean, money and status aside, the only thing that truly defines us is our integrity, right?

In the BPO world, wrong. It is all about money, status, and survival.

However, fortunately, some of the smarter people do cotton on to the fact that the promises of development and career advancement are simply an example of excessive carrot, and unfortunately excessive stick. And there is certainly no shortage of resistance and rebellion in such organisations, often even sabotage.

In relation to sabotage, this is frequently limited to the withdrawal of labour or a lack of care and attention spent on work often in the knowledge that errors are being allowed to pass. There are though examples of full-on and concentrated sabotage which we will discuss later. Having noted that the bum deal is recognised, it is often not however recognised for what it truly is. Employees frequently view the failure of organisations to support them effectively or when they renege on their apparent promises as failures on the part of individual managers or indifference to what is really happening on the shop floor.

It is however far from indifference and the senior management teams know exactly what is going on and moreover, that this is a direct result of their own covert business plans for the organisation.

The usual lines that are trotted out to employees who have been led along for an extended period of time will typically involve roles having to go on hold owing to budgetary demands or client requests or excuses that seem to have some legal justification, for example, if there are potentially other employees in the organisation 'at risk'. Effectively anything that will justify a delay in advancing somebody may have a plausible third-party justification rather than being the decision that the senior management would ideally like to take.

§

During my career, I had often wondered why employees did not take a full step back and reassess and evaluate exactly what was occurring. I certainly always acknowledged that the power wielded by employees was far greater than any of them ever seemed to appreciate. It was clear to me that knowing that service delivery for clients – and therefore billing which was the oxygen of the organisation – was wholly reliant on the presence of employees doing the work itself, the company itself was completely dependent on people doing their jobs on any given day.

It could be a very straightforward thing to arrange for all employees to fail to turn up to work on a given day which would completely scupper operations.

Totally wrecking service for a period of time and seriously undermining the confidence of clients in the BPOs.

And as long as everybody stuck to their story on return to work, there is no action that could be taken against them. This is because everybody has the right to self-certify their absence for up to 7 days. Therefore, everybody could elect not to turn up to work from Monday to Friday, call in sick and then reiterate that on their return to work during their RTW interview with their line manager. As long as they maintained their story, that it was, for example, a flu virus, no action could be taken against them.

It would also not be a feasible option for the company to discipline a whole body of workers in some sort of class-action disciplinary, nor could they reasonably raise the context of wider absence with only one person, because the question of employee absence and wellness is always an individual and private matter.

The BPOs concerned would not even be able to address that wider group of employees with their concerns as this would undoubtedly breach confidentiality provisions and may lead to a case being brought by the employees themselves.

It would be that simple – all it would take would be a degree of organisation, a very low profile, and the holding of individual nerve. And the reason it doesn't happen, is because people generally do not take that step back and truly evaluate the bigger picture and what is happening. They satisfy themselves that their hardships and challenges are the result of incompetent people who can then be the subject of their various moans and grumbles.

They do not take the time to consider that actually they are pawns in a game that has been deliberately thought through and that they are the victims of ongoing exploitation.

The development and advancement plan or 'people strategy' that these BPOs purport to play centre stage in their organisation is no more than a hologram, unashamedly projected at every opportunity onto every area in the business but which can be inoperable if enough light is cast on the site where it is directed.

It is unfortunate that most employees in these BPOs do not even notice its true nature or if they do, they feel powerless to act or are so deeply entrenched in the roles that have been carved out for them that they feel that it is a fight that is not worth getting into.

What you will find is that members of senior management teams in these organisations will bring in former colleagues in groups who will be well-versed in the aims of the organisation as they will be painfully familiar with the way in which their patron had previously managed similar businesses. I like the term 'patron' in this instance as these 'clumps' of personnel can survive only with the patronage of a senior manager who is keen to maintain the status quo – somebody who is wise to, and 'in on' the game.

Indeed, they may have already been complicit in the furthering of plans in those other companies. What this does lead to is the establishment of cliques and closed units of operation and decision-making in businesses which can be very difficult to change or to challenge.

In its own way though, this can lead to some absolutely outrageous appointments, particularly where people are shoehorned into senior roles that give good salaries when such roles are very different from any of their previous experience or expertise. In practice though, in terms of day-to-day operations, this probably makes very little difference because the work is typically done by those closer to the shop floor. It can however lead to some rather embarrassing situations, particularly during client visits or review meetings when the people concerned clearly demonstrate that they are indeed clueless.

An old saying from Denis Thatcher is one worth mentioning here (though others probably said it before) because it sheds a tremendous amount of light on the approach that such people should really be taking. When asked why he said very little in public, old Denis sagely responded that it was better to *be thought of as a fool than to open one's mouth and remove all doubt'*. And in my career, I think I have probably seen it all. I've seen divisional managing directors bring in their former partners as fellow directors and on mountainous salaries, sometimes doubling those of people in the same position. I have seen people join at the head of companies, bringing in family members on meaningless consultancy contracts where they are able to charge massive day rates over protracted periods.

But it is not just restricted to the most senior levels, because a similar process seems to have gathered much pace within BPOs which seems to have garnered almost universal acclaim and yet which is fundamentally flawed. That process causes issues that are rarely understood and certainly not appreciated. I am of course talking about the potential for the *recommend-a-friend* or *referral*, recruitment channel. Christ on a bike, could anything have ever been introduced into an organisation's philosophy of which the underlying thought process was more warped, screwed or off the mark? It is fundamentally straight out of the *Arkham Asylum*.

Now this is much championed by HR teams, primarily because on the face of it, they are extremely cost-effective in relation to the cost to recruit. When you consider that a half-page advertisement in a local newspaper would cost several thousand pounds and from that you may only receive a handful of applications. And potentially if you're lucky, one successful hire. With the recommend-a-friend approach, the idea is to offer existing employees a reward of £250 or a similar sum to introduce a friend to the company with payment to be made if the employee is successful with the application and remains in position for a specified time. The rationale behind this is that if an employee making the recommendation is a high-performing employee then they are more likely to refer high-performing friends. Therefore, the company at a reduced cost of recruitment can tap into a wide pool of high-quality employees.

And make no mistake, HR departments are absolutely wedded to this concept. I have never worked in a BPO where some sort of employee referral scheme was not at the top of the list in recruitment as far as their strategy was concerned.

Jesus wept – it is just one great example of why HR teams should not be let near people issues in *any* organisation.

As a way of tapping into the available employee pool, this is bordering on the insane.

Firstly, it makes a gargantuan assumption that the friends of an employee will perform to the same standard and have the same ethics or outlook towards work as the person who recommended them. I think we all know examples ourselves of friends that we may have who, while they may be good friends and decent people, may be hopeless at work, personal organisation, or reliability (continue ad infinitum with values of your choice). It is simply a wholly erroneous and baseless connection to make.

Of course, the success rate at assessment for referred candidates is very high, primarily because they have an inside track on what to do at their assessment centre and on what are the right things that the company expects to hear during all interactions.

So is not only a flawed approach in terms of the identification of candidates, but the recruitment processes are compromised, and they are able to enter the organisation with fewer restrictions. Completely random in terms of the narrowing of the pool and a disproportionately higher chance of success through 'gaming' the process.

And once they are inside your business, you have a different set of challenges which of course are entirely of your own making. Notwithstanding any potential problems with their performance levels, you now have a closer-bonded group of people in operation within your company who gain influence that is not so easily managed and who also have a tendency to leave in groups in the same way that they arrived in groups. So even if you have been fortunate to randomly recruit some good performers, you will run the risk of losing them again in one fell swoop and you experience sudden and immediate impact in terms of attrition if they all decide to leave at the same time (or in terms of their social lives if they are absent at the same time after parties or other events in the annual calendar).

This is one of the rare types of situation when attrition would be a significantly impactful issue because of the concentrated volume of leavers that might seriously cripple specific accounts within the business. This is rarely taken into account because as with all aspects of BPOs, it is the immediate bottom line that is the be-all-and-end-all. Very rarely is there consideration for investment over an extended period.

When using these referral processes, it is all about the unit recruitment cost and getting an individual into the organisation to fill a seat. 25 years ago, BPOs used to be all about putting bums on seats. Over the course of those 25 years, everything has been geared towards changing this perception; however very little has changed in practice.

It remains a volume capacity business with both eyes firmly on client billing.

So, if you are a client of an outsourcer and you are viewing a credentials presentation or visiting a site and you see a major play is made of the employee referral scheme or of the work community and how the staff are bonded together, think about how many eggs are being kept in one basket.

Ask yourself why these organisations which love to promote their MBA and HRM Masters credentials on their staff profiles, do not use more scientifically grounded strategies to attract and retain their staff. Perhaps, if you do wish to take everything right down to basics, the big question is whether you are content to work with companies that simply bring in their pals.

Of course, whether it matters or not will largely depend on what you ultimately expect them to deliver, and perhaps that consideration helps us to understand a little more about what these businesses actually want and how this relates to what the clients actually expect.

As we have already explored, perhaps the success of this policy and the almost complete absence of dissent towards it explains a lot about how this so-called 'industry' runs and is perceived.

If it were all about delivering a quality service, companies would not promote it, and clients would not accept it. Yet here it is and there does not seem to be any sign of it waning any time soon.

BPO organisations thrive on bringing enough kindlings to keep the fires burning. And whatever they need to promise, whatever performances they need to deliver in order to convince the staff that there is actually something in it for them, they will do.

And if they can get people to bring in similar people at a reduced cost and perpetrate the same old tosh to them, then happy days.

But ultimately, it is only ever one-way traffic.

One group of people on the fire, and one group feeling the benefit of the warmth.

Guess who gets to play which role?

11 – Organ Grinders and Monkeys

Having looked at a selection of some of the snidely arse-ferrets who scurry around the BPOs, eking out their livings, let us now turn to some of the main protagonists and some of the key roles that you will find in any BPO.

So, firstly straight to the heart of operational delivery if you can bear a further example of bewilderingly ironic double-speak. And let us start with the humble Operations Manager.

Operations Managers of various monikers are the people who manage day-to-day service delivery. Line management of people and ownership of processes. A common question from the rank-and-file is: *'what do they actually do?'.* And to some, it sounds like yet another moan to have a pop at the management team – and it is.

But it is in fact an inadvertent bullseye from an emotionally driven shot in the dark. *Operations Managers* in outsourced contact centres do very little of substance. But they are absolutely well-placed to cruise and to cover.

Of course, while they are not motivating you with lines like

'We need you to work hard – but if you'd prefer to go out and pick strawberries, then go and get a job picking strawberries'.

I remember hearing of that one at an induction.

On a par with Mel Gibson in *Braveheart*. Pumps me up even now. They must have been pulling up trees in the asylum grounds.

Anyway, we move on. We've talked somewhat about the stringent controls imposed on the rank-and-file staff in BPOs and also how at higher levels there is a significant void in this regard. While this can lead to opportunities for revenge and sabotage, it also presents a more everyday opportunity for managers to spend their time on tasks which are not those for which they receive their not-so-insignificant stipend.

Yes, my friends, the *skive* is not only perpetually on but runs at almost epidemic proportions.

So how do they get away with it? Only a marginally closer look is required for all to become clear. Almost all meaningful and delivery-related activity in a contact centre is electronically managed, from which copious amounts of MI can be derived. The swathes of staff are line-managed by *team leaders* and managers who do not only the legwork but are also the recipients of whatever the more senior managers choose to delegate. Even better if you are a third-line manager or more senior manager in the scheme of things – fewer direct reports.

So operational managers need only really hold 121 meetings with their own reporting line, read and interpret data and then communicate updates either on calls with clients or internally with other stakeholders. Once you have your feet under the table the reading of reports can be accomplished efficiently in minimal time. And very helpfully, the desire to pick up delegated tasks is almost universally lapped up by *Team Leaders* who are desperate to climb the greasy pole – particularly if, as a savvy manager, you are carefully projecting your promotion hologram. Furthermore, at a more senior level as long as the job gets done and the bottom-line results are where they need to be, those at Director level will readily accept your commentary on how everything is panning out.

As you become for familiar with the workings of your particular office, you will create more and more time surpluses that you can use as you wish. The tacit knowledge you pick up and accumulate is essential here not to gain efficiencies for the benefit of the business. *But for efficiencies for the benefit of you.* I remember one colleague who spent the best part of 5 months designing and building a website as a private project and later got a job with his client – all while ostensibly managing an operational team. Others devote their in-office time to the Open University or administering their own businesses. Throw in a few working from-home days for review of slide decks for MBRs and QBRs (already completed in minimal time at work) and some client visits (whole days out of the office for 45-minute meetings) and it becomes even more straightforward to continue to meet outside goals.

There are however some risks to this which can lead to an unravelling of this arrangement which primarily stem from the ambition of those at levels below you who readily pick up the donkey work.

In the first instance, they need to ultimately gain their promotion, so sooner or later they are going to become disenchanted with their increasing work level and the pain of being squeezed upwards and downwards. This is of course what makes Team Leader/manager roles in any event arguably among the most challenging. This is where you need to plan strategically and apply a combination of two strands of adroit manoeuvring. Firstly, you need to build a *context* for the benefit of the more senior management team. Along the lines of:

'*X is very capable but not really a team player*'.

'*X is very vocal about the way the company is run and tends to run with the horses and the hounds*'.

This one works brilliantly with *team leaders/managers*, particularly those who have previously been *Advisors* in the same company and who are larging just a little too much.

This will put the brakes on any further promotions because *X* will be viewed as a competent performer (this also helps to avoid any questions about why you would not have needed to start any capability process with them) yet also a troublemaker who is not pulling in the same direction as the others. In doing so, you perpetuate the discourse of the disrupter (in a negative sense) which is then repeated so often it becomes the *truth*.

At the same time, you have to tell *X* how much *YOU* value them and how you have recommended them. Make a few vouchers available periodically and give them occasional time off 'under the radar'. This second part is crucial as you have to make them *complicit in illicit*. Once they are party to some free unauthorised time off, they will immediately shrink back from any thoughts of raising concerns with anybody senior about the lack of opportunity. You thereby get them into the *'Us'* camp of a clear *'Them and Us'* situation.

Ultimately, when you see this kind of unrest developing, you know that it will indeed be only a matter of time before *X* leaves (you can indeed precipitate this, by making them aware of your own view that they are too good for the company – possibly even put them in contact with a Recruitment Consultant who might be able to help).

When that point comes, you have of course already warmed up the senior managers who will be relieved that a troublemaker has gone. If HR raise any concerns, you can point out that *X* had been with the company for a number of years without a sniff of further promotion *(true)* and that while you valued them *(true – and would be corroborated in an exit interview)*, they were not seen as a great fit at a more senior level *(true – and would be corroborated by the senior management team who would have adopted the discourse of the day as the truth)*.

And the kicker is that this is a contact centre environment where high attrition of all levels has become normalised. Almost certainly means that any scrutiny of the circumstances remains a mere scratch on the surface.

Once *X* has gone, repeat the cycle ad infinitum. You will never be short of willing participants, and it takes only a few weeks of supervision once the new boys are immersed in the operation before the stabilisers are off and you are 'free to freewheel', so to speak.

The second step that operational managers need to take when embarking on these techniques, is to constantly emphasise *how busy they are at all times*. This prevents any additional meaningful tasks being thrust upon you which would rather scupper any back-channel enterprise you may have cooking at any one time. Any circumstantial window-dressing you can muster should be adopted, whether this is blocking out time in your calendar for reviews, analysis, research, or over-exaggerating the time for actual bonafide activities, it should be done.

Thirdly and equally critically, you should ensure that you use some of the time surplus to demonstrate adding value to the business. If you take all the surplus time for yourself, you will risk losing an opportunity to pump up your own image and possibly raise questions about your own position. You may be seen as competent but lacking in ambition. In doing this (which should not be too onerous), you can take the opportunity to delight your clients with some free analysis, for example, and in doing so build up your own level of perceived indispensability.

It is a pattern of behaviours I have seen over and over again, and I would say that 80% of operational managers use these techniques to a greater or lesser extent. In some cases, managers have built up more than 30 years doing this – even to the point that they get repeatedly promoted with the most successful repeating the trick with 2nd line managers and beyond.

§

One indispensable tool for all operational managers who need to control their people effectively while keeping this modus operandi as free-flowing and as undisturbed as possible has become the most preferable and favoured in the last 30 years. And that is *'feedback'*. Oh, deary me, how deliciously useful this is. A way to coerce and control while legitimised under the seemingly omniscient HR-driven principles of self-awareness, personal development (whatever that might be) and continuous improvement.

The weapon of choice for the less scrupulous – under the guise of constructive and cooperative working, feedback has become the acceptable face of politicking and backstabbing. You have probably been there before. In a 121, after the jocular preamble of kid- or football-related chatter, your boss utters those classic words:

'I've had some feedback'.

Now this is great for the boss as they can give you what is actually their opinion without it seeming like it is in any way confrontational or with any risk that they may then be red-faced following any subsequent firm rebuttal. Sometimes it is not feedback at all but cited as such for these precise reasons. Other managers use it as a means of getting overly vociferous colleagues onto the back foot – throw some rumour their way and they may concentrate their efforts on repairing their public image rather than voicing their dissent. A useful tranquiliser.

More often than not though, it is the unsubstantiated opinion of some worthless snake who has decided to stab you *au Bruté or* use you as a helpful distraction from the discovery of their own crass ineptitude. It is all part of the bullshit that distracts managers from the real organisational challenges and somehow transforms into facts that then have to be addressed in the course of what BPO managers like to term *man-management.*

Frequently the feedback is that:

'you appeared disengaged in x meeting.'

(maybe it was because the leader of the meeting was unprepared, lacked knowledge of the subject, had awful presentation skills and – on balance, given that the operation was currently on fire, your mind was on other things than spending 2 hours on a Monday morning having to endure it).

Sometimes it is that you do not appear to be working closely with the group or, the oft-cited gem:

'not in the boat rowing in the same direction'.

It is a lovely way for the jobsworth to level the *'not a team player'* allegation. This, in a BPO, is a cardinal sin even though what is often held to be a team, is not a team per se. Just a loose group of individuals who often work independently on tasks and who do not need ongoing assistance to complete them, in accordance with the generally held to constitute the working of a team.

But to be frank on the rowing analogy, if the boat is careering over into the abyss, then that's probably why you're not unquestioningly pumping in that same direction.

What a shame that the mindset in these organisations prevents the respect for independent thinkers who might otherwise prevent disasters and take the businesses to new levels.

What a shame that senior managers, when offered feedback, do not challenge the givers that their information is often unsubstantiated, personal opinion. And they know the difference because when you have cocked up, the chat is altogether different. On those occasions, it is made clear that x error has been made which is evidenced by y outcome.

No nebulous and shadowy *'feedback'* there, old boy.

Wow, I almost felt indignant there – but there are no shortages of senior managers who have used the golden nugget of 'feedback' for no other reason than to protect their own freewheeling journeys down easy street. And I for one played a number of these cards very successfully over a very long time.

§

One final mention on control and power. While behaviourally and psychologically, these are clear strategies that can be employed, a savvy *Operations Manager* will also ensure that their people are tied down contractually to the weakest possible position. One common practice with employment contracts really does exemplify the landscape almost perfectly. This is when the BPO works with contracts that have imbalanced notice periods requiring the employee to give 1 month if they wish to leave but only 1 week if the BPO wishes to terminate. It is not just the inequality that stands out but the brazen abuse. A step to protect their service if the wind blows one way yet discards the employee at a whim if it blows the other way.

I know, I know.

What drives any person who takes pride in themselves as a leader, to want to deprive people who sweat blood and tears to build businesses on their behalf, of three weeks' salary in the event of a redundancy? Millionaires futureproofing in order to lop off £850 from somebody on minimum wage at the point they lose their livelihood.

Refrain from preaching to your people about your company values of respect and integrity or cite any people-centric Branson quotations while you are pulling these kinds of stunts. Yet such contracts are fast becoming the rule for BPOs, not the exception. In spite of all the spin to the contrary, is more challenging to find examples of when BPOs are *NOT* exploiting staff rather than vice versa.

These are the same tosspots who tried to make everybody take pay cuts during the 2008 credit crunch, to, so say, save the businesses even though it was their piss-poor leadership that never saw the crash coming and left their companies so woefully under-prepared. What a shame they never offered employees stock so that the sacrifices made by the people who took the cuts, might have been compensated at a later date. Apparently, some people were threatened with dismissal if they did not accept the pay-cut requests. Wow. How can people be so gullible to believe such tripe? I would have had them into a tribunal faster than an Ethiopian suicide kinder commando hits an available breast.

Filthy Lucre ain't nothing new – and neither is cash from chaos if you will excuse the *Pistolian* asides.

All of these tactics and approaches are indispensable in keeping staff on the back foot, fearful for their livelihoods and therefore correspondingly less likely to rock the boat. It also makes it so much more straightforward for the operational management teams to pull the proverbial trigger when there needs to be a swift parting of the ways.

§

But you do see some wonderfully comical situations when people are put on the back foot themselves, particularly when this is one publicly. Take the following example.

An email came out to the whole company to let them know that there would be sessions available to discuss pensions or the like. One wag replied (to all):

'Maybe you don't pay me enough to take out a pension.'

11 words that led to a meltdown of emotion. Full-blown, molten angst and toys jettisoned forth from the corporate pram. Volcanic eruptions and tantrums followed.

I laughed so much, a little bit of wee almost came out.

At the time that this off-the-cuff response was sent – and let's face it, it was sent 3 minutes after the initial communication, some members of the management team were (I do not jest) in a meeting discussing the results from the most recent employee survey and how to better promote *employee engagement*.

Someone from a different department sprinted across the office to immediately alert them (admirable dedication for one so deceptively rotund) and the meeting was adjourned, so the matter could be dealt with.

The author of the delicious eleven-worder was subsequently sent home for the day, and HR were summoned amid whispers of gross misconduct disciplinary hearings.

Where do you begin with an analysis of such a situation?

The employee responds to an email from HR, of which he is a bona fide recipient.

Presses 'Reply All', a legitimate function of the email system of which he has authority to make use.

Composes and sends a message which could in no way be construed as either offensive, obscene, defamatory, or discriminatory.

Asks a simple question, to which the answer might have been a simple 'Yes, we do'. Or alternatively, a 'You are quite correct – we don't'.

Sounded reasonable to me.

The most serious transgression was the omission of a question mark even if the question was rhetorical. Come on now, you have to have standards!

Crazy that in ostensibly trying to get to grips with employee dissatisfaction, a meeting was adjourned to initiate disciplinary proceedings about an incident that was just a legitimate concern being raised.

Flippant? On the part of the sender maybe. Shooting from the hip? After a 3-minute gap, yes, I think so.

The management team was embarrassed at being implicitly called out for no pay review in many years and for their failure to make a positive case for their team. Another possibility, perhaps.

So important that everything has to be dropped in order to screw somebody who had the temerity to voice an opinion? It would appear so.

Why not take it on the chin and let it blow over? The email would be forgotten by the next day. Invite the guy to have a coffee and listen to the underlying concern. Perhaps take the opportunity to emphasise what are the most conducive channels through which to raise a concern. Perhaps the sender might feel a tad sheepish.

Why not show some empathy at a minor display of frustration at a blanket email that was in the opinion of many poorly thought through in the first instance?

Show some leadership that management roles demand and step up to the plate. *And consider carefully who may be more guilty of misconduct in this situation.*

One poor management soul ended the day walking through the contact centre muttering:

'fucking gross misconduct...fucking gross misconduct',

then sitting in tears at their desk before having to jog off home early.

The next day an immediate reverse ferret was required when HR stepped in to explain that it was not misconduct, gross or otherwise, to simply ask a question.

Sad really, for anybody to be put in such a position that they end up having to thrash around in full view of an incredulous audience. Great entertainment though but crazy at the ease with which these so-called leaders can be thrown into disarray by any perceived slight.

They did still manage to produce a letter of concern for the poor chap. I wish that had been me – that letter may have served as an improvised tool for me to wipe the floor with them.

I would have called it an interest-free repayment.

§

The ineptitude of operational teams can at times be mind-boggling, no more so when confronted with multifaceted problems – most BPO managers have brains like Fisher Price computers, so can only retain a maximum of 3 pieces of information.

Ask them the time and they forget their name.

But it is not just the histrionics and the irrationality.

A near-complete removal from reality would not be unfeasible.

Allow me to recall the sad tale of Employees A and B and an allegation of harassment. It is a bonkers account that would probably be hilarious, were the subject matter not so grave.

Here we go:

Employee *A* (Male) was paying unsolicited attention to Employee *B* (Female) – constantly approaching her, sending gifts etc. Nothing horrendous in the contact itself but generally inappropriate. It gets bad enough for B to ask the company to call the police in. The company quash this, amazingly stating it to be an inappropriate course of action.

A is however asked to stop, but he persists, and disciplinary action is not escalated, after intervention by the head honcho who is concerned about any reduction in staff following a sacking, that might affect service delivery at a crucial time.

Employee *B* decides to leave the company because of this.

At a later date, Employee A who by now has completed all the informal modules required to be certified as a fruitcake par excellence, leaves of his own accord.

The organisation later hits a resource issue and decides to reach out to all former employees via its informal network and Employee *B*, as a fully trained advisor, returns after assurances that Employee *A* is gone and will not be re-employed.

HR confirmed this, noting that *A*'s file has been suitably flagged as 'Do not re-employ'.

All runs smoothly until *B* sees *A* in Reception.

Using the same re-engagement mechanism that brought *B* back into the organisation, *A* has also been rehired.

And placed on a team that is not only on the same floor as *B* but on the next pod.

Both then pick up where they left off, *A* in terms of his stalking and *B* in her permanent and escalating sense of anxiety.

B resigns again and *A* stays slightly longer until he momentarily loses his mind and screams at a customer, leaving the company no other option than to jettison the perve with immediate effect.

And once again, the organisation is 2 FTE down.

I wish I had made that up, but sadly *A* and *B* did exist and that is by no means an uncommon yarn, in terms of the wholesale absence of common sense, professionalism, and management skill...in fact, it lacked everything.

Welcome to the world, in which BPO employees are held hostage to high rents and the cost of living.

§

Some managers do however make an effort which is exemplified in the next example of *The Thank You Lunch*. I think I may have to offer some of these scenarios to Larry David for any future episode of *Curb Your Enthusiasm* he may be considering.

Operations Manager invites their two *Team Leaders* out for a 'Thank You Lunch'.

This is then cancelled and rescheduled. Cancelled, rescheduled, cancelled.

It is then again rescheduled, this time as 'Lunch'.

And then cancelled and (after a medium-length hiatus) rescheduled as a 'Planning Lunch' with an email to one of the *Team Leaders* thanking them for their work and for assisting the other *Team Leaders* while copying in the second Team Leader.

The 'planning lunch' was scheduled on a date during an extended period when the second Team Leader was on annual leave (which the Operations Manager had authorised).

This all followed a previous 'Thank You Lunch' when the Operations Manager and *Account Director* had proceeded to smash back bottle after bottle of wine and make all attendees split the bill. £50 for one course and a glass of wine? No thanks.

And there is a footnote to the story. The 'Thank You Lunch' never happened, but the same manager then sent an email to their team saying that it was their birthday soon and that as their partner was going to be working away and their friends would not be available, would they like to go out for birthday drinks? Gall level 10 on the gall-o-meter.

Unsurprisingly the take-up was low. Even less surprising when at around the same time, the annual appraisal cycle came around and the same team were invited to adopt an unrefreshingly creative approach to their meetings. That is to say that they had to fill out all sections in the review document (including line manager comments) and bring it to the meeting.

Should not have been too much trouble for one of the *Team Leaders* who had already for some time been sending manager communications to the client in *his* name but dictated word-for-word by the said manager. Obviously keen to have their thoughts heard but very keen not to take all the credit (or otherwise)!

I worked extensively in the operational field and met so many people like this who dared to call themselves leaders. And yet the strongest corroboration for the abilities that they bring to the table? Almost exclusively how many years they have been doing it. In BPO pitch responses, *PowerPoint* slides and brochures, it will be in there. The sad fact for these people is that their fifteen to twenty years of experience is simply rolling out the same old twaddle for fifteen to twenty years.

It really only emphasises how practised they are at being pisspoor.

12 – Client Surfacing

Now I have worked across the spectrum of roles in my largely undistinguished, what I like to loosely term, 'career' as well as meeting accomplished professionals in all those areas. In the world of BPOs though, you will not encounter a greater concentration of psychotic narcissists consumed by their life scripts than you find in account management or client relationship teams.

The world of client servicing. Sounds whore-endous which indeed it is. I always referred to it as client surfacing or client shore fishing (as Sean Connery would likely not say, ever), as the occupants of these positions would either be just skimming the surface or be at the peripheries, casting the odd line out to see what they might hook in terms of relevance to the business at hand. Never of course getting into a boat and venturing out into the ocean.

Now before I receive emails from those who feel that HR are in competition on this score – I will acknowledge that they are in terms of the psychosis – however when you add the narcissism and the vacuous twaddle, the account teams trump all. Black belts in *bullshido* to a man.

These are the ones who have the most to lose when the lights go out and the circuit breaks. *Client Managers* and *Account Directors* – whatever title they might hold – are characterised by perpetual anger and dissatisfaction, turning in on their colleagues (and therefore themselves) with predictable regularity when the absolute perfection they preach to their clients collapses into dust.

They will be the ones who explode and go over the edge at the slightest sense of client dissatisfaction, but not because the service has fallen short of standards. People who develop and manage constructive relationships do not flip out over single issues. On any level that is a dysfunctional reaction which would likely make the perpetrator a candidate for a therapeutic intervention.

When you see their apoplectic outbursts and ranting, that is the by-product of fear and exposure. At that point, such is the fragility of (what passes for) the client relationship that the house of cards must surely come tumbling down. It is the same fear that engulfs their direct client contacts who suddenly realise that the paper-thin charade of service is about to go *woomph* in the blink of an eye.

It is said that real relationships can sustain a setback – in these cases, they can be terminal. If the problem is not so severe, the client managers become client messengers. They take up a partisan position where they serve as the 'yes man' for the client, apologising without thinking on any subject, whatever the circumstances, and then flipping to face the operations teams where they fling it all lock, stock, and barrel, demanding immediate resolution.

And what else can they do? At the point the issue is raised to them, their trousers are well and truly down around their ankles. They will generally not be conversant with basic operational concepts, let alone the specifics of their own accounts. So, at that point, their moral compass will be set aside, and they will advance anything that keeps the dream alive. This has in the past been the domain of fake *SLA* reports, forged customer emails and even fraudulent invoices.

> *Ladies and gentlemen, no eyelids were batted during the making of this felony.*

There are a number of ways that this approach can come back to bite the outsourcer. As the so-called relationship is built on a desire to achieve unqualified happiness on the part of the client, anything that goes your way is gleefully accepted even if it might be potentially damaging or a risk in the long-term. An example of this is in relation to feedback on colleagues for the client (NB. a very different beast to the internal weapon, so generously enjoyed by operational managers).

This is the common scenario: someone may do something that is received positively, and, for example, there may be some excellent feedback to pass on. Now, the smart client manager should always take an even-handed approach here rather than just jumping on the bandwagon and throwing a party. This is because over-praising people for just doing their job means that everybody has further to fall when – just as fortuitously – things go awry. Keeping it real for the good news means that everybody keeps it real for the not-so-good. You then create common ground with everybody being, ahem, *on the same page* and likely one step in the direction towards a more trusting relationship.

When things do not go so well, the same client managers – because it is anathema to accept any fault or omission – will single out operational or project staff for blame, possibly even to the point that they will be (drum roll) *'moved off the account'.*

To clients, this seems like the ultimate sanction, but in reality, the staff do not care one jot and the BPO takes this as an opportunity to demonstrate compliance, the ability to act and of course, remove the source of immediate stress. As a forerunner to removal, clients delight in providing not only negative feedback but also overly exaggerated and gushing praise for another colleague in the BPO, preferably if the object of the praise is subordinate to the target of blame. This *punishment feedback* is designed to humiliate the real scapegoat; however, sadly for the client and client managers, it frequently backfires.

Firstly, because it allows the target of the abuse to back out from a quite weird, sadistic outpouring of self-loathing (never pleasant to witness). However, most crucially, it puts everybody in a position where they have placed the replacement on such a firm pedestal, that they are subsequently embarrassed when that person – who is often thrust into a role for which they are ill-prepared – makes a calamitous error themselves. It either reflects poorly on their own judgement when people remember their previous praise or their desire to sweep everything deftly under the carpet prevents them from acting and they are saddled with an incumbent poor performer. If matters cannot be adequately camouflaged, there is always as ever a wholly detached and power-oriented HR grunt who is only too willing to step in and remind everybody that people do not go from excellent to poor in a short period of time and will ensure that an unfeasibly resource-debilitating and time-hungry performance improvement plan (PIP) will need to be set-up.

Cue a fresh serving of 4 months of paperwork, 2-hour meetings, evidence-gathering, a nice project for said HR bod's CIPD portfolio, and a nervy client who will then shaft you with your boss for your alleged mismanagement. Top it with a cherry of it being raised (for the first time naturally) in your performance appraisal 6 months later when you have forgotten any salient facts that might have helped your defence. Garnish it with some hypocrisy from your boss who knew that it had been caused by your institutionalised tendency to be obsequiously compliant regarding a client account to which they would be magnificently indifferent and distant. Unless of course, it was time for monthly billing. In that case, they would be all over it, like bluebottles gorging on a silky turdette.

Seriously though, it is why the more reputable companies who run operations with supplier deliverables have generally moved towards roles with dual functional responsibility, i.e. account and operational management combined. These are where managers deal in tangible concrete deliverables and move supplier relationships onto firmer ground where *de facto* equates to *de jure*. However, in the outsourcing world, the split in function which has become more and more *de rigeur* means that the Account Managers are free to peddle their illusion so that the unconnected reality can continue to flourish unabated.

§

Now on the subject of relationships, this is a potentially controversial theme for some, it is probably worthwhile considering how the relationships between suppliers and clients work in practice. After all, there are many Account Managers and *Account Directors* assigned to the specific task of maintaining and growing the client relationship — some are specifically called *Client Relationship Manager/Director*. Talk about having to signpost that which should be naturally apparent.

As a starting point, let us consider exactly what a relationship is. The *Oxford English Dictionary* defines this as:

'The way in which two or more people or things are connected or the state of being connected.'

And also as:

'The way in which two or more groups regard and behave towards each other.'

Fascinating stuff when you consider the different contexts of relationships and how they work or how successful they are. The first point to note is that with the different parties, there will be different perspectives on what constitutes objectives, the degree of success etc. – a multitude of factors. There may even be discord in relation to whether what exists actually constitutes a relationship.

From a client perspective, the default position will often be one of command and control. They hold the purse strings and the outsourcer, desperately clinging on to the revenue and the wafer-thin margins, will do everything possible to keep the arrangement going. If this persists, the relationship will be deemed to be 'good'. When there are problems, the outsourcer will look to repair any damage with a solution. This is where it gets interesting. The solution will often not be credible, balanced or even viable. In fact, it may often not be real. For example, the number of times when there have been email backlogs or *SLA* failures the plan will be presented as *'we are drafting in more staff at our cost'*. The real solution will however be that we simply delete items from the inbox or provide a revised *SLA* figure that we have in fact invented.

And the clients dutifully accept this without challenge or investigation. It used to seem bizarre to me that people in such positions would lack even the most basic inclination to undertake some form of critical analysis.

But as time passed, I realised that it was not the solution they were interested in.

It was the story.

They needed a nice potted account for their bosses that demonstrated that they could contain and control – and that their bosses in turn could pull out of the bag in the event of an audit or the requirement to publish some *customer experience* data.

It was then that I learned that the relationship is a marriage of convenience where good equals a comfortable status quo that allows both parties a free pass and a feathered nest for continued operation.

What I always assumed to be client incompetence was in fact a misunderstanding on my part of the *de facto* relationship – a mutually satisfying relationship that allowed both parties to get through the working week. It explained why clients would accept *SLA* reports on Excel spreadsheets. Why they would allow the management of email through Outlook rather than via an auditable CRM system? Why do they never request transparency of staff lists?

It also explains a lot about the rate of turnover that exists in these supplier/client relationships. While the nature of relationships in the true sense is complex, detailed and often significantly based on intangible qualities such as trust, these are very different. It is impossible to examine these in detail owing to their variability and bespoke nature. However, we can observe reality and make a number of deductions that will provide us with a general picture.

By point of comparison, we are told that 1 in 3 marriages ends in divorce. If the supplier/client divorce rate were 1 in 3, we would be awash with medium and long-term account relationships. Now that is not to say that they do not exist – indeed for many of the larger more integrated operations, like with marriages, separation brings practical issues that on balance cannot easily be contemplated. In Freudian terms, the preferred state remains one of common unhappiness as opposed to hysterical misery. No psychoanalysis needs to be booked. Allegedly.

So, the tenure for many of these accounts is 1, 2 or 3 years – often the duration of one contract. If the so-called *Relationship*

Managers are developing relationships in the true sense of the word, why is this level of turnover so high? The answer lies in the fact that the relationship circuit is a simple chain or series. There is very often no parallel set-up of components that allows the lights to stay on when one part of the circuit breaks. When it fails, all the lights tend to go out because everything is based on the maintenance of an illusion.

If there is a great history of service delivery, continuous improvement projects and great customer feedback that drive a wider value for the client business, a one-off error will allow the client stakeholder to view a mistake as a small blot on the provision of an otherwise effective and valued service. For accounts where the history is transactionally one-dimensional and solely papered together by fictional narrative, the one-off blunder can be terminal. This is because the client stakeholder in sacking the outsourcer jettisons nothing more than the error and the problem – it does not give rise to further issues and be managed by an exchange.

§

In spite of all this, the *Account Manager* role remains popular even though the actual work performed could be by functionaries on a fraction of the salaries offered. More bizarrely (or not if you are now more acquainted with the lunacy that prevails in these organisations) is that those in the role remain incumbent even after a management track record that sees account after account lost. And for that, there is one very simple explanation. This is a group of managers whose sole output is a creatively viable story – they simply prepare an equally plausible version of events for the internal audience that reflects the inevitability of the loss, the market factors beyond our control etc.

So how is it that these yarns are believed? Well, they are facilitated by three factors: firstly, the ongoing *contexting* from relationship managers that emphasises the precarity of relationships and the work that they (as the saviours) are putting in to buttress the position of the organisation. This also at the same time builds a picture of their indispensability. NB. as discussed in other sections, this *contexting* plays an important role in many aspects of outsourcing industry situations and associated tomfoolery.

Secondly, the senior audience (preconditioned by the *contexting*) is usually so removed from their own business that they do not have the wherewithal to critique or analyse what is being presented to them. All they worry about is whether the gaps can be plugged with new numbers.

And finally — and this is the real beauty of these accounts for me — is that the whitewash does not need to stand the test of time. Once the losses are known and the stories accepted, everybody moves on. Nobody is remotely interested in going back to check the details, notwithstanding that they would not really know where to start in the first place.

I used to refer to Orwell's 1984 in relation to some of these matters. There is of course a parallel in contact centres with the panoptical position of 'Big Brother', in the sense that all activity is measured and monitored by all-seeing management. The further comparison that resonated was the one of 'doublespeak' (see numerous references passim) — though on reflection in outsourcing, there are so many more layers to it. Of course, you do have, a selection of examples — managers who do not manage, *Team Leaders* who represent all that is the antithesis of leadership and *Human Resource Managers* who have no interest in or care for people.

But the whole business of BPO contact centres is that they purport to deliver fundamentally what they cannot deliver.

Their clients know this but make demands of the outsourcers that they provide evidence that they *are* doing it.

It sounds outlandish, but these are precisely the comfortable roles into which each party has eased.

This evidence is delivered by means of an ongoing narrative illustrated by whatever will be accepted as viable. The clients then present this, if required, to stakeholders in order to demonstrate that activities are of the highest probity.

While this is happening, the BPO structures themselves internally by installing all sorts of working practices and procedures which are ostensibly best practice but which are also routinely bypassed and ignored. They however continually repeat that they are doing what they state and reiterate this to staff.

The staff know that this is a sham but comply and allow the corroborative material to be generated. This can then be produced to substantiate the essence of professionalism and best practice if need be.

And everybody believes – because they need and want to believe. And that (apart from love, of course) is all you need.

13 – Checkback Planning

Having tiptoed deftly through the charred embers of the whims and fancies of *Account Managers*, it may seem incongruous to mention the works of the Russian philosopher and semiotic Mikhail Mikhailovich Bakhtin.

Well, probably somewhat pretentious, but I promised myself I would shoehorn in some Bakhtin, so here we go. I will keep it brief, and I hope relevant.

For some background, Bakhtin's work remained largely undiscovered until the 1960s (he was born in 1895 and died in 1975) and is not widely considered outside academic circles. He wrote extensively on dialogue and goes into this subject in fascinating and illuminating depth which fortunately for you all is not relevant to our subject matter here.

He is however in this vein best known for his statement that:

> *'(...) The word in language is half someone else's. It becomes one's own, only when the speaker populates it with his own intention, his own accent.*[ix]

Never was this truer when you consider the way in which and the extent to which the cardinal blaggers in the world of client services appropriate words and phrases and bandy them around in order to blunderbuss a wider impression that they are *with it* and *on it*. Not to mention *full of it*.

We have all doubtless witnessed the way in which a favourite stock phrase catches like wildfire and spreads through the organisation as people jump onto its coattails to repeat and use it. Doing so helps us to categorise and present ourselves as one of the team. Somebody with influence, for example, comments that the project is *'a moveable feast'* and within two to three weeks even the cleaners are using the term to describe their work rotas.

Of course, there is a more subconscious mechanism working here – this works with humming certain distinctive tunes in the lift or in a queue. After a while, you hear everybody all around the office humming the same ditty. Lithuanian electricians humming *Rawhide.*

I used to muck about with these ploys, by taking an unusual phrase but changing it slightly – referring perhaps to a *'mobile feast'* – and seeing how far it would travel. Sure enough, it would merrily be sung out like a *Fraggle Rock* chorus even at board level. You see, it is almost instinctive to appropriate small details that either enhance you or make you seem to be part of the in-crowd.

Nothing is new under the sun, as Bakhtin notes, because no matter what you say, it will have been uttered previously. As such, words and phrases do not exist in any neutral form but always in other contexts, fuelled by other intentions. Bakhtin incidentally notes how the appropriation does not always work, how the words seem 'alien' when emanating from the mouths of those who speak them. Who remembers when Mrs Thatcher appropriated the royal 'We' with 'We are a grandmother?' Lead balloon city.

What is striking about the BPOs, is the way in which words are appropriated by people and used to demonstrate meaning and understanding rather than simply being decorative. What is all the more stunning is how the obvious nonsensical content is never challenged with these discussions and meetings continuing with the impression that everybody is engaged in meaningful business discussions.

A great example of this was in the way that 'Checkback planning' managed to permeate into the management-speak of a company where I worked. At the time, a BPO site I know had the misfortune to be dealing with some *VP of Global Bullshido* who was a typical product of the rapid growth in near-shore BPO activity of the 1990s. A whole career built on a vacuum of substance, flitting from job to job, a working week dedicated to ingratiation and vacuous twaddle. But here she was, on a conference call with the team in the US, and by virtue of my friend's position, he was giving everybody a rundown on the latest operational plans.

Now immediately before the call, it had been his lunchbreak and he had been on the phone with his mobile phone supplier about a cheque that he had not received, you see, he had taken out a plan that involved him receiving a 'chequeback' every three months if he provided copies of his paid bills to evidence that he was still a customer in credit. It was actually known as a 'chequeback deal'.

He had come off this call and straight back onto the work conference. Partway through the conference call, he was talking and, as I am sure most people will have experienced at some stage in their lives, he uttered a word completely out of context, that was sitting there still in his subconscious. Much in the same way that people make so-called 'Freudian slips'.

Accordingly, he used the phrase 'chequeback planning' quite inexplicably in a sentence.

There was a brief pause, and the conversation continued. *VP, Global Bullshido* commented on how positive the use of checkback planning would be and how advantageous other market leaders had found it. The US guys agreed and gave me 'kudos'. They actually do all go 'kooooooooo-dosssssss......'

My friend had to mute the call – totally bent up, hardly able to breathe.

Even for a domain where a lack of substance is normalised and almost mandatory, this had taken absolute toss to a new level or depth, depending on the perspective.

And so, it came to pass – *checkback planning* became cited more and more as the weeks went past (even featuring in email correspondence with its Americanised spelling). Nobody delved into what it was or what it actually involved, but everybody sure wanted a piece of the action.

To be seen as an exponent of 'checkback planning' placed you at the top of the tree. The next step would surely mean that we would all be licensed to don the blue shirt, chinos, and yellow/brown brogues.

The progression to the full-on US business dress never happened, apart from one relentless bottom-feeder who to be fair changed his entire wardrobe and, in doing so, achieved his most memorable contribution during his lamentable tenure – imagine the bizarre situation where you deliberately dressed in this pseudoformal way in order to pretend that you were one of the ones who pretended to be something they were not.

I am not sure I am clear on what that would make you. Other than a consummate brown magnet.

The whole checkback planning tale is a brief account of something that is, on the surface insignificant and immaterial. Somebody blagging and working their way up the ladder on the back of some gibberish.

But it is a microcosm for the whole damned shooting match.

Is it really that much different than spraying concepts like *NPS* and *CX* about? Do those relate and reflect *customer experience* or satisfaction, any more than *checkback planning* represents whatever of those cockwombles were suggesting it might? There really isn't that much difference.

When you scratch just below the surface in any area of BPO operation, they are all checkback planners.

14 – Guitar George and Sexy Sadie

Now I am quite partial to a little music, of all types. I have after all an eclectic taste. As well as an eclectic kettle which I put together myself from spare parts taken from lots of different kettles. But enough of that for now.

Coined by a colleague about a mutual boss who wore his appendage on his sleeve – in many senses, a true *Sultan of Swing* himself though sadly had very little to offer in terms of tangible deliverables. A real 'slopey shoulders', bereft of the ability to bear even the slightest burden and running for cover at the slightest whiff of trouble, he was to us – *Guitar George*.

He knew all the chords.

He knew everything about everything in his own mind. But sadly, very little when it came down to matters meaningful. When Putin was mentioned, he'd managed multi-site in Russia. On the subject of classical music, he was a virtuoso on the Bassoon. Yet he clearly knew little about the very matters for which he deigned to receive his stipend.

These *Guitar Georges* are like the *Sexy Sadies*[x] who appear with cyclical regularity in BPOs. Each year or so, these flavour-of-the-month wannabee C-suite shit-shooters rock up, and they have this Tony Slattery-like 1990s presence. Remember when every time you turned on TV during the mid-90s, there was Tony Slattery? At home when you opened up a kitchen cupboard, there was Tony Slattery. Like *Cato* in the *Pink Panther* films.

It's like that with these people. They are in every meeting, and every focus group, always working on their projects and workstreams. You see, they have to be given centre-stage as it is their outputs that will help to prop up the rep of the jerktard who hired them. They are, as John Lennon sang, *the latest in the greatest of them all*. All they do is *make a fool of everyone*.

And then decision-makers finally piece together the elementary puzzle that is:

> *new superstar starters + 1 year + no discernible improvements + some regression = not great*

And they start to contemplate the situation which will trigger a blizzard of references back to the carefully cultivated *contexting* of some toss-spouting director. You know, the one who brought in his chum the workforce planner and made him the HR Director before all these, *'inevitable events happened that were out of everyone's control'* etc., etc.

By then, George and Sadie are long gone, buzzing off to the next turd. After all, that CV won't add its next role on its own.

And you can bet your bottom dollar that when you compare the LinkedIn profiles of some of these people, they have worked with each other at several different companies over the years. Leaving a trail of, well nothing, in their wake.

No matter, I digress. Yet you can bet your life that anybody who has ever worked in a BPO knows their very own *Guitar George* or *Sexy Sadie*, probably several over time. A know-all, posturing fake, for whom the timer is in perpetual countdown to discovery and for whom the bell should certainly toll. However, the cringe-inducing fact is that such braggarts and hustlers have now lent their talents over and above the mere exaggeration of personal attainment even extending this beyond the field of low-level and local pumping-up of professional accomplishments. They have now taken this to a new level, appropriating a term and new perch for their posturing.

They are the *'Thought Leaders'.* Oh, my sainted aunt, what a concept. Fly me to the moon. Because you would have to go that far to find anyone who would find this credible, wouldn't you? Well, apparently not if you are tangled in the BPO web of intrigue.

Thought leadership has become a buzzword across a number of industries, yet nowhere is it more liberally used than the self-stimulating world of the outsourced contact centre. It is in fact quite manifestly over-ejaculated and with the advent of new technologies, there are plenty of opportunities for platforms on which to spurt forth, by means of blogs and other social media channels.

The *thought leaders* remind me very much of the super-intelligent folk you encounter on quiz evenings. They know Don Bradman's test average and that Juliet is a Capulet. They will with self-satisfied aplomb confirm that George Eliot was in fact a woman and the author of *Mill on the Floss*. Yet when you engage them in a discussion on the devices employed by Eliot to convey the tension between the spiritual energies of her characters and their determinist milieu, they are immediately dumbstruck.

Moving the conversation further to locate the text (this my thought-leadership gurus is 'seeing the bigger picture') to an examination of the novel as a fictionalised autobiography and they are shuffling uncomfortably and desperately willing for it all to end. Tentatively explore a comparison between her style and that of Dickens and you risk a meltdown. For the quizzers, their knowledge of Dickens extends as far as *Oliver Twist*, possibly to *Bleak House* and maybe even (but not guaranteed) to *Barnaby Rudge*.

Introduce the notion that Eliot centres on the psychology of the individual, whereas Dickens' focus is on the individual and society and all you will hear is an echo of your own voice.

And so, it is with the *Thought Leaders*. Their awareness of Artificial Intelligence is limited to the most basic summary of its features. Open up a wider discussion on AI improving on literal thought to the extent that it surpasses the cognitive skills of humans and the consequent implications, and they are, ahem, *going to have to get back to you on it.*

Actually, it is quite inadvertently appropriate to mention Artificial Intelligence as an example here.

The point is that the professed intelligence is nothing more than a loose collection of buzzwords blunderbussed at the masses in order to create the illusion of expertise. There is however no depth to this and scarcely any dexterity that enables them to apply it to the emerging twists and turns of a real debate. Take them out of their comfort zone and for a downhill run off-piste and it is sadly game over.

So how do they manage to keep the facade upright in the face of a real client scenario? The answer is a mix of careful scripting and cold reading.

Step 1 is to ensure that a comprehensive slide deck is produced that allows for a scripted story accounting for 80-90% of the allotted time. This will be delivered with consummate slickness with the minimum opportunity for interaction.

As an aside, where did the term '*slide deck*' come from? Horrendous – and it has even started to inveigle its way into my vocabulary. Straight out of the marketing book of absolute toss. But probably and subconsciously linked to the '*pick a card, any card*' routines of the magician. But whatever you call them, the slides will always be an invaluable standby for the connivers and deceivers.

In the event of questions, *Step 2* kicks in. This is where the presenter listens and allows the knowledgeable client to raise and develop points through their questions and the inevitable wider context and justification for questions that people invariably offer. This then serves as cue to the presenter to gain information they did not know and to play back information to the audience, often reaffirming what had been told to them in the first instance. Add in some praise for the points raised in order to bolster the importance and self-esteem of the audience and limit any challenges.

After all, who would criticise and possibly curtail the opportunity for one's ego to be stroked, particularly as it may be in the presence of underlings (making you appear even more superior) or senior colleagues (consolidating your apparent competence and position)?

No different technique from a psychic who will impress you with all that they know when in fact, alas, they know nothing at all. The good ones will however make you believe, by harvesting anything they can glean, twist, and assemble. It does however fill a gap in the market – as there is an inexhaustive market for piffle.

You will see organisations periodically producing presentation decks that they cascade out to client-facing staff and request that these be delivered to all clients in order to convey the united front of their particular flavour of *thought leadership*. The 'one-size-fits-all' delivery of a message that they believe will unlock all doors. However, what the organisations fail to grasp is that high-end premium clients are looking for consultants who are experts in the client industry and who, through their deep understanding and partnership, can then apply the specialist contact methodologies.

This is however very rare, and the presenters simply churn out their generalist fact-dump slides intertwined with their own company credentials. And of course, when it does exist, it is way over the budgets of organisations who are in effect simply engaging with the contact centre outsourcers in order to dump their trash.

The kind of expertise and skill that the outsourcers pretend to offer is sourced on a much less frequent scale by professional services consultancies. They charge big money and deliver big results. They have proven methodologies of discovery and solution design and select but do not dump useful wider examples that support and enrich relevant solutions.

Their slide presentations are sparse, but their industry knowledge is proactively delivered to the client and supported by a nimble and flexible application of concepts to underpin their solutions and whatever emerges as the discussions develop.

Well, that's when they do a good job – even these big boys drop some quite high-profile biggies that substantially fail to deliver the basics.

What is further cringe-inducing is that the BPOs absolutely believe that what they are doing is thought-leading and representative of excellence. They are quite literally getting high on their own supply and are obsessive about their junk getting dealt to every punter in town. They will even keep spreadsheets that detail which client has seen the presentation and the plans/deadlines by which they will be seeing it.

You couldn't make it up. They actually believe that this has value for clients and their little Excel sheets measure that value. It is truly tragic.

But in practice, as is so often the case, all is not what it seems. All parties have wildly differing perspectives – perhaps in the way that audiences see a very different game when watching the same match.

What our BPOs do is provide a show that allows the client audience to justify their presence in the business relationship. This added-value content helps to legitimise their position as suppliers. At the end of the presentations, people ask for copies of the slides. Now this is not so they can re-read the material themselves. It is so that they can send to their bosses to file away in order to provide corroborative material as evidence of expertise and therefore justification for the outsourcing decision.

In the outsourcing world, the slickness of the presentation slides outweighs everything – even the delivery of the tangible service. Do this and you will go far. That appears to contravene everything they purport to achieve but exactly matches the niche that they fill. It is a performance art founded on misdirection and sleight of hand.

Sounds outrageous? Many will read this and say exactly so vociferously.

But do not be so surprised. Look at pop music factories churning out crass computerised tunes with carefully manufactured star images. It purports to be art and entertainment and what the kids love. And they do love it, sometimes obsessively. Yet it is not done to improve well-being or to elevate art. It is simply to make the most of an opportunity that exists in society to create prodigious wealth. Do the record companies put out statements confirming this? No, of course not – the genie may be half out of the bottle, but there is no sense in allowing it to escape completely.

The difference with BPOs is that the bottle is still buried, and it suits everybody that it remains so. Well, everybody who is making money at least. But let us take the opportunity to reflect on what *'thought leadership'* actually means. There are many genuine examples of this – individuals who excel in their chosen field and who share their wisdom with the wider industry, illustrating their ideas and concepts with relevant examples of their success and achievements. These are recognised experts who have their position of authority in the field bestowed by peers and others performing at the same level.

Contrast this with the *thought leadership* demonstrated by so-called *'thought leaders'* in the world of BPOs. For these individuals, *thought leadership* begins with self-appointment and it is not fuelled by recorded personal achievements. There is a good reason for this. Much of what they are involved in has such a narrow scope that it is of little wider practical use to anybody. What they do in practice is simply scrape the Internet for anything they feel may be of remote interest to others and to whom they would hope to attract into some sort of commercial relationship in the future.

They then post these articles on their blogs or via their social media channels and introduce them as matters of potential interest. This information is frequently accompanied by a standard descriptor which is typically a re-hashed sentence from the article itself.

For example, there may be a piece that talks about AI being successfully piloted in a particular scenario and the introductory line would say something along the lines of:

> *'AI is becoming a hot topic in our industry with a number of trials taking place – but is this the new dawn?'*

It is just a dump of a raft of subject themes on the audience but with no associated analysis, critique, practical application, or even reference to the organisation's own capabilities or achievements.

And yet this is positioned as *'thought leadership'.* Just nothing more than a rudimentary scrape of the Internet via Google or some other search engine and to the readership it demonstrates no other capability than how to use a search engine.

It is the sort of quasi-plagiarism that would score fail marks at pre-GCSE level. But the BPOs themselves thrive on it. Some BPOs organise rotas where managers of a particular level need to source and post articles in order to keep the repository topped up. Some may even attempt to write blog articles themselves which unsurprisingly are often plagiarised pieces from other posts or are frequently taken way out of context and are remarkable for only their irrelevance and the grammatical crimes committed by their creators. You will also find internal communications distributed lauding the *thought leadership* of the contributors and encouraging others to share these via their own social media accounts. Many indeed do though the majority exercise sound judgement and refrain from this in order to protect their reputation and no doubt to maintain their self-esteem.

It is a loose, chaotic approach to what they believe is content marketing. In fact, it is a spray-and-pray, often while not even using original material.

And everything is *disruptive* – like they are some kind of revolutionary force, bringing you instant recognition of hidden truths that will change your lives.

Mother of God, you need to do the basics first and have those grounded in reality before you can even dream of disrupting the status quo.

Disruptive. It would make you laugh, were it not so appallingly weak. But they just don't see it. They can't stop doing it and can't stop banging on about it.

In many BPOs, thought leadership runs almost exclusively on the premise of *Google-skimming.* It is however no different to the buying and selling concept of *flipping* – where a product is acquired, dusted down, and sold on with minimal investment.

§

Others take a more subtle approach and go the video content route. Now have you ever wondered why *LinkedIn* is plagued by people posting shaky video clips of themselves reading from scripts and poring forth on random subjects? There are two reasons. Firstly, it helps one-dimensional folk with neither creativity nor the ability to bring some uninspiring text to life. Secondly, it is the most effective way to plagiarise the work of others as words through video form are not as easily detectable through a search engine if those words seem just a little familiar.

Sorry for blowing the lid on that one chaps, but the cyber world does need a break from your tedious home videos!

Anyway, back to blogging and naturally, in a world where quantity is everything, the crescendo of self-congratulatory backslapping hits an all-time high when a digital grunt reports that the latest blog has been seen by accessed by over 40 members of the public. Yes, 40 hits. I remember the moment well. Sadly, that means that 40 more potential customers of the BPO have been exposed to the chilling fact that *thought leaders* cannot spell 'anonymise' (*'annonomise'* anyone?) but thankfully do know how to search Google. So, it's not all bad.

Even more mind-blowingly, in a digital world where clicks need to amount in the tens or even 100s of 1000s before a proverbial eyelid is batted, 40 hits reflects either how low expectations are or perhaps how unaware the *'Thought Leaders'* are of the size of national, let alone global markets and their own position or status within them. I would hazard a guess that elements of both are relevant, but that misplaced self-awareness flickering against unwarranted self-aggrandizement is probably where, in *Google Maps* terms, one might drop one's pin.

You see, within these organisations, there is a truly bizarre de-sensitisation to the outside world. Becoming an *Account Director*, for example, becomes a life goal towards which your average career assassin will spend years, and I mean years, disposing of bodies and stooping to hitherto unknown moral depths. Just to secure that title and, as our US colleagues might force from their nasal cavities, kudos or koooo-dosss. It is such a crushing blow to discover that outside the walls of the BPO organisation, it means nothing. Just a pumped-up title in another shit-kicking, soul-eroding shysters' paradise.

What they do know – and some do have some particular skills, aside of course from the borderline psychotic manoeuvring and actual criminality – is often so niche it is not transferable and those who do manage to talk themselves into a role with a reputable company are soon found out. The only alternative for them is to slink back and do what they do best – back to the world of make-believe either to their previous BPO role or onto the BPO circuit where they will go around and around. The challenge then is to pace themselves and try to last longer than the almost obligatory eighteen months of the senior executives so that they can stretch out each lap to a full career.

In a sense, they become prisoners of their own pasts, recidivists who become so institutionalised that they can't carve out a straight life on the outside.

The self-appointed nature of *'thought leadership'* in these organisations is in itself worth albeit brief consideration. Like the self-declared Christians who have to keep reminding you that they are Christians because presumably you would not guess the fact through alone witnessing their actions, the *thought leaders* have to be explicit about who they are. Otherwise, you just would not come to that conclusion.

Similarly, there is a growing trend for members of operating boards to name themselves the *Leadership Team* because if they didn't, nobody would know that leadership was part of their roles and responsibilities!

One way to spot the aspiring *'thought leader'* though, is via their *LinkedIn* profile picture or how they appear on their company website. Standing speaking in front of a *PowerPoint* slide or with a headset or mic are the giveaways. I know of a few people who have had colleagues take iPhone pictures of them in internal meetings and they've used these closeups to give the impression that they are conference speakers. Another posted an entirely mocked-up picture of himself with an ear-mic.

Just one step away from wearing WWII medals at a Remembrance Parade. You wonder whether their *Facebook* profiles have them in full martial arts Gi and *Amazon*-purchased black belt.

It is sad, but is it really surprising? Real *thought leaders* have genuine careers that produce tangible results. When your working life is based on illusion and pretence, then maybe the sham reputations are a reasonable extension of this.

Perhaps they are a critical component of the whole picture.

15 – The Echo Chamber

So, we have considered *thought leadership* and also discussed that an illusion of service and delivery is maintained on all levels. Yet working on the premise that it is always easier to tell the truth than a lie, how can the facade be maintained?

Well, on one level it does not need to be. All the participants are compliant in the deception, ranging from the clients who need only the front to be maintained, to the staff who need their jobs and who (generally) could not care less after they have left as they will by then thankfully have real and authentic lives to lead.
But to maintain enough corroborative evidence that can be picked up and disseminated if questioned or posted and displayed for those who have no reason to question, there does need to be some sort of structure in place that applies sufficient control and regulates the free-thinking within the BPO itself.

Do not forget that the other side to the coin of reasonably well-educated staff who can read, write, communicate, and follow a script will always be free-thinking people who want to exercise choice – and they are dangerous.

Let them run freely and they will be digging for the genie's bottle and will not hesitate to pop the cork. Not with a view to necessarily causing intentional damage (though we can look at that later), but because the facts are there, and some people need to question and challenge.

§

It is now that I will do what I promised myself I would avoid at all costs – and that is to introduce some philosophical concepts that risk making this debate dry up to the point of whether nothing further can be comfortably ingested. I will however make it as palatable as possible before we move on. In doing so, I will risk combining the thoughts of two philosophers who in their day rarely seemed to agree on anything. Indeed, their public debates remained fractious to a tee, but both coined ideas and concepts that explain a great deal on this point.

The first is Michel Foucault whom I hope will not spin in his grave too virulently at the prospect of being coupled with the second, Noam Chomsky. I will keep this brief and to the point.

Foucault has been spoken about to some extent in relation to call centres as he was very keen on power and control and also referenced Bentham's Panopticon – useful ideas in relation to the all-seeing power exerted over others in the delivery of work.

It is all very interesting stuff and worth a read if you have several years to spare and have an undemanding personal life. But I should keep to the point at hand. What Foucault did further discuss, and it is this which is my point of focus now, was that those who have power at certain points in time, get to define the *discourse* of the day.

And if the *discourse* prevails and is repeated enough, it becomes *truth*. *Discourse* determines how subjects are discussed which defines *truths* in society. If enough people in the UK repeat that comedic virtuoso Allen Carr is a national treasure, then that is what he becomes. The institutions with power – newspapers, television stations, feature magazines and radio repeat it, and it becomes accepted and *'true'*. The same process works at a micro-level within organisations, and this is how organisations start to define how subjects are addressed.

If we park that for a moment and come to Chomsky who explored in some detail one of the frameworks for how discourses themselves can be framed and operationalised. This relates to the concept of *echo chambers*. Within organisations, *echo chambers* are maintained by creating a shared spirit and confining discussion confined within defined limits. Chomsky himself comments:

> *'The smart way to keep people passive and obedient is to strictly limit the spectrum of acceptable opinion but allow very lively debate within that spectrum – even encourage the*

more critical and dissident views. That gives people the sense that there's free thinking going on, while all the time the presuppositions of the system are being reinforced by the limits put on the range of the debate.[xi]

Through the headlines of the thought leaders and the values and behaviours that are propagated, a prevailing discourse is established in relation to key topics. Certain subjects like *Quality, Communication*, and *Service* are defined by the discourses used within the organisation. They are understood in particular ways, to a point where discussion does not extend beyond them.

For example, 'service' was for a long time viewed in terms of the 80% of calls answered within 20 seconds and the number of calls abandoned not exceeding 5%. That was '*service*' and therefore the '*truth of service*'. The fabled 80/20.

It was only when new discourses started to emerge on a wider level outside organisations, forcing a desire to change within them, that *customer experience* and first-time resolution started to emerge as new '*truths*'. These in turn were then propagated within the chambers within which they remained unchallenged until new ideas became irresistible to the organisations – ideas like the *Net Promoter Score (NPS)*. All the time, while the values of '*Openness and Honesty*' are championed, discussions are confined within these certain limits.

Now that is not to say that there cannot and is not opposition – but psychologically they are very difficult to resist. It means standing alone and effectively going to war against peers and colleagues at all levels in the organisational hierarchy.

It is, just not going to happen – at least, not very often.

Of course, those who do not agree and who are fearful of overt opposition to the ideas propagated within the *echo chamber* can opt for silence in meetings for example, while exercising freedom of speech outside the formal and regulated environments.

However, this in itself is challenged by a very straightforward tactic of being openly called out by requests for feedback/opinions. You know the scenario – someone will pan the room and ask you outright for your view or even more obviously will make a point of going around the table to ensure that all views are sought.

This is done in the knowledge that people who were either reluctant to speak or who did not feel strongly about something to proactively offer a view, are likely to take the path of least resistance and offer positive comments. Under the guise of open leadership and openness to a constructive exchange of views, the intention is very much to kill opposition by forcing commitment to a public position that the person will need to remain consistent in the future.

If you do resist, then as I have mentioned, wait for some emotionally stunted ex-retail worker who has been *punishment promoted* to head of department to subsequently confront you with some obscure piece of CRM data as evidence of your shortcomings.

Most people catch on and fall into line. Or resign.

One example of this is a BPO I know where 'Quality' is viewed through a lens of quantity. It is actually so bizarre and contradictory that I am frequently incredulous about how it can be maintained. But maintained it is to this very day. In brief, the BPO has a varied raft of clients and measures quality performance on all of them. The clients are very different though there is one single QA framework against which all calls and emails, irrespective of which client, are graded. Quality improvements are ascertained by the number of monitorings that are completed.

Now there is no examination of whether certain criteria are essential for client *x* or whether certain omissions might be critical for client *y*, while acceptable for client *z*. In effect, a qualitative view of, erm, quality is completely disregarded. Quality has become quantity. If 100 emails are monitored this month, compared with 85 last month, quality has improved(!)

Nobody has considered that quality systems are about defining a requirement in detail and then measuring adherence to that requirement. In a multi-client environment, this would of course need to be specific to a client and then individual service. Once we have a requirement that reflects what represents good for each client, we measure how our performance meets the goals. If they do, then performance is good. If not, it is below the acceptable quality. It, to any sane person, has nothing to do with quality. But just in the way that nobody ever questioned what an 80/20 service level actually equated to great service or why it was even 80 percent within 20 seconds (I still do not know the answer to that one myself), nobody challenges the re-imagination of quantity as quality.

It is staggering, but it happens to this day. Graphs are produced and there are cheers in the room when the number goes up. Actual cheers. But the prevailing discourse and the truth is that increased quantity equals increased quality. And so, it shall continue. Those in opposition who remain incredulous simply choose their battles and now go along with it. When all things are considered, if the aim of the game is to preserve one's position and relentless account churn has become normalised, why bother fighting it?

It is one of the vital building blocks that allow BPOs to maintain their insupportable logic and methodologies under the guise of *truth*. If *truths* can be maintained and never challenged, then change cannot threaten the status quo.

And in these organisations where resistance to change is ostensibly a cardinal sin, is it not a delicious irony that the prevention of change is part of institutionalised culture and practices?

I don't think I'll ever tire of the hypocrisy of the outsourced contact centre world.

Well, not now that I've handed in my badge and gun.

16 – Selling Close to the Wind

We have doubtless all heard of the *'pen test'* for potential salespeople at interviews. At some stage in proceedings, often at the very beginning, the *CEO* or Sales Director or whoever is leading the interview will nonchalantly pass the interviewee the said object and ask them to sell (them) the pen. For pen, substitute stapler, elastic band, apple etc., the specific object is not essential for the exercise.

The objective of this is to uncover whether the applicant for the said position has a valid process for selling, that is to say, a sales methodology. The trick lies in the ability of the salesperson to ask lots of questions which can be structured in a number of ways.

One approach might be to probe firstly about the seller's *situation*, then move on to questions that uncover potential *problems* that the potential buyer might be experiencing.

Then questions that highlight the *implications* of these problems take the buying to the verge of needing a solution.

The final step is the *need-pay-off*, the ta-dah moment that the pen is presented as the solution. The buyer has, via their carefully scaffolded answers, effectively whipped up and justified their need for the pen and in a sense simultaneously becomes both buyer and seller.

This is the *Huthwaite SPIN®* model devised after extensive research, namely a review of 35,000 sales calls. It is a highly effective model that makes sense and works. No criticism of the methodology whatsoever – it is a proven success and is used widely. I am personally an expert even though I have never strictly speaking held a sales position. I use it socially, interpersonally in public and even sometimes at home when I am trying to position things with my wife who invariably is always one step ahead of me anyway. It is a great model for no end of selling situations.

It is also the most prevalent technique used by the BPO selling machine and it absolutely pays dividends. In many BPOs, the top-performing sales managers will earn more than any other employee. I know of several who would top £250k in a year. They have little seniority overall, but they master this technique and deliver on it with such regularity that the high bonus payments that they command make them worth every penny to the organisations who employ them.

While they present themselves as affable, friendly, and loveable chaps, they are consistently and unswervingly applying this methodology in all of their interactions with both eyes firmly on the point where they will close their deal.

Yet, the sales process is not a single series of actions, and it most certainly does not involve the skilled salesman hooking and reeling in the unsuspecting buyer. Well, not entirely. Remember that in the world of BPOs, things are rarely exactly as they seem. Something is certainly being sold but what, to whom, and when are very different facets of what amounts to be an intricate process.

As a starting point, what is not disputed is that BPOs offer customer communication handling services and client organisations want to buy them. That is the headline statement and how everything appears on the surface. To the uninitiated, how could it be any different?

§

Let's look at who is actually doing the buying and how they do this.

There will be RFIs, ITTs you name it – all kinds of requests for information and responses. At this stage, all the standard credentials-heavy content is provided and frankly not very closely read (you discover this via the later questions you are asked about your organisation and capabilities).

Then you have the pitching and site visits which lead to the more formal closing.

As for the potential buyers/clients, there are generally two kinds.

The first is the less senior stakeholders who are potentially idealistic and who value their customers and their brand. They will be sent into the early stages of the sales situation, like canaries, often in the knowledge that their senior management team are leaning in favour of outsourcing though they themselves – being customer service savvy, have reservations. They will however be less seasoned regarding exposure to charlatans, so will not recognise the sales process as it is unfolding.

§

So, if you are a potential client and relatively new to the process of service procurement, take a brief moment to consider that at all times, you are being 'worked' into shape and steered down a well-trodden path towards that inevitable *need pay-off*. All the way through the process, the salesperson is constantly evaluating and re-evaluating what he thinks you are most likely to buy and that is the great thing about selling services.

It is not like there is a tangible product whose features you can see and for which you may already have some degree of opinion about the suitability or likelihood of purchase. The end product delivered in the payoff will absolutely fit like a glove when it is described to you. These are the stages where the sales professional understands exactly what you need and then malleably presents their organisation's services in the right way so that you are onside.

At this point, there are lots of *S* and *P* questions with a certain amount of *I* probing. The *N(P)* may be a little less explicit though often there will be full-on *SPIN®* and sub-selling to the minor stakeholders if there is a sense that there is strong competition, and the sale will need to be supported by internal advocates.

This is where *SPIN®* is the most effective and where the commissions are truly earned.

However, that is not to say that the selling BPO will possess the capability to deliver on a number of the key components. Of course, the sale is not necessarily the commitment to deliver what is promised. Remember that this process is about the salesperson formulating a sufficiently credible response that meets the documented requirement from the buyer. Once the two perspectives on the paperwork are aligned, the real sale can be completed between the parties – that will be the offloading of x or y service to the BPO who will then need to ensure that the delivery teams can deliver an ongoing credible story of service rather than any service itself.

This stage is about getting through to the next stage (unsurprisingly) with enough recorded/documented in order to justify relevant capability.

The team on the client side will likely have clear processes in place for recording the outputs from sales processes and reporting progress up through the line. This provides crucial corroboration for sales decisions as it emanates from managers who are, ahem, closer to the detail. It is their earlier-stage meetings that get the BPOs through to the latter and business-end stages of the process.

If you are wondering what role formal procurement teams play in these processes, the answer is that it is generally a selective one restricted to managing frameworks, processes, negotiations and putting together contracts. The real 'sell' happens outside of any such constraints or controls.

The second category of prospective clients themselves are not fooled by sales patter. These are the more senior clients, who absolutely understand the rules of engagement of the BPO sales process. They love it because a well-drilled sales professional is building a case (all backed up and documented in their slide decks and contact reports) that justifies the purchase to stakeholders.

It removes any suggestion of underhand procurement and protects the buyer from any comeback in the event that matters do not develop as planned. All decisions are of course backed up by the less senior staff who are exposed to the *SPIN®* and who report back favourably on the pitches that they attend.

Once the sales team get past the first hurdle having worked their *SPIN®* on the less senior team and addressed any questions or challenges (these can be comfortably addressed at this stage, as any site visits are likely to come later, so tough questions can always be glossed over verbally), everything moves to the next stage where the senior teams judge the pitch on altogether different criteria. It is here that the theoretical service and its credibility are tested along with an assessment of whether that commentary can be supported ongoing. If it can, then the presenting BPO is in with a chance of the contract.

Along the way, of course, there are other 'activities' that sometimes oil the wheels of a deal. I never had any direct knowledge of gratuities being offered or solicited, but then again such occurrences would unlikely be rolled out under anything other than the strictest levels of confidentiality. I did often wonder how people go about offering a bribe – after all, it would be a rather high-stakes proposition, given that if turned down by an affronted potential recipient, it could lead to immediate termination of all business and possible scrutiny from the authorities at all levels of your organisation.

I knew enough about the number of bodies buried in the various BPOs where I worked that outside scrutiny would be the number 1 *Kryptonite* for the senior management teams. Naturally, there were the usual corporate freebies – presumably piss-ups that would not have taken place in a brewery for obvious reasons – which I would guess were reward enough when you take into consideration the bonus structures that both clients (in relation to high levels of service reported) and BPO management (in relation to billings and, er, 'growth') could 'legitimately' rake in through a sustained and credible service commentary holding up over the course of the contract.

If these are in place, why take the risk of handling difficult-to-launder cash which might be exposed by anybody with an axe to grind? After all, nobody even wants to be in a situation where they have to defend themselves from such an accusation and the heat that such questions would bring. From an ethical perspective alone and I doubt they would even think twice.

You will hear of course of BPO personnel complaining about overselling of deals – it is the most common operational gripe about sales. Whenever I hear stories about sales managers overselling BPO services that operational teams struggle to deliver, I allow myself a wry smile – there is a delightful twist in relation to why this happens.

These are the occasions where unacceptable levels of integrity have leaked into the BPO's operational capability and the teams are actually attempting to deliver a real high-quality service (I know, I know – it's so difficult to get the right staff nowadays!).

It can happen when managers are recruited via an objective process rather than the *Facebook* methodologies and the BPO ends up employing a *mover & shaker* into a position where the wider organisation hopes that there will be neither moving nor shaking.

These problems will occur when the spectre of professionalism and integrity is not adequately kept at bay (it's a hard life in a BPO!). To regurgitate the Jobs quotation again, he said that Apple hired great people, not so Apple would tell them what to do but *so that they would tell Apple what to do*.

Of course, Jobs was a visionary who was motivated and invigorated by breaking new ground rather than somebody who simply wanted to keep cranking the wheel.

The first rule of BPO recruitment is to hire people who will accept what you tell them to do. If you do not do this, you will find that the double standard is not recognised, and people start to move and shake which takes the vessel off-course. It is therefore not an oversell at all but a complete strategic misappropriation by the account teams in question. They soon learn and fall into place, following the script.

The whole sales process is a carefully structured and layered series of actions designed to build the credibility of a story rather than that of the service being sold. Everybody plays their part without fully knowing the precise part they are playing. The manoeuvring at different stages creates collateral that builds a picture of credibility and propriety. In this way, confidence levels around a robust process are high and everything can roll out as planned.

To borrow an astute observation from Groucho Marx:

> 'The secret of life is honesty and fair dealing. If you can fake that, you've got it made.'

And in the BPO world, the sales teams can and do.

17 – Hey, Charming...

If you ever wanted to be a human resources officer and, having done your CIPD qualifications you needed to work in an environment where you would have plenty of opportunity to apply your theory to practice, the BPO would be your first and preferable port of call.

There is as a rule no shortage of personnel-related issues that will come up day after day, week after week, and seemingly endless opportunities to support and coach managers in best practices that are recommended by your professional body. That is the positive spin.

The reality is doubtless abundantly clear: BPOs are a mosh pit of vulnerable and delusional people suffering from a seemingly endless range of personal problems, not to mention medical and psychological ailments, who in turn are pressured into fulfilling repetitive and often meaningless work under chaotically conceived and applied management practices. Phew – no, I don't think I've left anything out there.

Now, that is a perfect scenario for somebody with a real love of human resource best practice to get involved and engaged and help to make the world a better place. It is quite simply a real opportunity for those who have such skills to demonstrate influence and leadership.

Alas, it is an opportunity that is rarely taken up. The main reason for this is that the so-called human resource professionals have a real reluctance to step away from their theoretical models and to actually step into the unknown and deal with real events as they unfold.

Back in the day, these were the people who were known as *personnel managers* or *personnel officers* as the concept of HR (whatever that actually means) had not yet come to the fore. To this day the whole area of human resource management remains a mystery to those involved in contact centres. One thing is for sure and that is that the so-called human resource function can actually be run on a very low headcount without the need to have numerous human resource experts focusing on every area relating to people.

Now I can understand why you need to have experts on employment law and the guardians of the various processes and procedures that support the way that staff should behave and interrelate. Unfortunately, in practice, those entrusted with this responsibility tend to play out whole careers on the fence, unable to commit to a particular piece of applied advice whenever asked.

The favourite position is to simply trot out the CIPD best practice and tell the manager seeking advice that it is their decision. Now I can absolutely get that – the manager is the business decision owner so that should be the person taking responsibility. However, your typical HR advisor will always ensure that they do not go even to the point where they would say what their recommendation would be under certain circumstances. That is however not to say that if the manager takes a decision with which they did not agree, they will not retrospectively position something as having gone against their advice. It's just that they are never explicit in black-and-white terms about what should be done. However, they will freely report to others what their advice would be or had been even though they had never articulated it in the first instance. Confused? Join the club because I was never able to work out why they were such opinion contortionists myself.

The position that HR folk typically take up in a BPO, is to enjoy the close interaction with senior managers and the status that this brings to them in terms of reflected authority while actually making very little contribution that their professional qualifications would suggest that they might. They absolutely relish that they are the ones taken into confidence in relation to restructures and potential redundancy situations and they absolutely enjoy the closed-door nature of the meetings that they can attend and decide on the fates of others, knowing that they do so from a position of relative safety.

It is one of those areas where posturing is everything and delivering rarely features.

You may see all of the certificates framed on proud presentation in the office, usually some master's degree in HRM from the University of Peckham or some other equally august institution, and that usually is the extent of it. As time has passed, I've come to the view that having an HR team is simply to add an air of credibility and propriety to personnel management issues within the BPO.

After all, while painting themselves as the guardians of propriety, it is usually in these departments that you will see the illicit affairs with colleagues (naturally with the company policies in relation to the declaration of any conflict-of-interest dutifully ignored) or the HR directors having their car keys wrested from them after several bottles of wine at a lower-level development centre. You know the sorts of shenanigans that pale into insignificance with the so-called indiscretions that they will be busting a gut to have you over with at the slightest opportunity. Having a poor chap sacked for making unauthorised calls on the ACD or some other such high crime.

In fairness, my analysis of the usefulness of HR teams does not seem to be inconsistent with the way that organisations are now starting to run them. In recent years they have become greatly slimmed down, and some of the activities for which they would previously have had responsibility have been outsourced themselves. These for example would relate to tasks such as reviewing disciplinary cases which in many BPOs were passing through insurers who would take the decision on whether or not a capability or disciplinary case would go to a full hearing. This way the quality of the decision is passed to somebody capable of making it and this decision itself has a much-mitigated amount of risk. Unfortunately, these insurers are so risk-averse in themselves – because they know that any costs for an unsuccessful case would need to be met from their own coffers – that some of the decisions meted out have bordered on the insane.

Just as an aside, it would cost in the region of at least £10,000 for a case to be defended, win, or lose, at a preliminary ET hearing if a Solicitor and counsel were engaged. For a full tribunal, you may be looking at double that.

Now, unless the employment tribunal at the preliminary hearing states that the case does not have a reasonable prospect of success, everybody will be in a position where they would need to cover their own costs. Anything with a sniff of discrimination is almost certainly not going to be kicked out at the early stages. As a result, I have seen cases referred to insurers, where employees were on final written warnings, and the decision has come back that they should be placed on a final, final written warning. I would love to be jesting, but it happens. Muppetry that would have made the legendary Jim Henson's beard tingle.

In fact, I am sure that one particular miscreant remained employed on a final, final, final warning. And a fully paid gym membership was provided, in an attempt to help the obscenely obese grunt improve his health to the point where he might have felt well enough to attend work. As that particular case unfolded, he expressed his gratitude by consuming 2 Mars bars in his return-to-work interview when news of this additional support was being given. You could not make it up.

This just brings the whole disciplinary and capability process wholly into disrepute, not just from my perspective as an outsider looking in but also in relation to how the employees themselves view the companies. And while all of this is going on, the BPOs concerned continue to use these staff, who can only be described as a gross risk to their clients' business, to deliver services for which they themselves continue to bill whoever is prepared to engage them. Now whatever the senselessness of this approach, it happens because HR professionals are seen as so ineffective and unfit for purpose.

But it is not just their fence-sitting and inability to translate theory into practice that has made HR professionals increasingly redundant from the relevant aspects of organisational life. It is also because, during their transition from personnel managers to human resource managers, the promise was that they would be adding more value to organisations.

Hmmm, now that was always going to be problematic!

What they tried to do was build up expectations around the ideas and concepts they wanted to introduce in order to facilitate the management of large numbers of people within these organisations. They talked extensively about *empowerment* and even more so about *employee engagement*. What a delightful concept which, like everything in the world of HR, is flogged to death relentlessly without any real appreciation of what needs to be done to make it happen in the real world.

In BPOs, any mention of *empowerment* and *engagement* is just *virtue signalling*, nothing more. Empty references with no commitment.

A former colleague of mine noted that every time they heard *about employee engagement*, a small part of them died inside. An over-worked and engineered HR concept that became a whole industry, instead of being simple common-sense everyday interaction with others, based on respect and understanding. In the BPO world, this is the sardine throwing to the seals, the transactional and immediate gratification that the shallow managers perceive to be job satisfaction and which they understand to be effective and respectful bridge building and the creation of a connection with their staff.

Those at the pinnacle of their own personal delusions have even styled themselves as *Employee Experience Directors* instead of the modestly absurd *Human Resources Directors* or *HRDs*. Who says that the chewing of khat had not crossed over from the Somali community? Well, if it is not that, then there must be a large number of GPs over-prescribing on the anti-psychotic meds. Whatever the reasons behind it, the HR gang are getting high on somebody's supply.

§

But back to the world of concept confetti. Unfortunately, their analysis and over-engineering of these grand themes have served only to alienate those who were intended to be the gleeful recipients of this knowledge. It was as if somebody had decided that the human resources industry needed to have some signature concepts, so they took some basic ideas and then tried to make them complicated enough that they seemed worth paying for. Something that elevated the mere personnel manager from their position of paper shuffling and form filling to, dare I say it, another form of *thought leader* who would define a new path.

After all, what does *engagement* mean? It is really not anything special or anything over and above what has helped to make the human race tick over for thousands of years. It is about respecting the views of others, listening to them, and understanding shared interests and objectives.

Yet if you speak to a human resource professional, they will sneer at you if you did not know how to set down an *employee engagement* plan in the way that their CIPD course lecturer would have tabled one. The most insupposable thing about all of this is that HR professionals rarely have any engagement skills themselves – this is one of the reasons why they love their position atop the proverbial fence. It is because they cannot handle objections and the fluid movement of an argument that might arise during engagement with another individual. It is why they like to point back to black-and-white processes and procedures rather than using the theories they have learned to inform a changing environment.

On occasions, they leave the whole consultation process to operational managers. Little wonder that Employment Tribunals then have to step in – as they frequently do – with some eye-wateringly poignant awards.

§

Empowerment is the other stock term that was used so prevalently in the 1990s that it felt like you needed a vaccination against it from your doctor. It was that pervasive, yet from our position as contact centre managers, it has been clear for a long time that *empowerment* is exactly what they *do not* wish to give their people.

Contact centres are about tight control of operational practices so that the uniformity of what is delivered is preserved. It is essential that what one customer experiences is exactly the same as that experienced by another. If you allow empowered decision-making, you will allow for variability. The cost models and the service delivery promises – in fact, everything about contact centres – are predicated on the elimination of variation. It is fundamentally at odds with free-thinking and empowered individuals.

Therefore, if you are a business that is looking to employ a BPO, and somebody presenting a seemingly endless *PowerPoint* slide deck moves onto the subject of *empowerment*, you know that what they are saying is absolutely what they will not be delivering in practice. It is the antithesis of the whole volume delivery model.

§

So, what is the future for HR professionals? Possibly not a bright one. More and more of their crazy policies are being called into question, including the hitherto sacred cow of the performance appraisal. As already discussed, is it feasibly possible to imagine a greater ball of toss? Many organisations have simply canned them in preference to summary statements and discussions at the end of the business year. Businesses are also frequently advertising roles under *HR Business Partner/HRBP* titles that do not require formal HR qualification, simply demonstrable knowledge of employment law and interpersonal skills. Finally, some common sense.

However, don't be too sure that this enlightenment will extend to BPOs. After all, this is the world of pretence and performance, so while the HR profession still retains some ostensible credibility, it will likely continue to be a feature of organisational shenanigans.

The issue for all you poor folk who continue to work within BPOs will be that you have to continue to endure the sight of under-achieving and mendacious, power-crazed, and sadistic, psychotic weirdos continually having their closet meetings where they can bathe in their proximity to authority and influence.

Or the desk-approaching, where they can squat down and have that special kind of conversation where you know they are putting the knife in. Remember when you see that – it is the prelude to poison. In brief, it is all about power by proxy – the kind of excitement felt by policy advisors in Government. Close the action but nowhere to be seen when the axes fall.

The occasional saving grace can be experienced in the smaller BPOs – that is to say, those who are likely to be acquired by a larger player. This is the direction of travel in the BPO world, as it always has been. Acquisitions of client lists, in the guise of the merging of companies per se. Then, almost inevitably, the subsequent joining of corporate worlds will see your existing HR slugs duly salted by the comparatively monumental HR miscreants of the parent company, leaving not more than the faintest of sliver trails in their wake.

18 – Hire and Hire

Recruitment is an area that is arguably worth a chapter on its own, given the volume of frankly incredible examples of ineptitude that have been witnessed over the years. However, as is so often the case, the essence of the problem can be summed up with reference to a number of key points of reference.

As noted previously, the idea of *Facebook promotions* vs those that are actually earned through proven skills and competencies is comically prevalent though even when companies do have documented recruitment processes and procedures, they are regularly subverted by a number of issues affecting assessors.

The most common one is when the hiring manager gives a clear direction to the lead assessor in advance of the process. This is more common than not and will range from the direct order or a more subtle expression of a sense of relief if candidate x – the clearly most suitable candidate for the position – were successful. I am sure that this resonates with most people.

In many cases, this is actually not required as candidates dropping the correct culturally attuned hints at an assessment will likely be scooped up without having to resort to anything so trite as providing evidence-based competency answers or even, as is now *de rigeur* evidence of their strengths.

This is because the list of 'Do-nots' for assessors is practically the unofficial handbook for assessors in BPOs. *Confirmation bias* is a favourite in most interviews where a pre-conceived judgement of the candidate fixes their score and outcome from the off. This can (and why not allow the whole process to be subverted by the literally superficial?) be driven by looking the part and by understanding the unofficial uniform of the BPO. At one place I worked, the middle and senior managers adopted the almost criminal US combo of blue shirt, yellow trousers/chinos, and chunky, tasselled shoes. Suits you, Sir.

Alternatively, this *route one* can be achieved by dropping familiar and jargon into the interview that allows the interviewer to judge the candidate as 'one of us' or somebody who knows their way around. I have seen interviews swing irrevocably on the basis of some lame examples about average call lengths or clients not willing to underwrite call forecasts on per-minute commercials. The almost now tiresome:

> *'Well, my view was that if the client did not have any faith in their own numbers and was not willing to put their money where their mouth was, then why should I?*

Yawn. Hired. Note to self that another shyster has just entered the building.

In the interview itself, this was commonly supported by what psychologists call an *affective heuristic* – often irrelevant but snap judgements based on a fact or characteristic that has little if any bearing on the role itself. A frequent one is when it is established that the candidate worked at a competitor (so they must know what they are talking about), knows a mutual contact, or is simply *white* and *middle-class*.

It is a sad fact to note, but how many BME senior managers have you ever seen in BPOs? Board members are practically non-existent or confined to token existence in meaningless or non-influential HR roles. It is unpalatable and unpleasant but borne out by the facts.

And the ones that do make it up the greasy pole to their token positions, do not last long. They are comfortably squeezed out in restructures, once they have served whatever purpose facilitated their elevation.

The senior figures at BPOs are reassured that the BME community are far too busy occupying the advisor ranks to be concerned with seniority.

While of course trumpeting their support for 'Diversity' in whatever *thought leadership* activity is currently taking their fancy.

In many respects, this allows some, albeit fleeting, picture of diversity to be achieved, but of course it never goes anywhere near a sense of *inclusion*.

Seriously though, the reason that more BME candidates are not elevated to positions of seniority is because selection decisions are taken by people who prefer to hire those who look like and think like they do.

Remember, BPOs are about exploitation, so those who feel the pain of this, albeit in other contexts are less likely to play ball and support these approaches in the workplace. So, it explains why these kinds of people are not readily hired. It is not unusual for BME candidates in the workplace to be termed 'vocal' which is code for 'problematic'. If they have an opinion, they may even be termed 'radical'. That is code for *'needs to be moved out of the business sharpish'.*

Hire a BME candidate who has experienced prejudice and oppression all their life and you had better believe that they will start to call out other injustices they see when in a position of authority. To most of us with a sense of justice and righting wrongs, that would seem reasonable.

In BPOs, it goes down like a vomit gazpacho.

Elsewhere in processes, pre-conceptions will also lead to common displays of *anchoring* – where a high anchor of expectation is fixed to candidates and then determines a correspondingly higher evaluation of any evidence presented. This will be applied as a way of upgrading responses where required, particularly if there are any unwelcome attempts from 'rogue' managers to inject any unwarranted objectivity into the process.

Intermeshed into everything however will be the ever-present and incontrovertible intuition of the experienced hiring manager who will *'know what good looks like'* and *'what is required to succeed'.*

This is where the *'business decision'* trumps everything and where the *'halo and horns'* beats all.

The bottom line is that recruitment is all about getting in people who will support common agendas and has little to do with fairness. Any established process that ostensibly guarantees fairness can easily be circumvented as hiring managers are well-versed in writing up compliant notes that can boost a poor candidate who is a good fit and can downplay a good candidate who may be a threat or a poor fit.

The way you hear some of the acolytes speaking in these organisations, these are the 'lands of opportunity'. Sadly, that is, ahem, a myth. The outward messaging says otherwise, but it is woefully the brand leading the bland, so to speak.

§

Let me take you on a brief journey to illustrate what life is like for an employee seeking to progress within a BPO.

When a role becomes available, internal candidates will generally have one of the following 3 experiences:

1) Firstly, there is the gold standard, reserved for the chosen few. To become eligible, people have to be unapologetic 'yes men/women' who unswervingly and unreservedly support the party line no matter how absurd or disingenuous. They will have sold out everything they purported to believe in for that next step up the ladder while outwardly projecting the mask of reason and professionalism. They will however have a surprisingly thin skin which betrays their awareness of their own potential vulnerability. They will of course be awarded the position without any objective process taking place.

Worryingly common, particularly at the more senior levels, but this route is reserved for the most sycophantic of colleagues who have spent years slithering up to senior managers, rubbishing others in their wake. So, unless people are prepared to share their pseudo-knowledge unashamedly and laughably or their hip social awareness at management dinners and the like, this route won't be for them. It is sickening ingratiation, not talent, that is valued and rewarded.

Invariably hopeless once in the role, they will try to piece together what leadership and their roles mean through endless *Google* searches and out-of-context articles after which their approach will be confused, contradictory and at times downright baffling. They will however paradoxically become unassailable as their removal would throw a bright spotlight on the clowns who had sanctioned their appointments. For the grassroots staff, these people are as welcome as cancer of the oesophagus.

2) Alternatively, they experience the 'Now you see it, now you don't' trick. A sleight of hand worthy of any skilled prestidigitator, the job is advertised for minimal time, in the hope that the favoured candidate will be the only one to apply. Sometimes just a working week with it included on the internal jobs bulletin a day before the application window ends.

This relies on the likelihood that strong candidates will feel they do not have enough time to submit a viable application. If more applicants do apply, the role will be removed for reasons of budget or the like with favoured candidates subsequently appointed anyway, ostensibly to a different job title and department.

Once appointed, it will be manifestly evident that the appointees will be stratospherically dim, and of course, majestically inactive when in post. Even the clown-like hiring managers will be baffled at their own stupidity with these appointments, so will try to reassure themselves by posting some articles on *LinkedIn* that reflect their desired status as thought-leaders. This might be an article suggesting that *'businesses are looking for the best talent'* or *'organisations want to make a profit'.* Or some other such ground-breaking revelations.

While these shenanigans are gaining airtime in the organisation, HR will acknowledge that it is all outrageous but will be relentless in their own pursuit of masterly inactivity. Well let's face it, it's difficult to have their endless stream of chummy huddles with people they are challenging even if that (i.e. supporting equality of opportunity) is actually a fundamental part of their roles. And so, it or rather nothing, comes to pass.

Meanwhile, the only movement in HR will tend to be the sense of a shiver, desperately seeking a spine to go down.

3) Finally, the remaining group of candidates apply and go through the full process but are not appointed even if they are the stand-out candidates with the highest scores. In these cases, scores will be moderated down and the favoured, but tremendously dense and wonderfully compliant colleagues will be appointed instead. Even if further vacancies become available, the organisation will wait for 6 months to pass so that the top candidates – if they are not confirmed acolytes – are still not appointed.

Meanwhile the Mr or Miss 'nice-but-dim' who are saddled with jobs that they cannot do have to rely on the true charlatans of the organization in order to step in and weave a beautiful tapestry of distraction for the benefit of all the clients who are impacted by this institutionalised mediocrity. And credit where credit is due, that is where these companies truly excel.

The clients – who for the most part just don't need the hassle and are really not close to what goes on – are expertly distracted by the swathes of flattering but useless content that is produced and sloshed around on endless online platforms. This is supported by the awards submissions that are designed to flatter the clients to the extent that it becomes the oxygen that pumps them up in the eyes of their own bosses and keeps the whole sorry ship afloat.

The dire and frankly abysmal social media marketing that the BPOs pour forth – we are drowning in it.

Name the bandwagon and they are all over it like a cheap tuxedo at an awards ceremony. It's all about shifting attention away from the pitiful services they frequently offer and giving weak clients every reason not to probe further.

Of course, you will be told that the BPOs are the source of opportunity. And of course, they are. Just not one of equal opportunity.

You will be told that people are happy and that they provide a great service – wow, some of the colleagues who work there even say so when asked. But anyone who seriously holds that up as credible has clearly never seen a video of a hostage reading a script.

In effect, these organisations have become the epitome of one where *appearing to be successful is the goal rather than actually being successful.*

They would rather fail than allow others outside the incestuous inner circle to be seen to be contributing something worthwhile. It is a warped, psychotic narcissism that eats away at all aspects of their operations.

Ultimately no amount of the vast swathes of gut-voiding marketing material, pictures of cups of coffee or views of the roofs of the environs that are relentlessly posted online (and you will be spoken to if you have not 'liked' them within 24 hours) or articles that the posters do not understand but nevertheless share in a desperate growth-hacking frenzy will deodorise the lamentable and inescapable truth.

The bowels of the BPO digestive system continue to excrete the worst contact centres in living memory.

§

You of course do get some classic situations with candidates appropriating the work histories of others even to the point of impersonation. I remember reviewing a CV where the candidate had – by chance – reworked their job history to include by the freak of chance a couple of positions that my own wife had occupied and one role that I had held myself. Companies and periods of employment cited matched our own (genuine) CVs. I probably should have invited him to interview to test him out, but it was simply somebody who was fortuitously rumbled doing blatantly what 90% of candidates do to a greater or lesser extent.

Interestingly the same candidate had applied for a role at another company where I had worked and had turned up for an interview without realising that he had previously worked for us when we had been known by a different name and been at a different location. He had left us under challenging circumstances 10 years previously and did not acknowledge me at the interview but had recognised enough people as he walked around on his site tour to ask one of the other assessors 'did this used to be called (company x)?'. When told yes, he appeared rather subdued as he must have been wondering whether he himself had been recognised and whether or not the fact that he had not noted his previous tenure on his CV might go against him.

Well, it did not matter too much. While he had and it did, he was on his own merit so poor that he would not have been allowed to run a bath, let alone a team. And that was coming from a company that was run by hustlers, for the benefit of charlatans.

It is just that you really do need to be good at being bad in the BPO world.

This was not the first time people returned to BPOs that had fired them – another Team Leader sacked for breaking into a senior manager's PC, ended up back in the same company following a later acquisition. Everybody was powerless though ostensibly they were all unaware.

Effectively though, internal BPO recruitment is simply a tool for the maintenance (and strengthening) of the status quo. It has nothing to do with talent, continuous improvement, or the enhancement of strategic competitiveness.

§

For the more senior positions, companies often rely on the service of specialist recruitment agencies. Now, such is the extent of their unscrupulous duplicity and immoral role in the so-called industry, I will struggle to find the appropriate words to convey the depths to which these individuals and companies will sink. But allow me to give you a flavour. I have had experience with these people from the client as well as the candidate perspective.

As a candidate, they are your very best friend, oozing positivity and always at the end of the phone, giving you every possible hint, tip, and insight into what the client organisation wants to hear. Note that most will never even meet their candidates though absolutely will tell the client that they interview and screen all the highest quality movers and shakers that they have on their books, so to speak. They are in fact large database repositories that are built up over time via their websites or via harvesting techniques such as Boolean and X-ray searching of websites.

They promote themselves as working their hides off to the *nth* degree to carve out the best opportunities for you and they flip it to the client that they are sourcing only the best candidates so that the process is time and cost-efficient and cuts through the trees in order to arrive at the premium pieces of wood.

The truth is less palatable. They just want to make a sale and will misrepresent the role to you, just as they will misrepresent you as the candidate to the client. They will try and get as many misfits to be convinced about the role as they can, in the knowledge that the majority of clients screw themselves over by being susceptible to the bias that the aforementioned traps bring forth. They do this in the knowledge that it is a numbers game where they need to be lucky only once. In an industry where managers are often not accountable once in a role their real skills only need to be their ability to 'play the game'.

Often though, the prep is simply to ensure that the candidates can bring enough credible answers to a standard competency-based interview so that the notes can be substantiated with the hiring manager able to gain enough insight into the candidate as a potential player. There are so many ways in which the approach can work – though rarely in the way it purports to. And work it does with it being a very lucrative business and with fees for more senior managers topping 30% of gross annual salary.

For the candidate though, once the client goes cold on them, the professional and attentive recruitment agency will drop them like third-grade French. Calls returned? Don't build your hopes up. You are a commodity to be sold on and have some healthy cash earned straight off your back. If not, you will be 'ghosted' faster than a *Deliveroo* suicide cyclist passing a red light.

There is a saying in the job market that the second worst thing to happen to you is to not get the job you applied for. The worst thing? To get actually get the job that you bullshitted your way into (or that somebody bullshitted you into) that you were ill-suited for. That will ultimately be more painful for you and for the company that hired you, than if you had received a so-called *regret* letter in the first instance.

For the recruitment agency, it is a win-win. The hiring BPO has to take responsibility for the hire – it is their decision after all and are unlikely to admit that they made a poor one. It will all be put down to the candidate not being able to hack it or documented as the mutually convenient *'personal reasons'* (when was any reason not actually personal?) and the cycle begins again – most likely with the same agency that will place their next candidate with you.

Of course, there is a silver lining here for those who despise the immoral BPOs – the specialist agencies are arguably even more despicable and ruthless than their clients. They moan about clients shafting them by going to introduced candidates directly, but they hawk their candidates to multiple companies to maximise the fees, often dropping the less lucrative client at the last minute and leaving them with no option but to take a weaker candidate or one who will likely not make the grade at the last minute. Often having negotiated 'exclusivity' on contracts but of course squeezing as much out of the candidate pool as possible.

But the height of agency miscreancy is the old phantom candidate scam. It is a beauty that works so well with heads of site who allow non-existent workers to be billed to their clients. Could these scams often work without the complicity of the agencies themselves? No, of course not. On more than one occasion, I was directly offered an 'in' into very sophisticated set-ups that would have given me very lucrative kickbacks on so-called 'ghost' agents. I do not recall working with any agency where such an arrangement – albeit on differing scales – would not have been possible or even readily available at the right level. Never with in-house operations though – only with outsourcers. The reason for this is simple. The cost of agency workers is passed through to clients with a mark-up. If the workforce management model justifies seasonal peaks of x, then clients will accept the scientific workings as justification for the spend – after all, none of them ever have their own WFM experts to scrutinise the workings, do they?

Furthermore, once billed, everybody gets healthy. The salary part is split between the agency and the site management in the deal – tax-free; the BPO takes the margin. Everyone's a winner baby.

The favourite identities to use are those on maternity leave who are without salary for an extended period of time and are happy to take a regular payment in exchange for the use of their identity. In some cases – for example, those who are married and who have left the job market – they may be completely unaware. The so-called work is of course reflected in the annual issue of the P60 – which of course is generated by the employer's payroll, i.e. the agency. Naturally, this is never sent on, and what is more never chased as the individuals concerned are not expecting one. As far as they are concerned, they have not worked. Any stray letters from HMRC that generate questions are typically whitewashed by the agency as errors. Agency employees typically use the agency as the one-stop shop for all queries even those related to tax. After all, who wants to pay phone charges for 40 minutes waiting on hold, followed by a painful 30-minute call only to be told that any matter then needs to be looked at in more detail before it can be fully resolved? You then need to repeat the process when you have to call them back if you miss their returned call.

One of my contacts who has been running these scams for the best part of 30 years explained that a combination of complex bureaucracy, operational inefficiency, and a general lack of awareness allow such ploys to run undetected for an indeterminate amount of time. It is the gift that keeps on giving. An opportunity to rely on the apathy and abdication of responsibility to others. Which is of course exactly how recruitment agencies come into existence. They do the jobs that organisations cannot be bothered to do and who are so keen to get out of their inboxes that they become completely removed and disengaged from them.

As a result, crooks managing databases become 'recruiters'.

The only redeeming feature of their work is that they are shafting the shafters, and in some ways it might seem a little like a form of divine retribution.

However, malpractice is malpractice, so it would be improper for me to not include these activities in our review of the BPO universe.

In some ways though, it is just another example of the exchange of cash on the money-go-round. The BPOs themselves would arguably not see any value in looking under the bonnet as long as the vehicle gets everybody from *A* to *B*.

Which is a recurring thread in this account. As long as the bottom line pans out as planned, neither ethics, professionalism, corruption, deception, nor any other chicanery will matter. Only the margin vs forecast.

It is on this premise that the recruiters base their skulduggery and earn their hall pass permissions from the BPOs themselves.

19 – Training at the Leash

In the grand scheme of things, I had not intended to talk about the next group of BPO actors as frankly, there is so little to say about them and what they do.

Nevertheless, in the interests of completeness, here is a brief exposé of another group existing within the broad umbrella of HR, namely Learning and Development or L&D if you are *on it*.

It will soon become eminently clear why, in my heart of hearts, I had not intended to include them. When you see the L&D team leaving a team meeting, it is like watching stiffs being pulled from a car wreck. Lifeless and soulless. Now that is not a personal criticism, just a recognition of the position within BPOs that they hold.

So, let us get this over with and cast our eye over their flatlining existence.

L&D professionals (as they do like to adopt this flattering self-reference) have emerged from the former Training departments, largely because the CIPD have sought to define the role of professional trainers in a broader more value-adding way (NB the transition of *Personnel* to *HR*).

This may indeed be creditworthy, in organisations where training staff not only teach employees the nuts and bolts of their specific roles but also plays a wider role in supporting them with their general professional growth with their softer skills and making them more rounded and capable professionals.

Ok everybody, back in the room. This is the BPO world.

Training does not – unless in very rare and bespoke circumstances – have its own revenue stream. Trainers are there to pass on the minimum required to get the job done and the time they spend (which is non-recoverable) is a straightforward cost. Training is therefore quick and dirty with no real 'learning' and certainly no 'development'. 'Courses' are slung together and delivered by trainers, often seconded or on, ahem, *'development opportunities'* themselves, who read line-by-line from slide decks and who often are seeing the material for the first time as they are running through it with their classes.

And when it's done, it's done – do not expect any ongoing involvement from the trainers, once you are in post.

Trainers themselves will be either the advisors who do not fancy advancement to a management role or will be the off-with-the-fairies type of hand-wringing lightweights who have parachuted in, thinking they are Mahatma Gandhi and will change the way we all feel, making us all emotionally intelligent or something similar.

You will also see more than just an above-average representation of claw hands and club feet in relation to the office holders. This is not by chance – it is a standard manoeuvre in BPOs to shuffle those who have ongoing medical absences into training roles. In that way, the revenue streams will not be adversely impacted when they are out of the business.

Furthermore, it moves the issue into HR who finally get to own some of the problems about which in any other situation they will be sitting on the fence.

In relation to the trainers themselves, the heights of their optimism will likely be matched only by the brutal put-down they will receive from some Neanderthal Site Director once they get above their station. The history of BPOs is littered with the puffs of disappearing smoke into which Training professionals evaporate.

Well to the BPOs, they are totally and immediately expendable. Just get another grunt in, give them a job title, and move on.

Now you will get properly accredited Training Managers in more senior roles in L&D. But for the reasons cited above, these will largely be the most demotivated and cheesed-off people in the company. If you had to rank the number 1 group of people in BPOs who are undervalued and who feel undervalued, it is these fellows. In the eyes of senior managers, they are even below those at advisor level – mainly because they do not have any earning potential.

Ask an L&D professional what it is like to get some training investment signed off by a *CFO* in a BPO. You might as well turn directly to face a hurricane while attempting equine-like urination. It just ain't happening.

Nevertheless, in spite of the charade, L&D managers and staff are still happy to play the L&D game – going through the motions and completing their CIPD coursework. For them, the endgame is qualification and a meaningful role in an alternative organisation. For the staff in the BPOs, there is basic instruction but sadly no learning or development. Unless, of course, they are learning about another application of doublespeak which is so prevalent in every aspect of the BPO performance. And given the resistance that can be seen in every BPO, it is highly probable that they are.

They do their best though, those L&D folks. For the benefit of their classes, they do try to come across as buzzing and bouncy, happy, and jolly. In reality though, they are terminally in psychological decline.

Essential for their immediate survival though are the so-called *happy sheets* at the end of the courses. Ostensibly to help them with the improvement and development of their materials but actually to validate their own positions as the providers of learning.

Learners will typically be asked to state their name on the sheets which psychologically gears respondents towards the positive as the path of least resistance because, in the British culture, nobody likes to complain.

They are then asked to rate the training in terms of its usefulness (how would they know until they have put what they have been taught into practice over several months?), the expertise of the trainer (again, how would they as the learners have any idea about that?) etc.

All part of the pretence, in organisations where it is more important to look successful than be successful.

Where the performance goal is to give an impression of growth of the individual, whereas the reality is that people need to be given only the essentials to deliver the minimum.

After all, remember the margins when you are charging £12 per hour and the fully loaded minimum wage in the UK will eat up 78% of that. And certainly, never forget that in the BPO world, nothing is what it appears to believe or is labelled.

Everything is packaged to make acceptance easier and questioning or challenges less likely or more trouble than they are worth. It is all about facilitating and greasing the path of least resistance. The lubrication on the invoice before it is deftly placed on the client P&L.

It must however all take its toll on the individuals working in these departments as their performance in role is the most transparent status you will encounter.

If the role of a Training or L&D Manager is on the one hand to devise organizational training strategy, oversee its implementation and assess its outcomes...

...and on the other hand, whose responsibilities include enhancing employees' skills, performance, productivity, and quality of work...

...then what they actually do in BPOs is closer to basket-weaving or jungle exploration.

Everyone knows that they are stretched beyond belief even to get enough under their belts to deliver their own charades, in practice often something just what they are frequently just reading from the projector screens. In most training sessions, the saving grace will be if they can get away with embarrassingly overplaying the knowledge of the participants to the extent that it is the trainees who effectively deliver the training. Regrettably even this is grossly apparent to the seasoned observer even if the rookies – who do not know any better – assume that that is how it should roll out.

But what must be the most galling for any Training Manager, is the absolute complete disregard in which they are held in BPOs. They sit in meetings and interject and are often just completely ignored, the disrespect is palpable. In some situations, it is all the operational teams can do to prevent themselves from walking out mid-sentence when one of these guys is addressing the floor (on the rare occasions they are afforded that privilege).

Even HR have more credibility which should be the death knell for anybody seeking some sort of self-respect or personal feelgood.

So, Training Managers determined to do something – indeed anything- viable in the professional world, need to stop straining at the leash in BPOs because there is a desert of opportunity.

Bide your time chaps, get your qualifications and de-camp somewhere you will just be recognised as a participant in the plot. Because if you stay, the plot will be what you have lost.

20 – Shhhh... IT Happens...

All BPOs naturally run on the basis of a far-reaching and often complex IT infrastructure and will have an in-house team of support engineers who will keep the whole thing up and running. Now that is their primary responsibility at the highest level.

However, in practice, what they are required to do is pander to the whims of often highly paid and supposedly intelligent staff who frankly do not know their *Adobe* from their *Windows*.

They are in brief the most overworked and put upon, and arguably undervalued members of any BPO set-up. It is often said of support engineers that they have very little in terms of people skills and talk to the internal customers as if the latter are rather dim. Well, the truth of the matter is most of the internal customers are somewhat dim and any slight sense of frustration on the part of the support engineer should actually be commended. The reason for this is that it is simply the tip of a very large iceberg that has been formulated and kept in check over the course of many, many years of trying to explain the most basic facts to idiots who lack the slightest iota of common sense and wherewithal to follow the simplest instructions that are laid out in support communications.

Breathe again.

I feel for the IT guys – they are dealing with incompetence laid bare though magically they are the ones within the BPOs who see the true colours of the abject morons who so frequently run the show. The puffed-up paper tigers with the scarcest yocto of cerebral capability between then.

However, in spite of the intellectual pigmies in high office, that doesn't stop most of these senior managers from bawling the IT guys out and tearing them a new one if it's taking them more than

30 seconds to untangle a series of errors and mistakes on the part of the user that has caused situation or problem to occur in the first place. Not only is that impolite and unprofessional, but it also reflects a lack of awareness of the bigger picture as users truly underestimate what your average IT support engineer actually knows.

For example, they know exactly what occurs online in an organisation. They know exactly how much time has been spent on non-work-related issues when users are logged in or indeed how many phone calls have been made or email traffic sent and received during the day. In essence, any activity that uses any of the company's systems, they have the access permissions and knowledge to see them.

So, you would think that giving them any motivation to delve a little bit deeper would be at the forefront of every user's mind when they were dealing with such people and would certainly be something you would not wish to stimulate. I say this, in the knowledge that most people in BPOs are regularly doing things that they should not be. Whether this is surfing the web on company time, listening to music or committing some of their more dubious practices to the written word via email, you can bet your life that there is a skeleton in every cupboard. The problem with BPO managers is that the majority of them think they are invincible and above the rules and regulations that they are so keen to impose on others. And of course, in many cases that is correct. There is a considerable amount of freedom to act with impunity, simply because the objective of those actions is welcomed by the more senior levels of management, so there is no reason to curtail the unprofessional and immoral.

However, when it comes down to malpractice in black-and-white terms that can be evidenced, it is sometimes possible to put the more senior levels of management in a position where they have no choice other than to act. This is most likely to happen when there is independent corroborative evidence that might in turn be produced to an even higher level, and which may then provoke questions in relation to why action had not previously been taken.

And over the years I have seen a number of arrogant and supercilious managers get taken down as a result of IT-related faux pas that just so happened to float to the surface. Now of course there are ways and means of doing this, and the IT teams themselves need to be very careful about how they are purported to have discovered the malpractices as HR teams will take a particularly dim view of any sense that individuals had been targeted. Therefore, the most common way of capturing somebody in the net is for a more general concern to be raised, for example around unusual traffic activity which allows for a more general investigation in the course of which the target individual will be identified as having breached company procedures.

Casting a wider net and capturing who you need in among the other, albeit smaller, fish.

This does sadly mean that there is typically a certain amount of collateral damage, but at the point that the more senior names fall into the frame, the IT team themselves can make representations in relation to the relative seriousness of actions that may be aggravated by a person's status and responsibility within the company. That may mean that some of the peripheral victims can escape with a slap on the wrist, whereas those who should have known better may find that their unauthorised access or usage has become somewhat terminal.

§

I remember one incident where a junior manager came into a department at the behest of a senior manager, presumably to inject some new blood into what was an already well-established team who were versed in the ways of the old guard. The individual concerned was not what one might call a conventional character and was quickly identified as being a 'spy in the camp' for some of the rising and competing management figures within the business.

It was therefore decided among members of the middle management team that he would have to go, so a colleague in the IT team reviewed his Internet usage for a time when he was managing the service shift. They managed to establish that he had been logged into the Internet at a time when calls were dropped during the shift while there was adequate resources to have answered them correctly. The evidence was then rolled up into a disciplinary charge of negligence and the said individual resigned prior to his disciplinary hearing.

In fairness to him, he did fire a parting shot of a seven-page letter that was highly critical of the managerial practices within the department and HR subsequently dispatched, I think, somebody from the Training and Development team, to act as an independent collator of the background facts so that everybody could be reassured that nothing untoward had taken place.

Well, clearly something untoward had taken place as an individual had been singled out in what was a thinly veiled, targeted attack on somebody who had been seen as an outsider, outmanoeuvring them by highlighting and punishing actions that routinely took place within the operation. It was at best tenuous to match Internet logs with lost call records and to suggest a charge of negligence. Nevertheless, with IT on board and pushing for action on a matter supported by black-and-white statistics and with HR sitting on the fence and not willing to challenge the operational decision to raise a disciplinary case, everything proceeded.

The individual concerned, exercising a judgement on the inevitability of the case, elected to leave with a positive reference.

The subsequent attempts by HR to recover the situation were scuppered by their own inactivity as they allowed another member of staff without a background in investigations to look into the matter, thus giving the operational team advance warning of the investigation and allowing them to tighten up their story to grade 1 copper-plated status. As it stood, the operational team being rather more well-versed in the management of disciplinary and capability cases, simply said little on the disciplinary offence itself stating that the facts effectively spoke for themselves. As for the extensive comments made on the management culture in the letter that had been presented to HR by the unfortunate leaver, the team collectively took a leaf out of the book of Mandy Rice-Davies – *well he would say that, wouldn't he?*

It is a classic example of somebody able to be effectively managed out by people with knowledge who can muster so-called hard evidence and support from quarters sharing the same cultural entrenchment. It also reflects how such behaviour and attitudes can remain unchallenged through the unwillingness of HR teams to get off the fence. In this case, even when they were pushed to act through a letter of grievance, they did not follow a formal grievance process and allowed a member of staff who was not well-versed in the operational milieu to address the matters in such a way that the perpetrators were able to strengthen their position.

I would like to think that such an incident would no longer be able to take place, and indeed in many of the blue-chip organisations of which I have experience, it would not. Yet in BPOs over the last 30 years, I have seen this type of targeting, cherry-picking of evidence and ineffective response on the part of HR teams over and over again. And there are no signs of things changing any time soon.

§

The IT guys carry on trucking through though as they are the ones who can wield some real power if they choose to. It is a shame that they do not swing the axe more often and once in a while aim a little higher because when the mighty fall, they fall hard.

One they couldn't influence one way, or another was in the case of an account set up so that the BPO was using the client's IT infrastructure, including their Internet access.

After a big brand re-launch, the said client ran a report to ascertain the top 10 visited sites, probably to test how much the customer service teams at their BPO were investigating the site and educating themselves. Only

Sadly, to their eternal chagrin, they found that the most popular sites accessed had been *www.ratemypoo.com* and another for pen pals for US convicts on death row.

Their own corporate Website was seventeenth on the list.

21 – Lame Duck PMs

The more I pondered on the panoply of BPO malefactors, the more I was keen to unpick the activities of a very special group within the contact centre outsourcing charade. The *Project Managers* or *PMs* as they like to be known and to which term the rest of us are completely ambivalent.

These people are the closest you will get to malfunctioning mutant droids in the workplace. They don't need Sherpas to guide them to the peaks of fuckwittery.

Holy shit, this school of fish out of water would turf any bumbling, blathering blaggards out of pole position in the Grand Prix of, well, pricks.

Project management is the blanket term to describe the oversight of anything with a beginning and end with all the little milestones along the way. But never will you see a more warped use of the term that is used in BPOs to describe the prevalent methodologies and approaches to set-ups and the like. It is another area that within a BPO truly does seem to take on a life of its own.

Without wishing to belittle the importance of a *PRINCE2* qualification, these individuals are tasked with ensuring that new projects are set up, delivering to the three core criteria of *Time, Quality and Budget.*

The role requires the ability to clarify a timeline and identify tasks, milestones, dependencies, ownership, and responsibility. Then it is about monitoring and chasing so that everything happens in accordance with schedule that what people produce is fit for purpose and that the whole thing remains affordable.

Project Management can be a very detailed and pressured business and requires a high degree of interpersonal skill, not to mention organisational acumen in the afore-mentioned areas in order to deliver the final product. Imagine what it is like to oversee the building of a row of houses or the implementation of a new CRM system into an organisation. Very detailed and multi-faceted work which may even involve multiple projects that are overseen by an überboss, a *Programme Manager*. Woo-hoo.

But let's face it, building a script and organising some training in the BPO world is hardly a project requiring too much hard work or even skill. Project Managers simply do the dogsbody means-as-an-end work that gives the enterprise a semblance that it is professional and organised, whereas in fact it's half-baked chaos that invariably will be shaped and largely designed by the operational teams after the launch date has long passed.

The PMs (get me!) draw up a project plan in *MS Project* (for which there are usually limited licences in the organisation, so nobody of any competence gets to see it anyway) and they then contact the operational managers as they go, to check whether deadlines have been met.

In brief, utilising PMs is largely — or certainly in terms of set-up activities — unconnected with the success or failure of the project. It creates an air of competence to the outside stakeholders and persons who can be largely ignored internally unless there is somebody to blame. Then, the PM is viewed as cannon fodder for *Account Managers* who need a ready-made and disposable scapegoat, which may be preferable to hanging out a reasonably competent Operations Manager who might after all be required to deliver something meaningful later or at least do some of the heavy lifting that the *Account Managers* will want to assiduously avoid.

When they are scapegoated, there is very little sympathy as they rest in a state of almost perpetual limbo. From a professional perspective, their views carry little weight, and they are seen as ineffectual jobsworths. They deliver little other than that which would in any event be achieved by other capable stakeholders but are fixated on their methodologies and their application even if these are likely to have very little impact.

They cling onto *PRINCE2* like it provides them with an almost biblical right to a seat at every table.

From a personal point of view, they are strikingly bereft of interpersonal skills, and they typically communicate by bluntly asserting their so-called project authority at every juncture. It is likely for this reason that such PMs end up at BPOs. These are the people who gained their PM qualifications but have nowhere near the required holistic perspectives or polished communication or stakeholder skills to head up a substantial project in a professional services environment.

So, where better to go if you are not required to do, only to seem to do? You've guessed it. At a BPO, you do not need to be able to deliver what you ought to or be the person you purport to be. It is enough to seem and to be believed by those who want to believe. Hence the reason why, for a comparatively modest salary, a PM can exist without too much accountability, working on set-ups that are projects only in the sense that they contain the components of the simplest projects you could imagine. These are projects, in the same way that a *Ladybird* story is a book. You cannot deny that they are indeed books, but you would not compare them to *Dickens* or *Dostoevsky*.

It is the most basic and amoebic form of a project that equally ironically requires little or no management.

Yet as with so many pieces of the BPO puzzle, it is enough that the relevant actors are on stage on their cue, at the point that the performance begins.

If as a client, you are introduced to a PM with *PRINCE2* qualifications, the message is that you have somebody qualified who will be delivering your project. The fact that you have very little, if any, insight into what they actually deliver or what contributions they make, is irrelevant. The reason they are there means that you will feel reassured and will not delve too deeply into asking questions. It is all destined to encourage the client purchasing the service to take a more passive role in the relationship.

And you wonder why so many BPO start-ups have almost terminal fatal errors? Why does almost every new project, in spite of the number of experienced and qualified personnel, always seem to experience these teething problems? It is not by accident. Allow me to provide some insight.

Were you to look at any BPO and establish how many PMs there are in the project management office within the organisation, you would find a handful of individuals. Yet these seem to be allocated to all the 'live' contracts that the business has. Any typical project manager may be assigned to 15 or 20 projects at any one time – way too many for any person to be performing meaningful work or to have a handle on all of it.

And of course, they do not – that is just the illusion. It works in the same way that Gym operators build their subscriber list without any further expansion of premises or purchase of additional equipment. They are banking on the fact that a large percentage of subscribers rarely turn up or do not turn up at all. It is the same for PMs in BPOs (and to some extent account management teams).

As a client, you get introduced to your PM who turns up for the odd call and produces the project documents. They do however very little else, but as a client you have no visibility of their workload or the full client list that they are supporting. You are presented with what you want to believe – that a professional and qualified team is supporting your project (they will likely be presented as your 'dedicated' PM) and you can comfortably tick it off your list – while of course your project sleepwalks into a challenging first few months or a crippling eternity.

What the BPOs are banking on is that 1) some of the projects, being relatively more straightforward and which did not need too much PM work in the first instance may go relatively well or will encounter issues that can be kept under the radar and that 2) client organisations have become de-sensitised to the notion of 'teething problems' and that there has been a normalisation of this.

When such issues occur, the BPO then plays its most skilful card. As the client, you have a significant amount resting on the success of the project – all the more so if it was your decision to outsource in the first place. The problems then become shared and if you try to focus the BPO on their sole accountability, they will point to any area where there might have been a lack of clarity. The risk here is that a client taking up an adversarial position against their BPO is opening themselves up for a shedload of brown to be deftly pushed their way. And clients do not like that one bit.

The real risk is that even if they win the argument, they will not come out of it undamaged within their own organisation. After all, outsourcing is supposed to be about trouble-free reallocation of work, not taking on a whole load of problems. If they fly off the handle and the BPO can demonstrate to the more senior people client-side that they themselves were set up to fail, then it may come out even worse for the client contact. Also, by this stage, the client is committed to the service and if the service is poor, then the brand reputation suffers with every minute that passes.

The end result is frequently that the client will magic up some supporting resource in-house who will work with the BPO to get everything back on its feet. In this way, the BPO can project the false image of professionals at the pitch stage to win the business and get commitment and yet can end up using client resources to set up the project and make it work.

The icing on the cake is that once everything is up and running (seemingly) well, the client will often want to forget that any bumps in the road were ever there and may be equally content to fall back onto the exculpatory *teething problems* discourse. This is in any event helped by the fact that once problems are resolved, people do tend to want to make the most of any feelgood period and are less willing to dig up any old and painful memories – particularly if there is a possibility that anything unpleasant may stick to them.

§

So as far as PMs are concerned, never let it be said that they do not have a useful role. It is simply that their role in BPOs does not really involve projects and very little management. No news there then.

But what they actually do can be breathtakingly shocking, to the point of comical ineptitude and incredulity. It is – and I am shaking my head while typing this as it is so bizarre – not unheard of for them not to even put project plans nor to set up any project review meetings prior to the set-up of a new campaign. Almost impossible to fathom.

In addition to this, many take the shortcut of exception reporting, using RAG status reports to highlight risks. Rather than a complementary tool for a project, they become the only governance. No wonder so many implementations go belly-up.

I know of one BPO where the company made its whole set-up team redundant immediately prior to a set-up (this would win the *Palme d'Or* at the Cannes Festival of balls-ups, were it to exist) and left this in the hands of a so-called PM. Now putting aside the rationale of disposing of so many key staff when there was so much deadwood elsewhere in the business (remember that protecting the *Facebook* crew trumps everything!), there was a genuine bafflement about why delivery issues were arising.

A little like your surprise that your car won't start when you have sold the engine for scrap.

Of course, the role incumbents hadn't been the greatest set-up managers, but it was akin to discovering some inappropriate priests and deciding to ban Christianity.

Baby, bath water, whoosh.

Anyway, the PM takes over the set-up piece in order to provide the set-up with some structure and rigour.

Yup, that was the thought process behind what is about to follow.

Unfortunately, they have no plan, do not interact with the client to clarify deliverables, and have no idea about what needs to be delivered, by what deadline or by whom.

It is naturally a complete and unmitigated disaster. Had someone thrown a bag of sugar onto the client, we would have had an instant candyfloss. They were incandescent. Frothing from every visible orifice. You know someone is angry when it appears, they are crying out of their ears.

And what was our response? Well, one month later after said clusterfuck- on the subsequent tranche of activity – we did it again.

A disaster recovery meeting ensues and the most senior of the most senior cannot fathom it. You couldn't make it up, and they really couldn't work any of it out. The PM is sitting there with a laptop open (this is a sign that demonstrates industriousness and tech-savvy and is a must for all PMs in meetings) but stays silent throughout, working through their inbox and everybody takes resolution actions. No deadlines were agreed though, along with no measures for success – just a request for enough feedback on progress for, you've probably guessed it, the *MD*s slide deck for a meeting in a fortnight's time.

No one seems to question that the PM is making no contribution to getting the project from *A* to *B*. In fact, there is no project. No one can understand why the client is unhappy and it seems that nobody for all the years of experience around the table can grasp that the failure to engage with the client from the outset is always the first and most important stage to take in order to set objectives and to demonstrate control. But then, these are the same senior managers who wanted new business growth but did not understand anything below the highest level of the requirements for delivery.

You can imagine them making the decision to remove the set-up team without even understanding what set-up meant in real terms. That isn't an exaggeration-they clearly didn't.

This should have been a harsh lesson that set-up is an indispensable step in delivering anything concrete. Sadly, it never hit home, and the process repeated itself. The survival of the PM corroborated the conclusion that the senior management bods had no comprehension of how their own business worked or needed to work in order to deliver even a moderately acceptable service. However, as we have already suggested, does it actually matter?

As long as the slide deck landed OK, that would keep everything ticking over...

§

So, while Project Managers don't do what they purport to, they really do fit in rather well in BPOs as they effortlessly blend in their own special brand of vacuous twaddle with the wider chaotic and rudderless leadership strategies (ho ho) that are employed (ho again).

And for that, their presence at the heart of BPO delivery (enough ho's for now, Ed) remains assured for the foreseeable future.

Which in BPO terms equates to tomorrow afternoon.

22 – Dodgy Figures for Dodgy Figures

The production of MI in BPOs should in theory be a relatively straightforward matter and one that resides at a central lobe of the BPO brain, if not exactly being its beating heart. After all, with everything closely measured and monitored via comprehensive automation, there should not be a shortage of data. And it is exactly this data that should provide management teams with the rationale for their strategic business decisions.

Of course, that is the theory which as a common thread that links all BPO activities, is several colossal steps away from what occurs in practice.

At the core of the matter is the challenge of transforming data – essentially hard numbers – into meaningful information that can be understood and appreciated by a competent end-user. The question and the potential challenges with finding sufficiently competent end-users is of course an issue in itself(!), but let us focus at this stage on the question of the transition of data into MI.

The first step in the production of MI is to have individuals who are adequately trained in the nuts and bolts of the management tool used (e.g. Business Objects) and appropriately schooled in the use of spreadsheet or database software that allows for the creation of the finished product. These are the rudimentary functional basics to the creation of reports and the essential criteria for employment as an MI Analyst, the job title du jour which predictably enough involves very little analysis. These individuals are little more than Excel monkeys who set up templates in accordance with management requirements and then ensure that the reporting tool delivers the required data in the chosen format and that the reports are run at the scheduled time.

And therein lies the first challenge. In order to turn the data into MI, the MI analyst must rely heavily on third-party knowledge of the delivery processes. This also further relies on the analytical ability of the delivery manager who must know not only how the processes on which the reporting is delivered work but also needs to have enough strategic acumen to adjudge what MI is actually needed and in what format in order to make it useful for the various business stakeholders. At the same time, the report requester should ideally have a certain reciprocal appreciation of the reporting framework in order to frame their requirements in terms that are a little more functional than the very typical moon-on-a-stick variety.

It is not a simple case of person *A* requesting a report based on *y* requirements and this being produced by person *B*. There needs to be some mutual appreciation of the other's world and understanding of their capabilities – some *empathy* – and then some constructive negotiations.

Dear me, I have just raised the question of mutual empathy – I must be losing the plot myself.

And this is where it breaks down. MI teams are notoriously functional and siloed in their thinking which effectively follows that akin to a production line. Operational and account managers, who are the typical report requesters, think only of the end product (*SLAs*, client satisfaction etc.) and hold positions in the hierarchy that allow them to make demands without having to spend time with (perceived) underlings in order to work towards constructive solutions.

This is in some ways beside the main point which is that they often do not really know what they are requesting, often asking for the type of MI that neither assists their clients fully nor helps their own organisation to put its best foot forward. If you imagine the skills that a lawyer or a doctor need to have over and above their technical expertise, they might be the greatest experts in the world in their field but the assistance they give will only be as good as what is reported to them. That is why they need to learn additional skills such as questioning, probing, making inferences, and reading between the lines, to quote but a few. Otherwise, the advice may miss the point, or the treatment may not be sufficiently curative or relevant, depending on the context.

In BPOs, there is very little of this softer skillset that allows the gap to be bridged between expert and layman. It is all very black-and-white based on interpretation and second-guessing.

Unless, of course, we are talking board-level composition, in which case it will almost always be white. But that is another story altogether.

With MI, there are naturally a few failsafes. Many recipients just 'don't do numbers', so for a large proportion of the time, the reports – useless that they are – do not actually get read.

Those who do read them often struggle so much with what they do actually mean that they gloss over their ignorance and pretend that they all make sense and are what is wanted.

The people who question MI are the ones who generally understand their numbers and are confident enough to raise a flag. The really daft recipients who ask questions are normally too incompetent to realise when they are given a fudged answer back.

The production of MI from data is very much like giving the finest ingredients to a bad chef. Or perhaps to a reasonable chef who has never seen the dish before and does not have a menu.

Of course, as I have mentioned before, MI reports are routinely falsified completely and ironically that is when – in the production of false reporting –the collaborative approach actually works. On these occasions, the requesting manager will know exactly what needs to be produced and will have a specific goal in mind that they need to deliver.

I recall one retail client who received fake call centre MI for at least a nine-month period and never once queried it. The beauty of that deception was that the reports never overreached themselves. They did not make any outrageous claims (e.g. that the 80/20 *SLA* was being hit) because this would have been at odds with other circumstantial evidence, for example, some customer complaints about waiting times or the odd test call put through from the client themselves. Just finessed above the level that would have caused any suggestion of a material breach of contract and deliciously at a level that would have justified the higher level of staff for which we were billing the client at an hourly rate. A crafted and delectable double whammy, tinkering a wondrous *ker-ching* lullaby on the ivories of the organisational P&L.

This same client was even coaxed into signing off a model that purportedly showed how many additional staff needed to be signed off and in situ for every additional percentage point that would be gained on the *SLA*. A frankly ludicrous proposition that ignored the realities of call distribution/peaks and the variance of handling times, but they trialled it, and it was signed off as it seemed to work. Well, it would, considering that the management team were fabricating the performance results.

Almost comically, this enterprise was shattered in a fit of pique by one of the managers who reported the true figures one week that saw the service level inexplicably fall by 20%. How the site leadership team squirmed on that occasion – 'puce' was the term used to describe the appearance of the site leader, which seemingly deteriorated as the week went on. At the time everybody feared for his blood pressure and seriously considered recommending that he abstain from salt for a few weeks. Titanic mortgage though (no pun intended), so he had to soldier on, albeit with a sodium substitute and abstention from using the stairs for a short period.

For those who were uncomfortable with the wholesale falsification of MI – and I did not meet many of these over a period of 30 years – the other effective tactic is to produce reports that have key columns of data missing. For example, not showing abandoned totals, just a percentage which can be rounded up slightly. This is a well-versed tactic as it prevents an analytical client from seeing end-to-end data and spotting where the numbers do not add up. It serves an additional and bona fide purpose though as it allows a dashboard to be produced that allows a recipient to separate the wood from the trees. A common problem with clients is that they often need to pass on MI to other more senior stakeholders in their organisations who invariably have questions that your client cannot answer.

The upshot of this is that the client will want more data added to the report or different views of the same data so that the report answers all potential questions. This leads to the dashboard growing arms and legs and often becoming quite unwieldy. To combat this – and to open the door for some nifty manoeuvring – clients are often steered into receiving slimmed-down dashboards, supported by, ahem, the BPO's commentary on the numbers. This is a surefire way to minimise queries on the veracity of the MI or on MI that does not tell a pretty story. It is just a matter of the right strategically focused wording and a little tender loving care.

Even formatting Excel columns to round up to the next whole number can deftly add 0.4 to a percentage that might just get you over the required line if the numbers are tight. A bonus if this is the difference between success and failure and it means that any further creativity – which always carries a risk even from the most incompetent of clients, downhill with the wind behind them – is not required. And when it comes to perception, awareness and general intelligence, the average client vendor manager is lamentably very, very average.

The favoured approach by BPO client management teams is to ensure that there is a combined layering of techniques that cumulatively deliver the right results, and which are fiendishly tricky to unravel.

It should be noted though that the process of fraud is hampered by the failure of the so-called MI Analysts to make their fake numbers add up and it is an often-witnessed performance trait that considerations of quality control are not high on the agenda. MI Analysts who check their work are few and far between. Those who even question the validity of what they do are rarer.

They are furthermore not the most cheerful bunch of employees you are likely to meet in a BPO. Hardly surprising when you consider that MI teams are usually in the firing line when some power-hungry, reactionary psychotic *Finance Director* decides to indulge in a round of short-termist cost-cutting and makes the whole function redundant.

This will invariably mean that they will need to join another BPO until they can safely return 12-18 months later when the wider business realises that they are no longer capable of producing any effective MI themselves, let alone any adroitly crafted reports that might help them to cover up any jiggery-pokery. On several occasions, in different companies, I have seen the *fire-hire cycle* with MI (it happens as well with Facilities), and it is as comical as it is predictable.

What a function to work in, MI. Having to often produce business-critical outputs and getting a proper brief, only when what you are producing is fictitious and knowing that the success of an account might fall exactly on your credible portrayal of a false situation.

And I used to feel sorry for them in the good old days when they were just flying blind and producing mostly accurate but mainly useless reports on our lamentable performances.

The *Les Dawson* piano players of the BPO world. But without the laughs.

23 – The Carousel and Other Rides

Irrespective of the context from my observations in working in outsourced contact centres, I have often tried to understand some of the underlying mechanisms at play which you see over and over again irrespective of the context.

One of these, I have termed The *Carousel*.

The concept of the Carousel came to fruition owing to how work tends to arrive at a delivery setting. For example, it may become apparent that a task needs to be completed on a particular account and that the nature of that task means that it may not readily fall under a particular jurisdiction. It therefore goes around and around, often by email to a group of interested parties within the BPO until somebody picks it up and owns it. On some occasions, an individual may pick the task up from the *Carousel* themselves, or it may be allocated to them by a more senior member of staff on the email chain who will make a preliminary judgement that they are the person who should be responsible for delivering it.

However, very often there is a crisis of ownership and a very clear reluctance for individuals to pick that challenge up and run with it – the immediate reaction is often to try and place that task or the responsibility of that task back on the *Carousel*, so it goes round and round and round until either somebody picks it up themselves and runs with it or the task becomes obsolete or superseded, in which case it is taken off and discarded.

The *Carousel* can itself be equally frustrating and amusing as people try to employ varying tactics in order to relieve themselves of the responsibilities of actually delivering something. One of the first tactics any 'at-risk' holder of the task may employ, particularly if they feel that the responsibility for the work will land at their door, is to set up a conference call with all the recipients of the email so that they can then decide who will do the work or how that work will be divvied up. It is on that call that you will hear such people posing the seemingly innocuous question:

'Would that be you, or would that be me?'

knowing very well that such a question invites the prospects of either somebody allocating the work back to that asker of the question or the acceptance of ownership themselves. In such circumstances, the odds are that the object of that question will take the path of least resistance and accept responsibility for the work themselves.

Another favoured response from somebody who is put on the spot and if it is suggested that they may have to take responsibility for the work is to declare that they are *'not that close to the detail'* and to suggest that somebody less senior who has a more hands-on responsibility should take ownership while they provide support and guidance. Of course, this begs the question or at least would beg the question in a normal organisation, just how much detail is that person close to and should they in any event be closer than they are? No fear of that though – this is a BPO where if you are savvy enough to recognize prevarication, you do not expose tactics that you are going to fall back on yourself in the future!

One that will always tickle my fancy – wonderfully transparent but predictably never challenged – is when a group of individuals are assigned a task and one of them volunteers to *facilitate* a subsequent meeting. Now when anybody suggests that they are the *facilitator* for a forthcoming activity, you can read that as a clear indication that they will not be assuming any responsibilities nor taking any actions from the meeting itself. There are very good reasons for this, primarily that the facilitator should be neutral and should assist and support discussion rather than taking on any position from a selected perspective. And that ladies and gentlemen, is precisely why that is a favoured position for the person who is keen to avoid any work.

Some of the cleverer individuals on the divvy-up call might employ a more subtle but well-honed skill which is to attempt a kind of *filibustering*, which will involve asking questions to all of the recipients on the email chain for clarification or for further information which will then exhaust available time, create spinoff lines of enquiry, or may even cast some doubt into the validity of the work. This may result in the work ultimately not being allocated as in doing so, they create a bigger issue than actually exists and may even be successful in diverging the main thrust of the response into a different department by changing the emphasis on what is interpreted to be the outputs. For example, the solution may initially be deemed to fall within *New Business*, but it may be steered towards a project management action as part of the probe into existing service delivery provision. On other occasions, I have seen the email chain grow to such immense proportions that it becomes so complex that the whole thing just runs out of steam, and nobody progresses it any further.

As a last resort, if somebody is unsuccessful at deflecting responsibility for a task, they might attempt to rearrange the conference call where they can really examine the roles and responsibilities and consequence allocations with a view to attempting to reallocate their tasks using one of the aforementioned tactics.

Sometimes, as I noted previously, the *Carousel* will go around and around without any of the above scenarios and fold with the result that as time passes the requirements to actually do the work in the first instance have passed. Something else will emerge that perhaps is more palatable or maybe even the initial requirements will no longer be valid, and no work will need to be done at all.

The golden rule of the *Carousel* is that you must attend the calls or meetings – failure to attend or sending a novice deputy will be like throwing your own carcass to the wolves. They smell weakness and vulnerability, and the well-versed reprobates will eat up your time and capacity with whatever dross they can offload from their inboxes to yours. That is a given.

You would think that the *Carousel* was a facet of an organisation's culture that senior management teams would be keen to eradicate – after all, it flies in the face of prompt service delivery and delivering solutions that are timely and relevant to client demands. However, you would be sorely mistaken. In the world of outsourced contact centres, what you would expect to be the desired and expected outputs are so far removed from the truth that even the most seasoned commentators need to take a second look.

As in most self-serving bureaucracies work gets pushed forwards, backwards, sideways, and round and round and it is the process of this movement and the activity that this generates that are in effect the core activity of the business rather than any meaningful delivery of tangible outputs that are valued by the clients. In this respect, the *Carousel* is indeed a metaphor for BPOs and the so-called 'industry' as a whole. Its direction of travel is not progressive in one way or another but is characterised by its continuing circular movement and by definition of its own existence.

§

The *Carousel* was not the only device that would be frequently witnessed in BPOs as a way of work avoidance. I knew of a BPO where the main contact centre was split into several floors, at the centre of which was a sizeable atrium where the site café was situated. It was there that you could look over from one of several floors and witness the performance of masterly inactivity. That I had witnessed in action many years before when at university, a colleague of mine would be forever walking around the department with a handful of books from the library in order to create the impression among lecturers that he was a self-starter and devoted student to a whole range of wider reading activities. When in effect he was simply poncing about and killing time. He was however a plausible actor though it must be said that my later colleagues in BPOs have invariably had this off to an art form.

So, owing to a shortage of meeting rooms, they would set the scene that 121s and departmental meetings would take place in the café or breakout area usually from 9.30 am in the morning to mid-morning or midday or during what was understood to be the dead time of the day, namely after about 4.00 pm. These managers would descend on the café area, books, and phones in hand where they would then proceed to congregate under the pretext of conducting valuable meetings in the company time.

In fact, they were often simply chatting and producing nothing, and in doing this would probably burn up to a full day of a working week simply sitting around and drinking coffee. To anybody passing by, looking out into the atrium, there would just be a snapshot of managers sitting together with books open, deep in discussion, because in all situations you see what you expect to see. In this way, the practitioners of the art of nothing were simply hiding in plain sight.

§

Another way in which additional free time was frequently added to managers' days was in how they managed their lunch periods. In most BPOs, everybody would have one hour's worth of unpaid break to take in the course of their working day. There would be an option to take one or perhaps two brief breaks at different stages in the day and then perhaps a lunch break of 30 to 45 minutes. Now what the clever practitioners of Team Leader level and above might do is take their full break allocation in the form of their brief breaks and their whole lunch break at the same time with the result that they would be clearly seen leaving the building and returning within their maximum of one hour. But on returning to the office, they would take out their lunch that they had bought when on their lunch break and would proceed to spend an additional 30 minutes eating their lunch at their desk.

The trick here is that nobody gets the full picture. To those who see the individual eating lunch at their desk, they see a conscientious employee who is seemingly ever-present, and they would not have an idea that that person when they're away from their desk was actually off the premises. For all they knew the individual may well have been in meetings. And that's one of the tricks of the trade in many different circumstances. It's an awareness that people cannot be in more than one place at the same time, so if you keep the ball is moving, it is less likely that one person may spot that you were taking from both ends.

§

Thinking about these tactics, it may seem to somebody who works in a normal or standard office environment that this level of, for want of a better expression, skiving, would not pass undetected or would cause the protagonists an issue in that they would never be able to get their own work done in the time that they were actually actively working. This however would not be the case for several reasons.

Firstly, the management of BPO contact centre operations, and indeed all relevant departments, does not require a huge amount of effort. It is not rocket science. The bottom line is that anyone with a firm grasp of what is required to be done can, after a period of several months, understand end-to-end processes and what is required and work very efficiently. The trick to protecting one's position in this way is to make it seem as if you are busy and to talk a good talk when managing upwards so that it cannot be clearly established that you have any capacity to take on more work. Never, ever betray that you have any *capacity*. It is all about creating efficiency so that *you* get the freed-up time, *not the BPO*.

In relation to the work that is done, this can be largely executed from behind a desk, and typically the more senior managers or those with responsibility for monitoring the performance of middle managers and the junior *Team Leaders* would likely be spending a large proportion of their days ensconced in offices poring over spreadsheets and evaluating and re-evaluating forecasts and the bottom line. For those managers, managing performance down through the line is a retrospective activity driven by the data that they read in reports.

There is very little to fear in terms of hands-on scrutiny of what people do day in and day out unless the numbers show that there are significant gaps in delivery and that those gaps are not being attended to.

While the number of staff members at different layers of management had been considerably shrunk from their position in the mid-1990s even the streamlined operations of the twenty-first century century BPO contact centres were structured from the distant perspective of managers who have very little idea of the true connection between assets required and outputs within the context of their own businesses. This is why they are constantly seeking to meet forecast numbers that are selected, often quite randomly by *Finance Directors* rather than having a true understanding of the potential of their businesses and driving performance to be the best that it can be. While there are many differences between the dysfunctional outsourced agencies and the established but reputable blue-chip clients who engage their services, this is one of the most striking. It is a lack of vision and a failure to understand potential in preference to the achievements of numbers on which they can get agreement from shareholders and the financial directorate.

Even when a workforce management plan is detailed and ostensibly on the money, you can be sure that some crafty old team manager has slipped in some assumptions or rounded up numbers that will inject a subtle layer of fat into the workings. That a) gives the managers some breathing space so that the work they have will be delivered comfortably and b), like being lax about soft drugs in prison, it keeps the population calm.

Once again, everyone's a winner, baby.

This is by no means the greatest tragedy of BPO contact centres who in the past would have just billed whatever they could get, and committed far greater crimes against commercial and organisational ethics but reflects the limitations of management teams with a restricted repertoire, in an ever-tighter economic climate.

These are organisations that are characterised by aiming low where employees in parallel are cutting corners so that the restricted aspirations appear to be stretch targets. It is comical and lamentable in equal measure, but I order to address it, they need to understand it. They have a long way to go.

§

On a final point, I would just like to say something about timesheets. You see, timesheets are seen by *Finance Directors* as an essential part of logging how people spend their working day.

The outputs even make it into the company accounts, in terms of reflecting costs that are apportioned to accounts in shared services or individuals working on more than one account.

But chaps, timesheets are actually used by staff *to hide* what they are actually doing on a daily basis. A few hours into '*Administration*' or a similar code (always the last refuge of a scoundrel), some more thinly layered onto multiple accounts, particularly into '*Meetings*' or offline client administration, and the well-initiated can make a whole day disappear as if by magic.

Done it for thirty years – never been questioned, never been challenged. This was all facilitated by an overall lack of control, in spite of a number of organisational changes in recent years. For BPOs, that really is a supreme irony, given their oppressive obsessions with close, dictatorial management and control.

They themselves are often so far away from actually controlling what goes on internally, you could even pity them.

In fact, on the weeks when I could only manage to eke out 20% of my time, I felt like I was under-performing. I went through some extended periods when I was spending 30-45 minutes a day reading and 'carouselling' emails – perhaps the odd, brief meeting – and otherwise free to do whatever I pleased (personal study and writing mainly).

Now that would be 90% of my paid time, so BPO contact centres were not *all* bad.

24 – Means Bugger All

I talked about the lack of direction of BPO contact centres and the lack of validation that they seem to have in relation to service standards and quality. Indeed, much of my argument centres on the fact that they are self-serving and simply fill a need to fill a gap in organisational commentary, both externally and within their own businesses.

Nevertheless, that has not stopped practitioners within BPO contact centres in seeking external qualifications that they hope will provide some credibility to those who purchase their services. Back in the 80s and 90s, when a number of BPOs were associated with marketing agencies, a few contact centre managers undertook the *Institute of Direct Marketing Diploma* or *IDM* as it was popularly known. Others took advantage of the *Chartered Institute of Marketing* certificate though why anyone would be happy at having *CIM* after their name, I do not know.

After contact centres entered the mainstream and it became much clearer that most organisations would require some form of contact centre activity or online presence, more workers involved in this sought more general management qualifications that would be effectively more transferable should they then work in an environment that was not necessarily contact centre or marketing based. Gaining in popularity were the *Certificate* and *Diploma in Management* and following on from that, the achievement of the Holy Grail of management qualifications – the *Master of Business Administration* or *MBA*.

Now I may be a traditionalist in terms of academia, but to me a university degree and a business qualification are essentially two very different things. A university degree is an academic qualification that signifies membership of the University at a particular level i.e. *Bachelors, Masters, Doctorate.*

So frankly when people are raving about *MBAs* and claiming therefore to have achieved a master's level degree – while this is strictly true in the sense that these are now recognised degrees – I cannot help feeling that they have a sense of attachment and credibility attached to them that is frankly not warranted.

As an aside, it is the case that many of the established universities, do not actually have business schools, and therefore do not award *MBAs*. Of course, we live in a new era when former polytechnics are now known as universities and have been given that right under Royal Assent so, for the purposes of argument, universities are. Perhaps I am now betraying a personal disdain, so should continue the main thrust of what I am discussing.

So, we now find ourselves in a position where a growing number of managers are presenting themselves as viable candidates for senior roles within organisations as a result of their attainment of the *MBA* degree. Such is the credibility of this award that I recall a meeting that I attended where we received a presentation from the *Group Sales Director* when he was discussing the various merits of his sales team, and he made the comment:

'we currently have six MBAs – at the last count'.

And the way he made this, and he didn't actually speak the words in a measured or matter-of-fact way. It seemed as if he was snorting them through the end of his nose after an acolyte had turned up the voltage on his nipple-rings. Not the slightest, sweet whiff of a humblebrag there. It kind of suggested that it was almost incredible to him that the quality of this team was so high that those MBAs just kept coming and coming. Possibly also that he needed to articulate this, such was our own ignorance. He was simultaneously orgasmic and contemptuous (a strangely erotic mix in many cases but sadly not this one).

To him, an *MBA* meant erect authority (*salutes).

It didn't resonate and my pants were unruffled at the thought. I recalled the wise old words told to me by a former lecturer who opined, that the meaning of *MBA* could be explained by the phrase *'Means Bugger All'.*

And he actually had one.

Now I am not saying by any means that what you would learn on an *MBA* course was not to be in some way useful for a career in management. However, the *MBA* seems to have acquired almost mythical open-all-doors status in BPOs, and the higher echelons of organisations seem to be increasingly populated by those who hold the degree. Now without wishing to be unscientific in drawing the following conclusion, I can't help feeling that there is a clear positive correlation between the prevalence of *MBAs* and the declining standards demonstrated by the delivery of organisations who provide outsourced call centre solutions. And I have good reasons for suggesting why this may be the case. I suppose it is inevitable that sooner or later, the industry would jump on the coat tails of what they saw as a meritorious qualification and try and adopt it as their own as the gold standard of achievement.

And there's nothing wrong in having a qualification that demonstrates the excellence and expertise of its holders. After all, that is the whole point of qualifications in the first instance. They are a certification that a certain standard of learning and achievement has taken place. This would apply in all fields, whether they are academic or vocational.

But I think the question around *MBAs* centres on what skills and attributes the holders actually bring to such an organisation. I should set this stage that my own belief in the value of an *MBA* per se is not without issue. Nevertheless, having undertaken a number of management qualifications myself, I would be more inclined to say that the competent senior manager in a BPO would be better off undertaking a basic management qualification, such as a *Certificate in Management* which will give a basic grounding in a balanced set of disciplines and then spend more time focused on the development of softer skills that might actually grow their teams and their capability towards sustained delivery.

Ok, ok, that is a theoretical perspective that hardly touches the sides of the smoke and mirrors of your typical BPO. How could I be so foolish?

Then, if you are looking at a senior leadership role in the commercial field, then take accountancy qualifications. As far as an *MBA* is concerned, I can see the value only for individuals who are at COO or CEO level, and even then, I see that the potential value in what is a bean-counting business to be limited.

After all, *MBAs* spend considerable amounts of time looking at cultures of organisations, focusing on balanced scorecards and even-handed management that takes into account people, processes, and customers as well as commercials. All pretty superfluous when it comes down to the management of an outsourced contact centre business, as everything is route 1 to the numbers.

It is almost as if we have forgotten that even with *MBAs*, you used to have had to have been at least 27 years old and active at senior management level (referenceable) in order to get on the course. The qualification was seen as a way to formalize the learning that had been accumulated via years of commercial delivery.

Now any old hoodwinker just has to pull out the money and some BPOs fund it, like they might fund an *Investors in People* crest to put above their door (Velcro® backing optional for the accreditation renewal dates). All part of the charade.

It would be much more appropriate for managers in these businesses, to focus on subjects like psychology which are fundamental to the success of their real agendas – if they had the freedom to pursue these approaches. There I go again, fantasising.

As an aside though, *appropriate*. I have just used the word myself, but in the BPO world this is a useful stand-by in all job functions. A wonderful word to show displeasure without actually having to back anything up with factual information. The mere use will throw into question *professionalism*, which in turn creates an immediate sense of vulnerability. Almost in the same way as *restructure*.

But I am again digressing – back to the world of MBAs and the like.

So, what would you say if in hospital and just about to go under when the surgeon told you that he was not qualified in medicine but had an *MBA* in logistics? Well, at least he might get you to your own funeral on time.

In a BPO hospital (if they existed) that sort of situation would not only happen, but it would also make it onto the Creds presentation and celebrated. You know what, I think it would.

It is certainly true that *MBAs* are seen as the key to the door and are required by all manner of junior to middle managers as a passport to success. They seem to be of the view that simply by having those three letters after their name, they have absolute entitlement within the business world. Not only are the syllabuses of such qualifications largely irrelevant to most business settings in practice, but they are also almost exclusively incompatible with the requirements of managers at most levels within a BPO organisation. The copious bags of wonga that people invest in these qualifications would arguably be better off spent on gaining an HGV licence or something more practical. But I suppose to be fair, if something does actually open doors and is valued in quarters within the organisation itself, then perhaps it is an investment worth making.

I have certainly yet to meet any holder of an *MBA* who is actually operating at a middle-management level who is able to translate the purported academic qualities of their qualification into practical delivery within their organisation.

It is simply theory and pseudo-academia and an invitation to accept what they are saying as gospel without any challenge to the rationales given, if indeed they are given. I certainly don't see what a business development manager with an *MBA* would have to offer over and above a business development manager who had a thorough knowledge of products and services and how they might be useful to fulfil a specific client requirement. And I say this in the knowledge that those in that role whom I have previously encountered with *MBAs* would not have given any consideration or at least very little consideration, to the factors I had mentioned – that is to say, understanding a client requirement and successfully applying the products and services in order to fulfil that need.

What I tend to see from *MBA* holders, is masters of the 'Creds' presentation – so whatever a client may say or communicate, the *MBA* man resorts to their well-practised and well-versed presentation on the products and features of the company rather than listening and offering something that is valid and constructive in practice.

In fact, the last one I worked with closely, openly acknowledged that they had plagiarised their *MBA* dissertation – and seemed incredulous when I highlighted that there might be an issue with that. Not sure how I would categorise them – as somebody who had faked a qualification that faked their suitability to lead in a BPO. It is so far beyond bizarre; you would need a bus to get back to bizarre.

When I encounter one, it is like taking a karate black belt of two years standing to a street fight. After all, anyone can buy a black belt on *Amazon* and put it on. Just like any one can produce some *MBA* coursework and scrape an exam.

What happens in the real world is a different story, as we all know only too well.

25 – (I Can't Get No) ESATisfaction

In recent years, one of the areas of interest that has become a focus for bulbous eyes in BPOs has been the conducting of employee satisfaction surveys or ESATs as they are widely known. In most organisations with which I am familiar, the ESAT represents one or two points in the year when everybody suddenly takes notice of what the general population actually thinks of the organisation.

Now let's be absolutely clear on one thing – the driver for the employee satisfaction survey is in no way from within a BPO, on account of a desire to ensure that the working environment is pleasant, interesting, motivational, or simply acceptable to the employee group. The driver is from clients who need to demonstrate to their stakeholders that their partner organisations, i.e. the BPOs, are meeting the same ethical standards of partnership and cooperation that they themselves need to demonstrate within their own (parent) companies.

NB. everything I am about to say here applies equally to *CSAT, CX* or whatever moniker you would choose to attach to it. BPOs contrive, using exactly the same strategies and techniques, to dredge up anything that makes it seem that their clients' customers are happy. As we have already established, *CX* within BPOs reflects a skimming of a slither of what an understanding of *Customer Experience* should be and the imbuing of all of this into single stand-alone questions. ESAT builds on this (in that there are generally more questions asked over a broader framework) but with the same goal: to capture limited information but pump into it as much meaning as will be useful to your cause.

So, when I write *ESAT* and *Employee*, also think *CSAT* and *Customer*. In true BPO style, they will flip what they have any which way – as long as it propagates the version of the truth that best suits them.

For BPO managers, all of this presents a considerable challenge. This is because at the point that the surveys are released the BPO managers are at the mercy of what employees will feedback in their satisfaction questionnaires. This in turn becomes reportable and there is always the risk that clients may get a whiff of how employees really feel and therefore gain greater insight into the practices that are *de rigeur* within the organisation.

Note that I am referring to practices rather than policies as the policies are absolutely beyond reproach in any BPO. They are typically well-documented and cast iron in terms of propriety. For all intents and purposes, for the outsider looking in, these organisations are respectable, ethical, and overall sound – exactly the sort of partnership organisations to whom one would feel comfortable informing one's stakeholders and owners with whom one was in partnership.

§

So how do they approach the question of *ESATs*? Well, the first step – and some might consider this to be the most important one – the questions need to be designed in a particular way. After all, as any expert in experience surveys will attest, you can only receive answers to the questions you actually ask. If you couch your questions in a particular way, it can shape, and in some ways restrict the answers you receive back. This is the reason why such *ESATs* are usually structured in such a way that the sections they cover, and the questions within those sections, are closed and centre primarily on perception and feeling rather than assertion of fact. The clue to this is actually in the title wording of *experience survey*. In positioning the surveys in this way, it provides BPOs with the opportunity to support any findings with a suitable commentary.

So, *Step 1* is to construct the survey in such a way that the range of options for response is strictly controlled. *Step 2* is to ensure that any questionable responses or percentages that exceed expectation in terms of negative experience, are mitigated by an associated commentary. I have extensive experience of being party to management meetings when experience survey results are being reviewed and they are master classes in re-interpretation, re-positioning, and re-casting of data. The most common tactic is to refute the experience reported by the data with conflicting evidence that suggests an alternative experience should have been reported or to suggest that the response reported was not what the respondents meant.

This reflects nothing but disdain for employees. If you so say respect people enough to ask them questions, respect the answers they give, end of. Do not be like one manager, I recall, who had to wait 6 weeks after results were in because they were so angry and then gave a presentation fighting back tears where every piece of feedback was denounced as *'fake'*. Yes, these individuals do exist, so take care people!

But back to our topic. Out of all the activities that senior management team would do in a BPO, the running of a survey is one of the most critical. In not running one, the risk presented by any resistance or leaking to a wider public of actual practices in place, would be considerably enhanced. By actually running the surveys and neutralising their message via a re-moulding of the response into suitable interpretations, they can demonstrate to clients and stakeholders that they are functioning as a(n ethically) high-performing business, and they can reinforce the decision to engage them in the eyes of the clients and their stakeholders. After all, who is best placed to comment accurately and effectively on the health of the business if it is not the rank-and-file employees?

If the hoi polloi is happy and content with the way in which the business operates, then the achievement of financial targets can be instantly validated as having been achieved through ethical means. Further to the re-interpretation of the data, there is often a limited acknowledgement of some weaknesses and areas for improvement which will be supported by an action plan and by a select group of employees who will meet on a regular basis to review actions. This may involve the commencement of some relatively anodyne features, such as newsletters or forums, which on the surface demonstrate a willingness to listen and act but in effect are nothing more than talking shops with no influence or authority.

Another subtle touch might in the first instance be to give a date for the completion of the survey and then if results are starting to look shaky, to close it down early. This removes a substantial risk of the more considered responses being submitted later in the timeline (experience shows that those who have more to say complete later and their feedback is statistically likely to be the more vehemently negative). It also allows managers to inject some additional submissions into the pot that will be more favourable to the overriding perceptions that the BPO wishes to generate (more on this to follow). All standard tactics that are employed to various degrees, more often than they are not.

The level of deception is breath-taking and arrogant to say the least. Yet this is the way in which BPOs have to survive. It is part again of that wider performance, the magical illusion. I do return to this analogy of the magic show repeatedly because I am astounded that clients would not know that this type of illusionary craft was not undertaken by outsourced agencies. Everything that they do know about the companies they employ simply points to the fact that the image of depth of quality and service and satisfaction, simply could not be delivered at the rates they charge and on the basis of salaries which they are known to pay.

Clients, as those who head up and run their own businesses, must surely be aware of running costs and the difficulties associated with achieving quality results themselves, in spite of the fact that their own running costs are higher and are not squeezed as outsourcers are. You can only really conclude that clients are complicit in the pretence because it gives them a viable account on the face of things that can be readily reported to others.

Is it truly feasible that clients *would not* see this all for what it really is? It is a fact that every activity in life produces waste. This in turn means that a function needs to be employed to clear up that waste. So, yes, the binmen did a good job in carrying the trash away. Great. Do we all fill out satisfaction surveys? No. No need.

We don't need to make anything more out of waste disposal than the fact that it is waste disposal.

Some councils used to call their binmen *hygiene technicians* which used to garner a wry smile, sometimes a chuckle. At least they stopped their bullshit at the name only and did not extend it into falsely *bigging up* a whole industry.

Sometimes my exasperation with the whole charade leaves me struggling to find my next expression of outrage at this whole sham.

Breathe – and relax.

Perhaps it is on a parallel with other experiences that those familiar with outsourced partnerships may have encountered in their dealings with vendor managers. That is to say, in the event of a service issue, vendor managers may sometimes simply request a detailed report, not because they themselves wish to investigate the issue, but because they wish to have a watertight summary of events that they can simply pass on to their senior managers so that the matter is dropped without further ado. That is a very common scenario, and I have done this extensively in relation to the management of many accounts in different BPOs. In effect, simply providing the script that supports the position of your contact – often because they are themselves incompetent and not sufficiently, dare I say it, close to the detail to evaluate your delivery as something for which they feel comfortable taking you to task.

If all else fails or if managers are particularly nervous about the outcomes of an *ESAT* survey, they can always exploit one of the favourite loopholes that again can be set up on the back of a principle that is emphasised in order to demonstrate the ethical nature of the process. That is to say they can take advantage of the fact that the *ESAT* surveys are deemed to be anonymous, and that individual respondents cannot be identified.

What this means for the unscrupulous manager is that he can arrange for extra survey responses to be entered with very little chance that this will be discovered. One of the advantages of this is that respondent levels are typically below the 80% mark, so there is headroom for the void of the non-responders to be filled by some favourable responses that the management team may need to insert into the body of data. In the course of my career within BPOs, this was the norm rather than the exception. This rather sheds a different light on some of the questionable results that did actually materialise from the surveys which otherwise would probably have been catastrophically appalling rather than the familiar strain of simply piss-poor.

Some companies claim to employ the services of third parties so that absolute confidentiality and integrity of the responses are maintained. Trust that at your peril – 1) there is a vested interest in who said what and 2) a further requirement to get the results they need to support the ongoing business.

If you think they leave either to chance, you are a very trusting person.

On one occasion however, a little massage of the numbers did fall into question when the supplementary responses formed by the management team ended up causing the respondent rate to exceed 100%. Therefore, it was clear that more individuals had responded to the survey than were actually at that time employed within the organisation. Helpfully, this was explained by the *HR Director* as individuals refreshing the final page after submitting which may have duplicated some entries.

Absolute tosh but a rare example of an *HRD* actually adding something of value to the business. This was the sort of rationale that made right-minded individuals spit out their Gold Blend in a mix of exasperation and disbelief at the audacity of it all and that at the lengths that senior managers would go to covering up malfeasance, particularly those with overall responsibility for the conduct of personnel.

But as I've stated many times in the course of this exposé, no falsehood is too brazen to offer, and no depths are too low that those in senior positions will not hesitate to resort to them in order to protect their positions and the illusion that these organisations are credible and deserving of respect. As Hitler and Goebbels said

– and I reference them only because their gang were the ultimate purveyors of spin and deceit – *lie big and stick to it.*

The theory being that if the lie of distortion is so impudent, nobody could conceive that it might be false. Goebbels actually attributed his inspiration to the English, which was really not cricket at all. Probably another example of lying big. Just say it and run with it.

ESATs for public sector organisations are a slightly trickier prospect, in that any information requested or logged is potentially something that could be subject to a *Freedom of Information (FOI)* request and disclosure or at least liable for disclosure within the client organisation itself. Therefore, public sector organisations who deal with BPOs are usually savvy enough to avoid the prospect of requesting the results of an *ESAT* and BPOs are equally comfortable in not citing *ESAT* measures when they are pitching for public sector business. In a sense, they attain a taboo status, and for good reason.

Underpinning all of these surveys though, and notwithstanding all these diversionary tactics, is a common position that in turn is based on a culturally specific premise. The goal of satisfaction surveys is not to find out what's going on and to fix any problems – anybody with half a BPO-cultivated brain knows what's wrong in their organisation.

The goal is to front employees up with a proposition and to get you to say '*YES*' to questions regarding our satisfaction levels even if everything around us in terms of reports and data is screaming '*NO*'. We live in a 'no means no' culture. The 121 with your manager when they know you're unhappy because of all the unfair and crazy practices and policy is geared towards one outcome. All they want is for the meeting to end with you saying that you're feeling happy or happier. It's never about an open and honest, introspective view of the insanity. It is about a box being ticked that can then be presented to others as evidence of how things are even if every other piece of evidence that they can experience with all five senses tells them something different.

Now is that not a fantastically astounding example of double-speak?

Running a process ostensibly to prove something that you know for sure is not happening.

It's so obscene, it's delightful.

Or is it not more incredible that it would be so much more straightforward to channel those not inconsiderable efforts into simply running the organisations more ethically and constructively and simply letting the ESAT reflect a more positive reality? Clearly that revolutionary concept has not yet dribbled through the cracks in what has always been a crumbling testament to employee happiness in the BPO space.

The most twisted part about these satisfaction surveys is that what is being surveyed is akin to a situation of domestic abuse. The victim suffers because there is no discernible way out for them, and to the outside world they have to keep telling everyone that everything is *a-ok*.

And the BPOs point to the positive survey results and proactively trumpet how happy everyone is,

The supreme irony being that employees may even stick up for the abuser if the abuser is challenged by a third-party.

It is a painfully difficult cycle to break as those who have to support abuse survivors will tell you.

If, of course, they do survive.

26 – The Empire Strikes Back

As researchers and scholars have become more interested in contact centres and the organisation of work within them, the subject of resistance has come more and more to the fore. Indeed, this is a subject that Woodcock (2016) starts to explore in his work 'Working the Phones'[xii], and he indeed identifies a number of examples of ways in which his erstwhile colleagues would exert certain ploys in order to prevaricate or squeeze out additional drops of personal time from the rigidly structured day or even prolong any activity that might delay an immediate return to the shop floor and the relentless cycle of call after call. Much of what he said resonated emphatically with me and reflected much of what I had experienced during my long career. It is a very worthy text and a recommended read for anybody interested in an ethnographical or sociological understanding of contact centre life.

At this point, we should perhaps define resistance more clearly. There is always the sense in some quarters of resistance to change and any manager or project leader worth their salt will have considered how to address this kind of reticence when implementing new ideas and processes. Ironically, the management teams see this reluctance to change as a fear of change itself.

In reality, the staff are usually unenthusiastic about new approaches because they can clearly see how impractical and senseless much of it is.

The (in fact double) irony stems from the waste of resource employed in objection handling in relation to ineffective initiatives that are often geared at driving efficiencies. As the staff appreciate, they just need to be better thought-through and more relevant ideas in the first place. But I digress. What we are really concerned with is the spectrum of activities and actions undertaken by staff in order to deliberately circumvent controls to the point where they move into the realms of sabotage.

I can myself recall the days when waiting for inbound calls which would be delivered in sequence, colleagues would flick out, then back into *Available* status just before a call would be delivered so that they moved to the back of the queue and handled fewer customers. At times it was the only way to gain limited respite from the 60-odd brochure request calls per hour you would otherwise be destined to pick up. Sometimes in order to alleviate the pain, we too would run competitions to see who could fit the most random words into their calls – often with ingenious solutions when words such as *'Jellyfish'* or *'Quim'* were sophisticatedly engineered into Army recruitment conversations. At other times, we answered calls using extraordinarily camp voices or in the style of a *Gestapo* Officer.

Thankfully, this was in the days that preceded the era of call recording, so you would do so only if you had not heard the pips in the ear that signified that you were being remotely monitored. My personal favourite was a colleague who would – when faced with a particularly obnoxious caller – thank him at the end of the call with a, *'fuck you very much, sir',* delivered with such aplomb that you would think, *'did he say what I thought he said?',* but then when you ran it through your head again, you were equally convinced he hadn't.

§

In a similar vein when working on a home shopping line, I remember this guy had a real yokel on the line and was playing him on loudspeaker, such were his unmelodic tones. At a point in the call, clearly interested in basted chickens, the customer asked:

> *'Ere mate, you got any of they bastard chickens?'*

To which my colleague responded (after deftly applying the mute button):

> *'No, but we've got some fucking amazing turkey crowns'.*

On another call, when asking the typical media question, an advisor asked:

And where did you see our number to?

To which, the obviously paranoid customer responded increasingly agitatedly:

'What number two? I haven't seen a number two. Just tell me what number two you're talking about?'

Well references to number 2s and BPOs, that is wonderfully Freudian. But we must continue.

The decision to resist, itself often kicked in before employees joined the company. In the late 90s/early 2000s there was a sharp increase in companies outsourcing large end-to-end functions, not simply small parts of the services. This led to 100, 200+ seat account operations for which some of the training was more in-depth and took up to two weeks. Not that this was required, but the BPOs over-emphasised the criticality of the proposition and fed on the natural reluctance of companies outsourcing so extensively for the first time.

If a client is nervous about letting go, you can agree that the work is complex and lay down a reassuringly detailed training plan. The investment that the client is prepared to make is or should be, directly related to the value they place on their business and customers or the fear that something will go awry, and they will be exposed to their bosses. And when the training is covered on a fully loaded hourly basis, the proverbial boots are filled.

Great news for the BPO but equally great for the opportunist. We then started to see people joining the company, completing their training, and then leaving before they had to go onto the shop floor and into the 'live' operation. In some cases, where there was a training graduation bay, they could sit around on 9-5 shifts with three calls an hour for another six weeks before they left to go into another trainee role elsewhere. Even better if they came in on the Recommend-a-Friend scheme as their sponsor would make a cool £250 on top. A nice cherry.

Another way that the rank-and-file would rebel was to expose the incompetence of managers. I always stated that were you to rank all staff in the order of intelligence, none of the management team would make the top 10. I cannot for that matter think of a company where someone at Director level would make the top 25, but let's not dwell on the obvious. What this does mean is that the agents see better, analyse better and by virtue of their roles are closer to the proverbial detail. By contrast, managers are less so (they are after all criticised for micro-managing if they get too close) and they are concerned with the higher-level oversight and performance. For everything to work effectively, managers need to build a strong psychological contract of respect and trust with their teams so that each can focus on the right detail and at the right level, in the knowledge that all are doing the right thing in each other's as well as the company's interests.

And that is where it can all go horribly wrong. In the BPOs, the gulf between management grades and the agents is often either wide or as is now the trend, hypocritically wide. The latter is where they talk a good game in terms of *respect* and *empowerment* while remaining even more dismissive and cold. At least in the glory days of the 90s, it was not something that was particularly well hidden or deemed important enough to hide.

What happens in practice, is that when the agents spot something that is not right, they sit back in blissful ignorance and wait for the balloon to go up. I have seen a whole operation remain silent on Boxing Day when the lines did not come back up after Christmas Day and thousands of callers waiting while the phones rang and rang – all while the shift manager remained blissfully unaware, doing whatever disengaged people do when they are rota-ed into work on a public holiday.

Moving from strategic ignorance to outright crime, I've seen £5k wedges of supermarket vouchers for customer 'gestures of goodwill' skimmed and loosely accounted for, and at times falsely accounted for. Colleagues filling their cars with client-funded Easter eggs, wine and bizarrely, razor blades.

A burglary on the safe in the staff café that held £2k – all on an inside tip-off that gained more in terms of strike-back adrenalin than the £500 they pocketed for their troubles as their cut. Everybody being in the know and nobody lifting a finger to inform on the culprits. They loved the buzz it gave as a slap back in the face of authority.

And there was also a tremendous wallet swipe, reminiscent of Matt Damon's 'best take yet' on *Ocean's 11*. A senior manager's fat wallet lying on the desk in all its resplendent glory when in one fell swoop a cheeky chappie strode past and whipped out £40 without breaking his stride. Now dexterous that that one was, it was actually witnessed but nothing ever said. The victim's appalling history in the workplace made a normally reprehensible petty crime seem a tingling delight for those who came to learn of it and who saw just a glimmer of justice in the act.

Even the managers were at it with their mileage scams for either journeys that didn't happen or regionally based *Account Managers* who would register their home address as that of a family member, then move closer to the office and their client base. The latter would then claim business mileage between their registered address and final destination. For an Account Manager out of the office three days a week and a forty-mile difference between registered home and actual miles, that's the best part of an additional £5k per year on a £0.45 10k band.

Others book premium rail tickets and claim for them but then cancel meetings and claim the refund (minus the £10 administration fee) – another variation of the so-called double-bubble. The list is endless, but the above scams were institutionalised at every BPO I worked at. In many cases the travel costs for *Account Managers* are assigned to job numbers and are invoiced out to clients, so everyone's a winner.

Seriously, any documentary on the BPO industry would have to have *Hot Chocolate* singing that as the theme tune.

Well, everyone apart from the clients themselves who I am sure never dreamed of working these sorts of scams themselves. Some very daring directors have even managed bathroom and kitchen refurbishments on expenses, presumably jumping from company to company in order to make sure that their domestic makeovers might be completed comfortably under the corporate radar. By the time, the expenditure does float to the top of the toilet bowl, you've guessed it, the rogues have safely hopped into their next BPO role.

Expenses claims jiggery-pokery in BPOs are often however a lot more simplistic – junior staff on company benders put claims on their cards which are signed off by their immediate bosses (who are also present) and are never again checked. This is the standard way to achieve authorization of claims within a closed circle of chicanery.

Others take public transport and claim taxi fares with bent receipts (easy to make up and usually only an amount to write in, so little detail to check – after all, how many *Financial Controllers* are going to phone up a taxi company to see if they can verify the validity of a fare. It is just not going to happen.

§

So, what makes these companies prone to such behaviour?

A lot of it will come down to the fundamental requirements to operate using very slim operational structures with very little in terms of direct and detailed supervision. A lot of these organisations operate on the basis of trust, once you step away from grassroots operational activity. And in many respects that makes sense as you invest funds for complex IT measurement to focus on the area where you have the largest amount of staff activity, i.e. on the operational floor. When you appoint first- and second-line managers, there is an inherent assumption that those people will be given high levels of responsibility and associated with that will be corresponding degrees of trust that you place in them.

The problems arise when the very senior levels of management within the company decide that they want to screw a little extra out of the managers themselves. Now it is a basic rule of any kind of Machiavellian manoeuvring that you do not attempt to inflict a wound into the back of those who are doing your dirty work for you. And that is because if they survive or get an inkling of what has actually happened, you have created enemies among those who know where the bodies are buried. And in BPOs, there are a lot of dead bodies – indeed a lot of mass graves.

That is why revenge does not however always emanate from the rank and file – sometimes the management team get in on the act and damages the companies in a way that really hits them where it hurts – in the balance sheet. As it may by now be obvious, these organisations are entrepreneurial in nature and as the client base is constantly changing or changing shape, there needs to be a rather loose and adaptable structure to support it. In many ways, they reflect a rather incongruous mix of stringency in operational delivery where staff are mercilessly scrutinised and measured, to an almost cavalier approach adopted at the higher levels of management. Unlike regulated environments, whether there seem to be processes and procedures for everything, the outsourced contact centre is very much focused on the ends rather than the means. This can give people quite a lot of room for manoeuvre. And the irony for BPOs focused on revenue is that while they control the production lines tightly, they have very little to rein in what goes on to the line or how this might be set up.

As a perfect illustration of this, I knew of a senior manager at a company, holding the position of *Head of Site*. Now the company organised itself in such a way that incumbents in this role were effectively general managers of their site with a considerable degree of autonomy. Of course, there were company-wide initiatives that needed to be carried out by all sites in the region, but at a local level there was a considerable degree of latitude.

Now following a breakdown in the working relationship with the regional directorate, the site leader, who owned all of the senior client relationships relevant to the site, started to take a rather cooperative and helpful approach in relation to contract renegotiations and, for the majority of clients on the site, allowed significant price reductions at contract renewal when they were tentatively pushed (as they of course always are) – and in some cases even proactively offering them. The message that he was relaying back to the regional directorate was that the clients were ready to take the business back in-house or go out to tender. A classic line mainly used by clients in order to lever a few extra coins from the outsourcers which has a meteorically high success rate particularly close to the point of contract expiry. As it happens, the site in question had previously had a lot of spare capacity following the loss of a major client, so had been filled with new client accounts when they arose.

As a result, a lot of renewals were coming up at the same time. The net result was total discounts of about £250k per annum for the next 2 or 3 years disappearing from the company's billings without a clue being had about what was really going on. Similarly, a client was also given a piece-by-piece rebate of over £100k after it was discovered that the Euro-to-Sterling exchange rate had pushed up the costs of services (they used to pay in Euros at the time). All under-the-radar arrangements about which the wider organisation remained oblivious.

It was a beautiful piece of *contexting* that was swallowed hook, line, and sinker by precisely those for whom *contexting* was part of their everyday repertoire.

They probably need to add that to the *MBA* syllabus — there are always other people who are as clever or cleverer than you.

It almost seems incredible on one level that such activities could take place. But consider the context. These outsourcers need to grow and grow often so that they can generate the pound notes profit they need in sufficient volume on tight-margin business, so they therefore acquire other businesses or set up new sites in areas of the country that are favourable in terms of available manpower, wage, and accommodation costs. That can lead to a quite varied geographical footprint which must be managed regionally. Now the task is simply too much for individuals at a regional level to control closely, so the power is devolved to the local sites with the regional and national managers doing — after all what they should be doing — the strategic stuff. Investment in information technology allows the numbers to be monitored.

The key component that you need to have though is trust. When you devolve or delegate, there will always be a certain amount of information and detail that you cannot, nor cannot hope to know. There are likely to be no extensive resource procurement and legal teams of in-house commercial lawyers. You have to trust in the person in situ and understand that they represent the actuality. If they do not, then the wholesale courses of action can overwhelm and transform what happens next.

The situations described above took place during an unprecedented period of financial scrutiny. Regional teams looking at margin on a daily basis with the sites. Controlling the production line. However, the control over what went into the line sat with the person in situ who was talking to the clients. And if they said that the client would pull the account if a 20%-unit reduction was not agreed upon, who would be there to dispute it? In this situation, by the time the notion of the discount became known at the regional/national level, it had been discussed so frequently with the client in positive terms that the discourse of the day equated to necessity. Therefore, even if questioned by the regional/national directorate, it would have been to no avail. One short circuit of the series and all the lights go out.

Imagine a bank with the most sophisticated security systems available. And then the teller just hands out the money over the counter. The bank loses the money without there needing to be drama or fireworks.

In other cases, more senior managers very au fait with contractual detail would 'assist' clients in their interpretation and understanding of terms so that rebates and refunds would be firmly on the agenda. Watertight ways in which to inflict damage to the bottom line. Some of the BPOs just did not help themselves – making employees work notice periods in the event of resignations and even redundancies, sometimes even after dismissal for misconduct.

Now any HR leader sanctioning *that* should just be fired. That is lunacy of the highest order and tells you that any numpty who sanctions such an act does not deserve to be employed – *anywhere.*

It is just fanatical short-termism and bitterness at any sense that someone might get paid for sitting at home. Instead, the employees spend 3 months or however long, finessing their own plans for how they are going to cost the BPOs 10 or 20 times more, allowing accounts to suffer irreparable damage, copying whole servers to disk, and walking off with sack loads of data. It happens and it happens with frightening regularity.

§

Of course, when the subtle and deft touches are not possible, the remaining options can just as easily be route 1 – and with the advent of new technologies, this is becoming even more straightforward to execute with often instant and impactful results.

I have seen this with blogs where organisations and their less than favourable employees have been surgically dismantled in public view with impunity. One published by a BPO employee was particularly enjoyable to read and done with precision and care – even with hints and tips to other potential bloggers in relation to maintaining anonymity. In that blog, it was clear that attempts had been made to unmask the said wordsmith but to no avail. Clearly, a well-informed and intelligent person who felt that they needed to blow a few lids off some rather unpleasant containers and who did so with relish.

It is that double-edged sword that comes back to bite these BPOs time and time again. They hire the smart people who need the work and treat them badly. They seem to forget that the clever ones are the most likely to analyse, internalise and have the wherewithal to respond in a way that will be felt.

The reaction to that blog, which was as you might imagine that some members of the site management team lost their air of condescending invincibility and recourse to HR in tears, reminded me of how quickly and seemingly effortlessly these paper tigers do get shot down. They simply cannot handle the exposure and fold up almost comically. It is as if they have no defence at all and interestingly never address the claims that are made – they just get angry, tearful, and bent on discovering and punishing the culprits. And the reason for this is that they cannot defend their actions.

They choose to do what they do because they can, because it's easy, and because they enjoy it. And in no other type of office organisation, where there are large numbers of people being drafted in to perform basic work, tied in by their own precarious situations, will there be the opportunity for psychotics to get knee-deep in power and subjugation?

So, when the fightbacks begin, it is gratifying to witness the total tyrannical meltdowns – the hero-to-zero moments of the most brash, arrogant, and aggressive, who become the tearful, pale saps.

Now the description of these people as tyrants may seem extreme – after all, nobody (directly) dies. But the psychological impact on their staff is huge which ends up causing significant long-term damage to a lot of people who simply want to come to work and do a good job. There is probably another book on that subject alone, but for now let us look at some of these examples of resistance.

§

In a number of cases I have encountered, email is the weapon of choice for a targeted and explosive thunderbolt that can quite literally shake these organisations to their core.

The first time I saw email used effectively in this manner was when an employee sent a company-wide parting shot to the business that was memorable not only for its content but for the manner in which the message was delivered. The background to this was typical of the type of interactions that employees and organisations used to have. Typical in the sense that employees exerting their rights would be ostracised and browbeaten by managers who were either ignorant of the entitlements of others or simply affronted that so-called underlings would have the nerve to challenge their position or simply act in a way that was contrary to their own expectations or wishes.

In this case, I believe the situation was that the individual concerned had returned from maternity leave and then wished to take the holiday that she had accrued while on maternity leave prior to the end of the financial year as was the requirement in accordance with the company's own holiday guidelines. As this meant that the management team then had a gap in the rota that they otherwise would have found difficult to fill, this was met with a certain amount of resistance.

Ultimately the company had to give in and authorise the requested holiday, but it was not without cost to the employee. The employee was then completely ostracised by the management team and steps were taken to ensure that her career progressed no further. This involved an order from the very senior levels of the company that an application she made for an alternative position should be scuppered. This involved direct interference in the application process, resulting in the individual not getting the job for which they were arguably well qualified. The individual concerned, obviously reading that the writing was on the wall, decided to look elsewhere and was successful in securing an alternative (external) position.

What they did as their parting shot, was to compose a rather well-constructed email that, while not naming names did make it very clear that they had been grossly ill-treated and that the way the management team were performing was manifestly not conducive to employee well-being, operational effectiveness, or anything else that remotely approached best practice. However, the twist in the delivery of the email, was that it was not simply sent but was using one of the advanced features of Outlook – sent with a delayed delivery. As the employee concerned finished their final shift on a Monday evening, this meant that the email was not sent immediately and prevented the company IT department from having the opportunity to access the email system and remove it from everybody's inboxes. What happened was that the email was delivered at 10.00 am the following day so that it landed squarely in the middle of one of the busiest days in the week, at one of the busiest times. It had maximum coverage. Within twenty minutes it had been removed but not before practically the whole company had read it.

Nothing came of the email as it was dismissed as being unprofessional with one senior director responding to the message (however he did respond directly which went to her company account, which of course she would never have read herself, having left). The email emphasised that in effect we all write our own references and that in what is a small world, it would only be a matter of time before somebody encountered her and remembered her for the wrong reasons. Now had that advice been seen by anybody other than those who were subsequently investigating the email accounts of the perpetrator, such advice may well have saved this particular company some challenges and heartache in subsequent years. A simple use of '*reply all*', which incidentally seems to be the bane of people's lives generally with the use of email (how many times do we see a simple thanks response being copied into 30 recipients?), would have ensured that a cogent response that criticised such email outbursts would have been seen by a wider audience. Alas, probably by accident than by design, the said director for once did not *reply all*, and the opportunity was lost.

What did happen subsequently in relation to the perpetrator is that a smear campaign was undertaken by more senior members of the management team in relation to her which involved disclosure of confidential information about the woman and her partner, which was potentially extremely upsetting and damaging. This involved information being leaked from HR, undermining the integrity of the business not to mention significant breaches of the *Data Protection Act.*

This information was then duly enhanced by the less scrupulous members of the management team and disseminated via a slanderous campaign of defamation. Even to the point that anonymous communications were sent to her new company that for a time interfered with her referencing. Whether it ever did any damage to the individual we never discovered. But it served to remind many that a well-propagated message would certainly hit a raw point while at the same time, a cloak of anonymity would be recommended in order to safeguard those taking steps to redress the balance.

On a corporate note, this also prompted a tightening of procedures that meant when an individual left the company, all IT accounts were disabled, passes cancelled etc., so at the point of leaving employees became completely cut off. Up to that point things had been so lax that leavers might continue to have access to company systems for months, sometimes even years after ceasing to be an employee.

What this incident did provide onlookers and observers with was an example of a potentially effective way to strike back. It just needed some embellishment and refinement. And that was where the attraction of the anonymous email came to prominence.

§

I think the first time I ever encountered the application of an anonymous email/tactical missile (i.e. that was different from the parting shot of a leaver), was when a disgruntled manager decided to contact their clients to make them aware of a number of alleged malpractices that were taking place in the management of their account. Now the motive for this was purely a heightened sense of personal dissatisfaction with their lot, nothing more. In brief, nothing more than you would get in any everyday situation in any type of job. Most well-adjusted individuals simply brush off that kind of dissatisfaction either with everyday coping strategies or if they become too a regular occurrence by looking for alternative employment.

Now the context of this situation was that the client was paying an hourly rate for dedicated personnel to manage their service and sales. Now at the time, the service bureau and the business were shrinking considerably as more and more clients were looking to move their business into larger dedicated teams. So, it meant that we had a bureau contact centre department that was suffering in terms of agent productivity. It's an age-old problem – you need work volume in order to justify the staff, but at the same time you need a baseline number of staff in order to justify the existence of the department.

So, a number of organisations in the situation will resort to the good old 'double bubble' of routing bureau service calls, which are chargeable at a per-minute rate, into dedicated teams where the cost of staff is already covered by a different client. The outcome? All the calls that you handle with the dedicated team members and are able to bill for in relation to the bureau service go straight to the bottom line.

In brief, client x is paying the cost not only for their business but also for the business of client y. In turn, client y is also paying for the cost of those calls, but everything they are billed for in effect becomes profit. It's a classic ruse from BPO contact centres and can sometimes be the difference between success and failure for lower volume operations.

Now in this instance, the manager concerned was clearly aware that, in spite of the playacting that goes on between these organisations and clients, nobody likes to be ripped off. So, what they did was put together a very brief but pertinent email, and in the knowledge of who the main client contacts were, knowing exactly the message and the tone that would get the maximum results might be, and having access to the relevant contact details, they made arrangements for an anonymous email to be sent.

A straightforward matter and straightforwardly executed. Simply the creation of an anonymous webmail address and an hour's worth of time purchased from a cyber café. Then, all they had to do was sit back and wait for the reaction. Now the reaction was probably more than that person could ever have expected. You would think that anonymous communications even if they contain little truth or at least very little that might be evidenced in fact, would simply be brushed aside. At the most, it might be raised by the client to their senior contact at the organisation, perhaps just test the water and see what the reaction might be. And this is where the reaction in BPOs differs from the real world.

Most organisations would react by saying that it was obviously a *'disgruntled former employee'* (that is the stock answer for any leak) and would of course open their doors for a further examination of policies and processes so that any fears might be allayed. They may then look internally to ensure that client contact details remained confidential and to ensure that managers were not allowing potentially damaging information to filter down through their own organisation, that might be used as potential ammunition in the future. As with a misbehaving child, it would be essential to ensure that no discernible reaction might be detected by the perpetrators because it would be highly likely that the perpetrators were simply seeking a reaction. In this way, lack of effect would serve not necessarily to deter but to remove the motivation for any repeat and potentially explosive communications.

What happened in fact, was that the client did indeed relay news of the communication back to the BPO who played it with a relatively straight bat at first and to the client, but who were so flustered and shaken by the experience that they almost started to venture into 'protest too much' territory. As a result, the matter was not wrapped up as quickly as everyone would have liked, and the effect of a message that was wholly unsubstantiated became much greater and much more impactful. In terms of effect on the BPO itself, it considerably exceeded expectations.

It frankly shook them to the core, leading to numerous internal investigations and an emotionally charged response that led to the whole matter being described as a *kind of terrorism*'. I laughed so much; a small amount of urine temporarily escaped my personal control.

The consequences of this episode were manifold. In relation to any commercial damage, there was not any immediate fallout. Probably at worst, it left the client with a feeling that there may be no smoke without fire; however, also the BPO would be on notice now that it had been raised and that any nefarious activities would likely not continue. What it nevertheless achieved for the perpetrator was a tremendously high degree of satisfaction as it had caused so much disruption and had gone straight to the heart and soul of the very people who had been antagonising them.

It was seen very much as entertainment for them, and absolutely thoroughly enjoyed by the wider employee population who had very little sense of corporate loyalty and identity. Even though their own jobs depended on the success of account service delivery, this was an incident that boosted morale to no end. The reason that it boosted morale, and in fact in itself was the most significant consequence for the BPO, was that it demonstrated the vulnerability of the senior management team.

It demonstrated how easily damage could be inflicted by employees, not only to the organisation but also damage on a personal level that went to the very heart of the individuals who wielded so much power on a day-to-day basis. The way it was done, the reactions to it and how it was addressed emboldened a whole section of dissatisfied employees.

Easy to do with limited resources. *Knowledge is power.* And these missiles absolutely hit home with their impact magnified by the incompetent way in which the BPOs themselves deal with them.

In relation to that particular incident, the perpetrator was never formally identified. However, as the years pass people become more relaxed about disclosing what they know, and loyalties change over time. It later transpired that the perpetrator had arranged for the email to be sent by a friend of theirs – a sensible precaution as it placed a layer of distance between the actual perpetrator and the company which would make it even more challenging for the BPO and to have unmasked them. The person concerned remarkably used their own name, perhaps because the name itself was not uncommon although perhaps because they got a certain kick out of the double bluff of masking their identity by using their real identity. Who knows? What you can see though is that all those years later, that very person appears among the *Facebook* friends of the manager who orchestrated the communication.

And even more amusingly the orchestrator ultimately received glowing *LinkedIn* references from one of the very managers who had referred to this incident as *'an act of terrorism'.* In fact, that person was even subsequently promoted within the same company on the recommendation of the very same senior bod.

I love this example because it demonstrates the fragility of those who hold power, it reflects the narrow scope of their awareness and knowledge and also shows how those who resist can manipulate decision-makers to weaken them and ultimately achieve what they seek to achieve. In this case, the perpetrator started from a position of considerable dissatisfaction with their lot and ultimately gained promotion and positive references for future employment. Not only that, but the person who pulled the trigger was hiding in plain sight. For a seemingly insignificant and minor incident, it is rich in its implications.

At the same BPO, the anonymous e-missile became a favourite feature of the resistance for a good number of years. Once the reaction had been seen for the first time, it became a reliable way to set the cat among the pigeons and to ginger things up somewhat.

§

At a different BPO, the email bomb was similarly used after a period of transition when the company had been bought by another organisation and the new business was going through the process of establishing efficiencies, removing duplicate roles, and dovetailing into one larger but streamlined new company.

This time though, the tactic was used in a targeted manner to take down a specific member of staff. The motive in this instance was simply that a member of the target's own team had been dissatisfied at having been overlooked for a promotion. What they did is they wrote an account of a conversation that had taken place when the takeover/merger had allegedly been discussed and where a senior member of staff had reportedly been disparaging the new company owners. It was further reported that this conversation had taken place in the café area within earshot of the less senior members of staff with the inference offered that senior members of staff were inciting rebellion against the company's new owners.

Now that conversation never took place – that is a fact.

The target of the communication never said those words and was wholly innocent of any allegation that they had. In fact, the person concerned was a very experienced and competent departmental head with a very credible track history in their field. In fact, exactly the kind of person who, in implementing best practices and rigour in such an organisation, would undoubtedly make enemies. This was exactly the type of person who would pose a threat to the kinds of manipulative managers who represented the majority of those controlling the status quo. On this occasion though, the real venom came not from the wider operational population but from a member of their own team, who day-to-day would be part of the inner circle of that department, taking a cheerful part in office activities and socialising with what was seemingly a close unit. And yet at the same time who, having secretly smarted over being overlooked, used their knowledge of previous incidents and inside information on personalities and the practicality of organisational relationships at that time to make a very effectively targeted intervention.

Now this particular communication caused a great deal of upset. This was evident from an eyewitness account of a manager who saw the victim and another senior manager enter the lift at the company headquarters, apparently after news of the communication had been broken to them. Apparently, as they entered the lift the person concerned looked visibly distraught. The new owners of the business ordered an investigation, and it was doubtless quickly established that there were no witnesses to a conversation that clearly had not taken place.

But for the target of the attack, it must have been deeply unpleasant and unsettling to know that within the organisation somebody somewhere had the knives out and was prepared to use them against an individual who was otherwise highly placed in the business. There must have been a realisation that irrespective of the office and of the responsibilities afforded to them, that individual was not immune to attack from those who were unlikely to be caught and who were therefore free to strike with almost impunity.

After all, any investigations into such matters would necessarily require suspects to be spoken to, which in turn would mean that the matter itself would become more widely known. And in the knowledge that people often see that there is no smoke without fire, it was counter-productive to make the incident more widely known. That itself allowed the incident to pass without a definite response or a statement of defence to be made on the part of the victim. After all, it is one thing to prove that somebody has done something but very difficult for an innocent person to prove that they have not done something, particularly when their hands are tied, and they are prevented from having a wide-ranging investigation into all the circumstances.

There was an internal investigation of sorts which quickly turned up that there was no evidence to support the claims and the matter was quite rightly put to bed. However, two aspects of this really struck a chord with those who gradually learned more and more about the incident as the years went by. This is when guards are dropped and in different circumstances, secrets of the past are slipped out in general conversations about business as people feel that the need for tight confidentiality is no longer required.

The first matter concerned the actual perpetrator. It became clear that when the matter had broken and when the victim was at the height of personal distress, the perpetrator had been one of the first people within their own team to provide support and encouragement. It just reflects the level of duplicity and subterfuge, not only that takes place but takes place with such ease and absence of concern. The fact that people can act in this way with such confidence and then later after the passing of a relatively short amount of time start to discuss their role and their duplicity in more detail – without the slightest compunction or sense that they would be criticised.

That gives as great an insight as you can possibly imagine in relation to the true cultures that develop and flourish in BPOs.

The second came from the mouth of one of the senior managers in the BPO at the time who recounted the whole incident as one of the most enjoyable moments in their entire career. Again, at the time that senior manager would have been instrumental in providing support for the victim and reassurances that the company and colleagues would be providing them with their fullest support, yet all the time they themselves were extracting maximum amounts of enjoyment and entertainment from the predicaments that a colleague found themselves in as the unjustified victim of a smear.

As an aside, it was mentioned in the years that followed that the matter had actually been reported to *Inspector Knacker* who themselves had instigated an investigation but who had been unable to uncover the cad who had been responsible. By the time it became more widely known who the perpetrator was, the main players had moved on and I guess even if stronger suspicions on the part of the police or any other person with interest in uncovering the truth had come to the fore, there would no longer have been any public interest in proceeding with any further action.

Delightfully, the perpetrator later left the organization and gained a promotion. And it is at that level they have remained for more than 15 years, never reaching the same level as the individual they had defamed in this instance. It speaks volumes.

Moreover, both the victim and the perpetrator are to this day friends on *Facebook*.

§

Sometimes these malicious communications have a wider net, and I recall one that somebody had sent directly to the Board of the parent company of a BPO that had widely lambasted the managing director and the senior management team, criticising their competence, alleging cronyism, and generally painting a picture that the whole business was going down the pan.

This had been a very tightly constructed message that had been sent from '*concerned employees at business x*'. Now while the business was sold nine months later, there is no evidence that this email was ever instrumental in precipitating that sale. But what is certain is that all of those who were mentioned in the communication sent at Easter time, were gone and the business sold by Christmas. And with all of these incidents, it is not ultimately what the message achieved; it is about the fact that people knew a potential soft spot of the company at that time and understood how effortlessly they could exploit that by creating disruption, discomfort, and unease, simply by taking some straightforward precautionary steps.

It is simply a matter of accessing a public computer terminal or Wi-Fi spot, creating a webmail account, typing some words, and leaving. But by the time the message hits, the perpetrators are home and dry and can sit back and watch the drama unfold.

When such a message lands, it must create a sense of overwhelming vulnerability to know that somebody is there within your very own organisation who is prepared to attack you by gunning for either senior members of staff or aiming their communications at the most senior decision-makers in the business.

The invincibility or shield from attack is in one fell swoop shattered when these types of activities take place. I referred to these matters rather over-emotionally being referred to as a form of *terrorism* when they first started to happen. But in some of these BPOs, that is exactly what unfolded. There were ongoing campaigns – albeit with a variety of unconnected perpetrators – that created a pervasive sense of fear and suspicion that made the more senior members of the management teams almost perpetually seasick at the prospect of opening their email or answering the telephone. It created a sense that no matter what they tried to build, there was somebody there on the inside who was collecting information and intelligence which they would then use to discredit and undermine ongoing business activities.

It sounds almost incredible that this kind of subterfuge could or would take place in a business. And quite rightly so, because in most organisations, there would be neither the inclination nor the opportunity to do so. But these BPOs are founded on words, not deeds. Where the whole product is over-hyped and made into something that it is not, it is equally easy as possible to undermine activities through the creation of a competing discourse. Now this is done regularly, almost as a business-as-usual activity within a BPO itself. For example, the deprecating asides from *Team Leaders* to their staff about a company initiative and the sarcasm of managers when referring to a decision made at higher levels. It happens frequently and is almost exclusively unchallenged.

In other organisations, this type of culture would not be accepted and would be self-regulated by colleagues at all levels. The direct communications to clients and other more senior stakeholders are simply examples of unofficial mailshots that work in exactly the same way as the corporate credentials that these BPOs spin out to raise their profile in a positive way.

The fact that this occurs is a recognition that anything can be marketed but that marketing is not always positive and brand-enhancing. You only need to look at failed marketing campaigns to understand that sometimes activity with the best intentions serves only to damage the brand. Disgruntled employees and those with an axe to grind can use exactly the same techniques in order to damage and destroy businesses and reputations.

At the heart of this though, is the question of why people would want to do this in the first instance. And that's what makes it unusual. It is because employees in organisations who act in good faith, which have a purpose or an essence that is meaningful or admirable, would not need to conceive of such resistance. Of course, there are dissatisfied employees in every company for a variety of reasons, many of which have nothing to do with the company itself. They are reasons that come from within and arise through an individual's position or personal context in life and those individuals move on or change their approach and become either productive employees at the company, or move elsewhere with no hard feelings.

The difference with BPOs is that the organisations themselves rarely produce environments that are conducive to recovery or improvement. The way they operate is that they exacerbate and compound already existing personal issues or they create them from scratch through their fixed gear towards exploitation and denigration. Through these examples, we can also see that any attempts to bring in quality staff well-versed in the standards of professional services will be met with resistance that transcends acceptability, often bordering on even teetering into criminality.

And I think at this point it is worth revisiting the candidate pool of BPO hiring. The goal is to get as many people as possible who are sufficiently literate and possess effective communication skills in order to converse with members of the public on specific, so-called technical themes. In many instances, these will be people who have finished A-levels, are undergraduates or are graduates or postgraduates. In brief, relatively well-educated people who understand how to analyse situations and make sense of their surroundings. They may be Psychology or Criminology graduates who can read into behaviours and who have an understanding of the limitations, not just of themselves but of others and can undertake risk assessments. Not necessarily in the formal sense, but they can plan effectively and securely.

What then happens is those people come to work in BPOs and while being poorly paid, are controlled, subjugated and at times abused. Now you do not need to be a graduate yourself or indeed a risk expert, to deduce that in taking this approach, BPOs are creating a potential cocktail of something rather unpleasant that in time the whole business may be required to imbibe.

A lesson from the schoolyard is that if you feel like bullying somebody, make sure you pick somebody who isn't going to hit you straight back. And that is an elementary schoolboy error of the high-volume Pound shop BPOs. Whether it is fuelled by a lust for power or a misplaced sense of invincibility, they underestimate who they are dealing with when it comes to the way they treat their own staff.

Whenever one of these anonymous communications or apparent attempts at sabotage comes to light, BPOs routinely refer to them as the work of '*disgruntled former employees*'.

Sounds just a tad exculpatory, doesn't it? *It's them, not us.*

Now, as a statement, this may often be the case as people may feel a little safer dropping a bombshell when they are clearly sitting outside of a company's internal disciplinary procedures. It means that they cannot be forced to participate in any subsequent investigations, in the knowledge that the only chance they are likely to be caught – if they have taken the right precautions – will be if they give themselves away. Here, the name of the game with any subsequent investigation will always be to say as little as possible.

Of course, those familiar with the technique of the television detective *Columbo* will know that one of the bedraggled Lieutenant's favourite ploys is to latch onto his key suspect and enlist said suspect in assisting him with his investigation. This serves to draw the malefactor into talking excessively about possibilities which then gets them tangled up in all sorts of ridiculous interpretations of what may or may not have happened. In turn, this invariably strengthens the case and makes the suspect look even more desperate and ridiculous.

In the cases that I have outlined, there were some instances of senior managers approaching possible suspects as if they might be a shoulder to cry on where they could be an effective listener to the woes of the victims or those investigating the cases of apparent sabotage. This added of course an additional element of motivation for the perpetrators as they got first-hand or second-hand opportunities to taste the pain and discomfort of the victims while taking care to not say anything that may have made them vulnerable to detection. Of course, these individuals went about it with no strategic plan, so it just became a window to the torment of the senior management team.

When you do *Columbo*, don't do *bad Columbo*.

The essence of *Columbo* is that he is a super-smart detective who acts dim. Most senior BPO managers and directors are super-dim but act smart. The concept doesn't work that way around.

But again, I digress. The impression that '*disgruntled ex-employee*' gives, is that people left the organisation in an unhappy state and almost let off an impromptu parting shot at the company once they felt it was safe to do so. From my research over a period of years, I think I can safely say that such actions are rarely off-the-cuff. They are often thought-through and prepared for in detail, often way before they are delivered to a wider public. Now there is an apparent contradiction in terms here because sometimes information that is disclosed has an impact primarily because the salient facts are immediately relevant and are likely to hit a raw spot when they are referred to or when a particular spin is put on them. What I am referring to when I talk about preparation, is the methodology and the preparatory steps that are thought through in detail with the up-to-date information that sits at their heart, serving to be simply the final piece in the jigsaw.

Sometimes though, particularly when there is a secret or a piece of confidential or damaging information that needs to be suppressed, it will not matter when that information is released as it will cause maximum damage. In those instances, disgruntled employees ensure that this information is captured and safeguarded for future use, and you can bet your bottom dollar that in these cases, the relevant anonymous communication is prepared well in advance to the final letter so that all that remains when they feel that the time is right, is to pull the trigger.

§

Now while I have managed to discover quite a fair deal about the motivations of these actors, mainly because I have good sources of information within specific companies and because some of these perpetrators have become increasingly relaxed about revealing details of their activities as time has passed – and of course because people do like to boast about what they have done when they feel there is no comeback – I have very little insight into the detail of the modus operandi employed by these individuals. They simply do not go into that depth when referring to what they have done as they are much more interested in focusing the attention of those who might be prepared to listen to the impact of what they have done and how they have delighted in this and got away with it.

I have however been fortunate enough to gain insight into an incident that took place many years ago with a well-known BPO.

The background to this was that an email had been sent to hundreds of clients and business partners of the BPO concerned, causing havoc and mayhem. One of the reasons why it piqued my interest, is because by that time, I had already been toying with some ideas for a book which at the time was going to be centred around employee relations and the psychological contract within organisations generally.

It was reported that the email concerned content numerous unfounded allegations about the BPO and its working practices and was sent to hundreds of recipients.

The Directors of the BPO were naturally outraged and had initiated a wide-ranging investigation to find out who was responsible, supported by offers of rewards among other incentives in order to discover who was responsible. Nevertheless, in spite of the drive to unmask *Oscar*, all roads led precisely nowhere.

To my knowledge, the perpetrators were never formally identified, and nobody was sued in relation to the claims.

I have no real interest in the allegations that were made in what became a quite infamous email and frankly the content of that communication is of no interest.

What interested me at the time was why those allegations were made and the methodology employed by the perpetrator(s). *Oscar* clearly had an axe to grind and set in motion a device to cause maximum disruption. But he obviously felt motivated to do what he did, and I wanted to understand more about his perspective and his mindset, and how he went about this apparent act of resistance. Back when it happened, I had a psychologically based interest in the affair. Now I wanted to understand more in order to assess whether I might then get a greater insight into the preparations that such individuals take when contemplating their acts of corporate resistance and revenge in the outsourced contact centre world.

My hope would be to gain access to *Oscar* and to gain some insider angle on his motivations what he hoped to achieve and how he did it. If I could do that, I may then fill in some of the gaps that I had hitherto been unable to fill in relation to my investigations into the BPO world.

It was a stroke of luck that I managed to gain access to the *Oscar* story at all.

A number of contacts within the BPO domain know people who know people. Therefore, when I was investigating different aspects of this book, and it became clearer to a wider circle what I intended to produce, the person behind the *Oscar* communication made contact.

The contact was made through a mutual acquaintance though in fact it transpired that I knew *Oscar* personally myself – in fact not only professionally but also via mutual acquaintances outside of the work arena. One of these mutual acquaintances explained that *Oscar* would be happy to contribute to the book if certain conditions were met. Primarily this meant that his anonymity would be preserved, not simply in ensuring that their real name would not be disclosed but also by guaranteeing that any circumstantial facts that may have served to narrow the focus for anybody wishing to work out their identity would be excluded.

I readily agreed to this, and this position was reinforced by my assertion that I was not interested in an examination of their detailed motivations for doing what they did but wanted to focus more on motivation at a high level, coupled with planning methodology and execution.

I wanted to know more about what it takes for an employee with a certain degree of disgruntlement to a position where they think through and prepare an act of revenge. From what I already knew of the approach to the drafting and delivery of this communication, it seemed to have been very similar to the way in which others before had inflicted or attempted to inflict damage on the BPOs who had been the subject of my own investigations up to that point.

Upon discovering *Oscar's* identity, I was not shocked in the least. If intelligence and drive were components of a successful resistance, then this person would potentially always have been in the frame. In talking to him, I was able to gain a very clear picture of his approach to his very particular brand of revenge. It transpired that whilst *Oscar* was indeed a fabled '*disgruntled former employee*', his actions were by no means off-the-cuff.

Indeed, *Oscar* had contemplated his actions for up to 9 months before he actually pulled the trigger. He clearly knew what he was going to do though at that point had not firmly decided exactly what. The idea for the anonymous email had first dawned on him when he had been a recipient of an email that have been circulated within the business that included a large number of internal and external contacts. These were the kind of *thought leadership* industry update emails that are quite common in BPOs. Nothing unusual there and quite normal for people in managerial or support functions to receive. Such emails for example might just alert everybody to conference events that were taking place and asking people to book tickets or confirm their attendance.

For *Oscar* however, this highlighted an opportunity to harvest a relevant database of potential recipients for a message. He therefore did this on a number of occasions until he had a list of close to one thousand external addresses. Now the challenge for *Oscar* at the time was how he would ensure that this list could be scooped up and sent outside the company so that he could work on it without detection. Given the Swiss-cheese IT security strategies employed by many BPOs, *Oscar* comfortably found a loophole that allowed him to remove the list undetected, giving him a reliable distribution list of relevant recipients to whom he would be able to send the damaging message of his choosing. Now all he needed to do was compose his missive.

Of course, what he did not want to do was log in to the account that he was going to send the message to the first time and have to sit there and wonder what he was going to be sending.

So, what he did was open up a webmail account and compose the message over a number of weeks and save it to the drafts of that account. Let's call it *Account 1.*

Then, on the day in question, he opened *Account 1* to access the draft, then opened a new Webmail account under the name of *Oscar (Account 2)* and simply copied his draft message into a new email on the *Oscar* account and sent it.

Oscar did not delete the account after sending as he believed that in keeping the account open anybody investigating the sending of the message might expend resource in monitoring the accounts in the hope that he may access it again and give clues to their location or identity. For example, sending an email with a *clear pixel* embedded into the message that might have disclosed his real IP address had he opened it. *Oscar* had at that stage however resolved never to go back and login to the account that he had used.

Investigators succeeded in gaining more information on the account used by *Oscar,* and at this point further evidence of his detail in preparation became apparent. The IP address that was finally disclosed was an overseas government-owned proxy – inaccessible even if logs were available. It was in fact the final stage of a proxy chain operating in much the same way as the TOR onion router. Multiple layers of IP addresses preventing tacking and detection as the missive pinged from country to country before it scorched into one thousand very relevant inboxes napalm-style.

And, ouch – it hurt.

Oscar himself had furthermore accessed the Internet by piggybacking onto an unsecured Wi-Fi connection in the next street at a location to which he had no known connection himself. When he sent a message, he was using a laptop which he had arranged to fix for a colleague as a favour after which he immediately reset it to factory settings and ran a military-grade hard drive wipe.

By the time news broke of the email, the equipment used was already back in the hands of its owner who remained blissfully unaware of the part their equipment had played in transmitting such a destructive message. The message itself had been sent as the 10th link in a chain with the final stage virtually inaccessible in terms of weblog with a first stage unidentifiable in terms of user identification as it was an unauthorised access of little more than one hour in total.

According to *Oscar*, the email was planned to be sent a week or two before in order to coincide with the announcement of some forecasted results which were not anticipated to be positive. The intention of *Oscar* was to provide some added impetus which might see dismissals from the Board. In fact, some changes were already announced before *Oscar* had the opportunity to press the red button, so his grand design went on hold while options were reconsidered.

The communication would initially have been sent with recipients blind-copied in order to create the effect of recipient enquiries to the BPO itself continuing to pop up and accumulate in the course of the days following its receipt. All to create the sense that the ripples would seem endless during the immediate aftermath.

However, this was abandoned and instead it was decided to make all of the names very visible, so for immediate shock factor the range of recipients was wide and also known to each other.

In the course of our conversations, *Oscar* acknowledged that the content of his message was entirely false. In fact, he delighted in the fact that the information and allegations contained in the message were wholly untrue because in his mind that would increase the sense of injustice and frustration felt within the BPO once the contents of the email were received.

Oscar's preparation went even further than simply the act itself. He was indeed a *'disgruntled former employee'*. While a stock phrase used by the press when describing such situations, it was indeed factually correct in this instance. As such, *Oscar* would not immediately be able to understand and relish the impact of his actions within the target organisation as he would have no direct way of seeing and experiencing it first-hand.

Of course, he knew, having so many contacts within the BPO, that they would undoubtedly be able to get the inside story in due course. However, given the anticipated level of investigatory activity that was likely to take place, it was equally likely that his contacts there would be particularly careful about being seen or associated with any likely suspects, particularly those who had left the organisation and might be considered to harbour a grudge or sufficient motivation for carrying out such activities.

So, what *Oscar* did as a test of whether they were under suspicion was ensure that there were a couple of social events in the diary for the days following the sending of the email. As expected, nobody turned up as previously arranged and there was an immediate radio silence via mobile phone which at the time were company-issued.

This told *Oscar* everything he needed to know about his position on the list of suspects. He was, if not at the very top then one of those who heavily featured at one position or another. Similarly speaking, *Oscar* anticipated that there would be a flurry of friend requests to social media accounts that had been associated with criticism of the company as people would be chasing any likely reward and would be keen to make friend requests in the hope that they might glean information about his identity or perhaps unearth an email address that may have been of interest to investigators and would secure a reward. *Oscar* was proven absolutely correct and in the aftermath of the communication being sent, one social media account that was actually associated with him had received 172 friend requests.

As a precautionary measure, *Oscar* had already contacted *Facebook* to raise a concern that the company was stifling freedom of speech by threatening to issue court orders against *the social media company themselves*. Even though he knew that he had taken similar precautions in relation to his social media activity, he wanted to ensure that company resources might potentially be expended in following up on red herrings. Therefore, the view was that if the BPO did indeed make a court order to *Facebook* that was then challenged, they might feel that they were onto something and might expend effort and expense in pursuing it even though he knew it would lead to a dead end with any disclosure.

The running joke that *Oscar* used to propagate was that any investigations by the BPO would likely lead to an empty *Linux* box in The Ukraine. Further to this, other employees at the BPO, unconnected to *Oscar*, hold an annual drinks event to commemorate the event, such was its legend.

It was an absolutely fascinating insight into the workings of one of these so-called '*disgruntled former employees*' and the lengths to which the planning and preparation would be examined prior to sending out one of these communications.

I do know however that the individual behind the *Oscar* email was never taken to task for what he did – and from what I have heard about the detail of the preparation in relation to what he undertook, I am sure that those two facts are not unrelated. In the knowledge that none of the perpetrators of the anonymous emails and communications in the BPOs had ever been formally unmasked, I can only assume that they too have planned, considered, and mitigated the risks involved in a similar manner before undertaking their actions.

I am further convinced that given a situation where somebody took an off-the-cuff action which was fuelled by emotion and anger, such perpetrators would make mistakes and betray enough evidence for them to be identified. All my experience in managing in operational settings leads me to conclude that impromptu actions lend themselves to the appropriation of evidence and proof by those who seek it on detailed investigation.

This did not happen in the *Oscar* case for reasons that I have now had the opportunity to examine in detail, and I draw the same conclusion with the BPOs who are the subject of my more detailed study and concern. Those acts of resistance in BPOs are not those of people who see an opportunity and take it while they are still bristling with anger or indignation. They are cold, calculated decisions that are taken well in advance of the acts themselves, and they are planned, well considered, and coldly executed in order to create maximum discomfort and uncertainty.

In themselves the substance of the messages is almost immaterial.

It is not even necessarily the potential sense of discomfort on the part of the clients and suppliers and stakeholders who are involved in the relevant industry that these perpetrators are pinning their hopes. It is in the actual act of resistance against which BPOs have very little at their disposal with which to fight back. At the point that the messages are delivered there is almost a lack of preparedness in how to address them.

And that is not a criticism of the BPOs, it is simply a statement that recognises that as businesses they are concerned with producing their products and services, how they interact with their clients and suppliers and with the engagement of employees on contracts in order to perform the work. How do you defend yourself when employees or ex-employees decide to breach contracts, betray trusts and to attack you behind a cloak of anonymity? How can you, from a standing start, deal with an action that is complete following weeks, possibly months of preparation where every element has been thought through like a game of chess?

And at the moment it hits, you have to protect all of your interests in one instant and all the different levels, in relation to all relevant angles and to the satisfaction of all the varying stakeholders and interests. It absolutely demonstrates the level of vulnerability of BPOs and how employees can very effectively strike back *if they so choose*. And those four words import so much. As it matters not whether there is any justification whatsoever for the actions that are taken. It is simply a question of choice, and it is that on which reputations can rest or which may help to tip the balance if there is a generally precarious set of circumstances.

From the *Oscar* example, we can see that the reputation of a company can potentially be adversely impacted through the exercise of choice by a determined, knowledgeable, and motivated individual. If you have the distribution list and some credible sounding knowledge, you will be in a very powerful position.

BPOs are filled to the brim with such people who have the skill, the knowledge, and the motivation to strike back against them, the organisations who in their minds, take everything and give nothing. Unfortunately, the appalling cultures, managerial techniques and twisted philosophies of outsourcers do little to encourage any positive change in direction of mindset for those who work within them.

§

As some of my examples reflect, there is a certain irony that the recruitment of progressive and forward-thinking senior management team members with a view to taking such BPOs to the next level is often a spark for resistance among some of the less adroit members of the old guard who seem insistent on clinging to the status quo of the 1990s and carrying this forward well into the twenty-first century.

It is perhaps a revelation to some who have investigated the points of resistance within BPOs that resistance while existing at grassroots level is often arguably more devastating and negatively impactful when driven by first- and second-line managers. It is only when the managerial philosophy right up to board level changes, will this resistance subside and BPOs will finally move into a more elevated status within British culture and industry.

It seems unlikely – though it may come to pass that the survival of the BPO work sphere will in due course occur only if contact centre outsourcing is taken under the wing of larger professional services organisations who regulate services and demand the standards that effectively define them.

The pattern of acquisitions is already moving in direction that suggest that this might be the most logical step. If the only rogues left are these amalgamated, post-merger giants who can no longer fall under the radar, they may need be forced into sales to corporates, who by definition are accountable and auditable.

The next 10 years may prove to be game-changing.

27 – Michael Fishing for Compliments

As we have already established, as with any business, bottom-line pound notes are the name of the game though with BPOs the financials cloud all decision-making, to the extent that any process-driven view of performance is swiftly abandoned. By this, I mean where businesses look to put sustainable infrastructures in place, enabling well-trained and supported staff to thrive and necessarily deliver efficient and high-quality services for customers that in turn will provide a healthy financial return.

The alternative (and the default position) is a finance-driven view of cutting costs, reducing investment etc.so that a very lean business might squeeze past its immediate financial target but with such an emaciated operating model that after a short period, an athletic and muscular business, stutters, and shudders to an unrecognisable state of permanent disability.

This is where businesses are operating on an iron lung which those of you familiar with BPOs will recognise all too readily. While a principal cause of this is a paranoid resistance to long-term strategy and investment and a need to formulate means in purely financial terms, the deciding factor can be found in the budgeting and forecasting processes that determine the agenda for the year.

Put simply, *FDs* and *CFOs* (who are often under stratospheric levels of pressure from stakeholders themselves) are only too keen to start with top-down forecasts for the business rather than looking at and understanding what the business might realistically deliver or stretch to and working from there.

In brief, they look at the aspirational number that they would like to hit – or are told to hit – and then divvy this up into targets for each team and department. And that is where the pain begins. To add insult to injury, the budgeting is often done in the absence of input from the *New Business* teams who will realistically complain that apart from the odd piece of growth from existing clients or emerging situations that may require immediate capacity and bring forth short lead-time opportunities (think *Bird Flu* as an example when every BPO would have received a quick turnaround ITT), most contracts are relatively long-burn for any realistic billings to hit the P&L.

Once the number goes in, everyone will be committed. As they say, *FDs* write everything in pen, never pencil. But the lunacy does not stop there. As the months progress, the management teams will go through a seemingly endless charade of pretending that they are on course to hit the mythical numbers, dreaming up no end of rationale and new opportunities which 9 times out of 10 they will have little chance of converting into pound notes.

It seems unfathomable, but there is method in the madness. It allows everybody to have an easier life, as opposed to the meltdowns that would occur if anybody stated the cold truth of a realistic projection. We all know the typical mindset of an *FD* – continually raise the volume of the shouting until resistance evaporates. *The beatings will continue until morale improves.*

Just playing the game and going through the motions to pretend that it might all be possible distracts everybody from the implication that most leadership teams are so far removed from their own businesses and so inept at drawing on the expertise (where it does exist) of their own teams that they might as well not bother turning up at all.

And for days on end, some of them actually don't.

There is of course always the chance that a client may suddenly cut the budget or pull a service, and these are the strokes of luck that the management teams are praying for.

It may sound odd that managers are pinning their hopes on business setbacks, but these really are the situations where the waters can be muddied so that all of the madness of the terminally flawed forecasting and subsequent playacting can be explained away. It is the ultimate rug under which all the sorry mess can be deftly swept.

As an aside, it happens frequently in operational settings. Balls up the resource plan? Have an appallingly high level of attrition and sickness? When service starts to dive, the teams will be praying for a product disaster, newspaper splash or some other debacle that will lead to an inundation of incoming queries in excess of forecast. It allows all the other bad news to be buried.

It again typifies the doublespeak of the BPO world. Forecasts that tell you nothing about what will happen, management updates that are wholly unhinged from material reality and management teams whose responsibility is to drive the business forward, willing for their accounts to stumble so that they cannot be held responsible for failing to hit targets that were always going to be unattainable. Crazy times? No – normal times.

Sometimes these client decisions are deliberately fabricated in order to create an exculpatory situation. This is done by furnishing regular updates with deliberately exaggerated information regarding potential business development. For example, a £50k gap in a budget may be smoothed over by the assertion that a conversation is taking place about bringing in an additional x agents for y period of time to support a new product promotion. This may not be entirely fabricated – the promotion may exist, and it may have been referred to by a client as a potential piece of activity that they (but not necessarily the BPO) may be undertaking.

This number may then remain in the numbers for a period of time and then subsequently removed, under the guise that the client 'pulled the plug'. This is then accepted as a *'white loss'*, e.g. a gap in delivery for which nobody BPO-side could be blamed. A decision that was entirely client-driven which was out of our hands. *Inevitable*.

BPO forecasts up and down the country are finessed in this way and have been for years and years. The concept of *inevitability* again – it just absolves all sins and washes away the pain.

You might think that it would make sense to have bottom-up forecasting and meaningful management of numbers that was driven by joined-up, synergised intelligence. Many would agree with you. But equally, perhaps in a perverse way this approach actually makes sense? If the essence of the business itself is based on smoke and mirrors, perhaps it is fitting for any supporting activity to similarly derive from a fictional base. Perhaps it is simply an extension of the wider and well-practised charade. The fact that a whole industry can be built-up on the basis of a series of client- and customer-facing performances may make any associated activity necessarily unreal.

If only *Shakespeare* had realised that the 'play within a play' might one day cease to be the stuff of fiction, to the extent that it translated so aptly into real life. Life imitating art. Not sure what the Bard would have made of BPOs though – probably as mind-boggling for him to understand as indeed his works are to most of us.

But BPOs and *Shakespeare* do have something in common. Whole hosts of people claim that they are great. Yet most have never even skimmed the surface of what either have produced.

28 – Office Whoring

If you are by now clearer on the grotesque nature of outsourcing of customer services, then the concept of *offshoring* takes matters to a new level – or depth, depending on your point of view.

As a starter for 10, I remember vociferously slating *offshoring* to India as a betrayal of customers in terms of service and security. I was accused of racism but with verified accounts of outbound fraud mills openly acknowledged, it seems perverse to be comfortable that in overseas countries with not even a fraction of what is generally accepted to be the right levels of data security in place, anyone would feel too comfortable about *offshoring* away from compliant and secure infrastructure and operations.

Given the range of blue-chip organisations who now refuse point-blank to engage in any enterprise where *offshoring* plays even a minimal part, I think my previously opined stance has now entered the mainstream.

Put simply, if outsourcing demonstrates a lack of regard for service by blue-chip organisations and a play-acting conspiracy on the parts of all stakeholders – and if the activities of BPOs demonstrates a subsequent double-cross of their clients – then *offshoring* is the double-double-cross. Imagine a dubious undertaker stealing pennies off the eyes of corpses and you will be on the right track. And for the corpses read *customers like you and me*.

I have always found it perturbing how client organisations can knowingly betray their customers by engaging with BPOs and the whole outsourcing charade. Faintly amusing that for all their supposed business acumen, they are then shafted and betrayed by BPOs who rob them blindly with their deceptions and falsification of accounts, reports and indeed everything and anything they can get away with.

When the BPO introduces *offshoring* to their client, it almost takes matters to a farcical level. The BPO has engaged a client organisation in a conspiracy to short-change and deceive customers. The BPO then double-crosses and rips off the client. The BPO then convinces the client of an even better deal by introducing them to the *offshore* solution. Ostensibly this is to turbo-charge the commercials of the outsourcing arrangement, but in fact it serves only to place both client and customer at greater risk. I liken the actions of the BPO as a fraudster who puts the client on a *'suckers list'*. After all, they fell for classic scam of going with the outsourcer, so it has to be worth a try to get them to believe the *offshoring* hype.

Of course, the customer remains firmly rooted to the bottom of the food chain ion this arrangement. As always.

I refer once again to the Goebbels principle of the 'Big Lie'. Goebbels also incidentally was a supporter of the notion that the repetition of a lie, as with any discourse, will eventually become the 'truth' if repeated often enough. Now while BPOs are largely criminal in their approach and actions, they are not on the scale of criminality employed by the Nazi regime. But some of the propagandist techniques are everyday similar and certainly comparable.

The *'truth'* with *offshoring*, is that the service can be scripted and delivered in English for a fraction of the cost. It is that simple. Nothing will make any idea closer to flying with a client organisation than pure pound notes. And nothing connects a BPO more to any plan or concept than the pound note. Everything else can go swivel.

When you unpack it (and it does not take much analysis), it is a frightening oversimplification. Imagine seeing an advertisement for a garage that announced expertise in servicing and maintaining cars that had a motor and 4 wheels. If you had a 4-wheeled car with a motor, would you be convinced that they were the right garage for you? Clearly, you would not, because there is a lot more to delivering the right service than an organisation focusing on core functionality that may be relevant to you.

You would not get your car serviced at a garage that simply claimed to service cars. You would want to understand their competence, skills, and expertise – the quality of their service.

Why on earth would you want to entrust the care of your customers to organisations that have no other claim to stake, other than they have staff who speak English? The care of those who buy your products and services that pay for your business to exist and who trust you to look after them and to keep their data secure.

Yet that is the premise on which *offshoring* takes place – the purported ability of advisors in India or South Africa, to speak English and follow scripts. That is it. And our BPOs absolutely present these services as being imbued with all the qualities that they claim to have (and do not!) without any justification. It is almost as if they are vouching for a friend who wants admission to a club membership. It is the *Recommend-a-Friend* methodology being taken to an extreme and frightening scale. The implication being that if you can trust us, then by extension you can trust these people. Astounding enough for clients to be prepared to accept but catastrophic for customers who have no idea about what is happening behind the scenes.

I remember the decision-making process behind *offshoring* an outsourced service – *'margin is too low – let's chuck it offshore'*. And we put it out without tender, to a provider we had never used for that kind of work. For the remaining 15 months I was at the company, nobody made a visit to the location, so we had no real idea where we were directing our client's customers. It sounds outrageous, and it is. But that was and is the norm.

Customers of these organisations are becoming instantly vulnerable to groups and businesses on the other side of the world who are accountable to nobody and on whom no checks can be made, or scrutiny applied.

The customers firstly get a poor service from the outsourcer without getting a choice in the matter – they are then downgraded from that to an even worse service when they have a demonstrably higher prospect of not just receiving an even more lamentable service but also being the victim of a crime.

For not only are the *offshoring* services largely of unfeasibly dire quality – a fact quickly recognised by the customer base who are regularly and frustratingly faced with an inability of most advisors to speak comprehensible English or perform any meaningful or relevant service once the conversation goes off-script – but a backdoor into the murky world of data and then identify theft and fraud is unceremoniously opened.

Offshoring centres are notorious for – at best, their lax approach to data security – at worst, their provision of an organised channel to alternative operations where inbound enquiries are *'flipped'* into fraudulent outbound enterprises.

In the lax security scenario, customer details are copied to paper or photographed and then taken away and used for low-level fraud. It is a common scenario, and a high percentage of card frauds take place when customers have been exposed to an *offshore* service, often without their prior consent. Some BPOs who are concerned for the survival of contracts are wise to this and send out auto-responses to customers who email queries, warning them that they should not divulge information like card details of passwords on their communications.

In the more sophisticated situations, whole centres are compromised by rogue managers who access customer databases and harvest data off and provide this to their criminal partners who use this information to target innocent people. One effective method is to zoom in on customers who use email contact forms to raise queries. From the Internet logs, the *offshorer* can identify information about browsers and operating systems used and match these to customer records held. These can then be used to perpetrate the so-called technical support calls where the callers know what PC the victim is using and persuade the recipient of the call to grant remote access to their PC.

From here, more data can be harvested, or ransomware can be placed on a user's machine. It is simple to orchestrate and many of the more effective frauds are only possible because a victim has used a service where the customer service is outsourced and then part of the service *offshored*. A further development of these scams is that data is now being exported back to the UK so that British criminals can deliver the frauds more convincingly than a caller with lower quality English who may not be able to pass themselves off convincingly as *'Colin'* or *'Martin'*.

The customers and victims in these scams will often not know that their data and records have been compromised and hijacked until they have been defrauded. At that stage it is a ceremonial pain in the neck to unravel what has happened and to get compensated for loss. Sometimes there will not be compensation and the customer will have to suck it all up.

Any opposition to the notion of *offshoring* will typically be met by accusations of racism which has become the weapon of choice to put dissenters onto the back foot. A gross simplification that misses the point that customers simply want good service and personal security. Criticisms of *offshoring* do not stem from a belief held by UK customers that non-UK-based services will necessarily be poor, and that this low quality is a necessary product of the ethnic background of the service providers.

It is from a knowledge that the quality is poor and that the risks are high within operations where staff are poorly trained, have little cultural awareness of the UK and where secure processes and adherence to UK regulations are often minimal.

Set against this context, it is also statistically more probable that where high numbers of staff are living and working under significantly greater socioeconomically disadvantaged conditions, these staff will be more susceptible to compromise. It is a combination of motive and opportunity that, while will not be inevitable for all staff, will certainly lend itself to a higher probability of incidence.

There is nothing controversial in drawing these conclusions. In many organisations in different industries in all geographies, staff may need to undergo financial vetting. Why? No other reason than a recognition that individuals with high levels of debt or poor credit may pose a higher risk of compromise by those who might provide an alleviation to those problems in exchange for an advantage. Such risks are as old as Jesus and the subject matter of any security expert worth their salt.

Ignore them at your peril.

Of course, notwithstanding the fraud risks that are interwoven within the very fabric of *offshore* operations, let us not forget the shockingly appalling service that the providers deliver. Putting aside the inept and inappropriate discussions in which *Sharon from New Delhi* will attempt to engage you in relation to the latest goings-on in *EastEnders* while commenting on the current weather in Newcastle (if that is where you come from), they will be so hopeless at addressing your queries that you really will be better off just hanging up.

I can recall being fifteen minutes into a cancellation call for a mobile phone service, only to be asked who my provider was. I then gave my reason for cancellation as the fact that the SIM card was a free offer, and I had never activated it, only to be met with a poor attempt to upsell me with a better deal. Matched possibly by my call from my mobile to a landline service to complain that my line had not been installed on the agreed date, only to be asked to call back from my landline.

Just classic scripted responses from people who are not listening, do not understand and who frankly should not be undertaking activities that fall so short of the minimal standards of 'service'. Yes, I appreciate the argument that states that offshoring creates jobs and an improved lifestyle for these who would otherwise not have opportunities but at what cost? Surely it would be a more viable option to simply increase foreign aid or at least discover something that people in these locations could perform effectively and explore whether there was a way that other services might be effectively offshored. But this should not involve customer service and the wholesale abandonment of quality, security and integrity that is essential for it.

Businesses across the UK have been slowly but surely waking up and inhaling the potent fumes of their morning roast, by publicly recalling their offshoring operations and using only UK contact centres. Now why would they so unequivocally make the point? Only because the toxicity of *offshoring* is now so clear that survival of brands will depend on the clear disownment of it as a concept.

In their own inimitable way, BPOs have attempted to soften the blow of *offshoring*, by, ahem *'near-shoring'*. This is the use of Ireland and Northern Ireland but usually refers to the latter in order to take advantage of lower operating costs and development grants to run their service operations.

Now I have seen some very positive services run in this way and they do ensure that the services are more culturally attuned and more relevant. The issue with these services is that they absolutely keep pay to a minimum and the staff in the NI call centres are often ground down on minimum wages, by the English organisations who are skimming millions of pounds for the privilege of having established job creation in areas that have been laid to waste by a succession of UK governments who had no interest in viable building and investment in Northern Ireland, or Scotland and Wales for that matter.

In a similar vein, increased contact centre activity among outsourcers has taken place also in Wales and Scotland which is absolutely more beneficial that putting these operations in India. The BPOs now just need to ensure that wages are at an acceptable level that rewards the communities who are now helping them to reap the rewards for geographical diversification. From what I saw in one near-shore location where the detritus from nasal cavities was added to the walls of the toilet like some yellow-green crispy mosaic, I think that the disdain of the staff was continuing to be suitably conveyed. I won't be holding my breath for a swift turnaround.

When surveying the BPO landscape, be vigilant also for references to *'right-shoring'*. Yes, you couldn't make it up. The new way to convince customers that BPOs will provide them with the bespoke *'shoring'* solution that is right for them. You know, keep your simple data capture tasks in Milton Keynes but *offshore* all that personal banking work to Bangalore.

They just never give up, do they?

The advice for customers is to do some preliminary investigations in relation to your service providers – find out whether they outsource and whether there is any *offshoring* involvement.

If there is, seriously consider taking your business elsewhere.

Your data, and therefore your personal security, will be at risk and you won't even know it.

29 – Deign to Protect?

Having talked now at length about some of the clearest absurdities of BPO life, it would certainly be remiss of me to exclude some discussion about the *Data Protection Act (2018)/The General Data Protection Regulations (GDPR)*.

While not wishing to spend any more time than I need to going into the detail of the *DPA (2018)*, I will for the uninitiated simply flag that this is a *United Kingdom Act of Parliament* which defines the law on the processing of data in relation to identifiable living people. In brief, it is the principal piece of legislation that governs the protection of data held by individuals and organisations. Now there are many facets of this law, and a number of key terms that need to be understood by businesses.

These include but are not limited to, *'fair and lawful', 'use for limited specifically stated purposes', 'a way that is adequate', 'relevant and not excessive', 'accurate', 'kept for no longer than is absolutely necessary', 'handled according to people's data protection rights', 'kept safe and secure',* and *'not transferred without adequate protection'.*

Protection for information that is even more sensitive than simply personal, i.e. information that relates to an individual's ethnic background, political opinions, religious beliefs, health, sexual health, or criminal records, needs even greater protection.

Now, that's a lot of information to get your bonce around, simply to understand the true nature of data that you hold. And that's before you even start to think about how you can protect this data efficiently and effectively and meet the requirements of the legislation. Added to this, there is a certain amount of uncertainty regarding the roles of individuals within an organisation when they need to manage this data.

For example, there are specific definitions of *data subjects*, *data controllers* or *data processors*. What can further complicate matters for BPOs, is that they then become unsure as to who the controllers and processors are and have a very unclear view on what they should or should not be doing. And that is probably quite a clear assessment of the position in which a number of BPOs find themselves. Not only do they not have a clear view of what data, or rather personal, or sensitive personal data means, they do not know unequivocally who should be processing it and how.

It is a very complex area of operation that requires a high level of technical expertise in order to operate within the requirements of the law. Now, this theoretically presents a significant issue. I say theoretically, because in order to provide a technically sophisticated and competent service in any circumstances, one needs to employ the services of experts. And this is where BPOs experience a significant dilemma.

On the one hand they are handling – and by this I use the term handling to reflect the everyday understanding of the word – enormous amounts of personal and sensitive personal data every single day, and yet their business models are premised on the low cost of their operations which makes their business models feasible and allows them to be in the game as far as blue-chip organisations are concerned.

Quite simply, if such organisations employed data handling experts to advise and to build robust operations that would protect data in the way that the law required, the cost of providing their services would make them too expensive an option for clients who wish to outsource services. They would in effect, price themselves out of the market.

So, what is their solution? Well, put simply it is to ensure that data is held, technologically speaking within an infrastructure that contains discernible and demonstrable safeguards so that ostensibly this data could not be accessed readily by any member of the public who decided to chance their arm at gaining unauthorised access. Having worked in a number of BPOs, I think I can safely say that data is held on servers which are secure and sit behind firewalls and have a degree of anti-hacking measures.

Of course, as a number of high-profile organisations with considerably greater IT budgets than your average outsourced service centre would testify, there are still risks, not only from state-sponsored or organised criminal enterprises but also the real experts – precocious adolescents operating from the confines of their bedrooms.

To be fair, your defences are only as good as how they measure up to the individual skill of an infinite number of individuals who are out there and connected to the Internet. So, the first point is to make the comparisons between outsourced contact centres that are run on a shoestring and their ability to protect data with the behemothic commercial conglomerates who are so easily hacked and about which we read with no monotonous regularity in the newspapers. I will leave you to draw your own conclusions in relation to how safe you think, and outsourced contact centre could protect your data when those who spend billions more are so easily and so routinely hacked as if at will.

Of course, for lots of people, who are not familiar with how outsourced contact centre services work, they might be oblivious to the fact that their account with a major high-street brand with whom they feel their data is relatively safe and secure, becomes considerably more vulnerable when their customer service records can be accessed by a contact centre outsourcer about whom they had no idea might have an existing relationship with that organisation.

And this is one of the issues with the illusion of outsourcing. You may be convinced by the data retention policies, for example of your bank. However, if you do not know that your bank is outsourcing to a third party, which in turn is spending a fraction of the bank's budget on data security, you are allowing your trust in the bank to extend to a company about which you know nothing and adopt the same trusting approach to them without even realising you're dealing with a third party.

Now that is not to say that BPOs have access to your bank account details. But they do have access to a wealth of information that could be used for identity theft and other nefarious activities. Think about it from a point of view of how you approach trust in your everyday lives. For example, you may have a good friend who you would trust implicitly. But does that mean you would afford the same level of trust to their acquaintances or the acquaintances of their acquaintances?

If the answer is no and if that seems to be an absurd idea – after all, why would you trust people whom you've never met? Think about how comfortable you would be if you realised that the business with whom you had built up a trusting relationship was now connecting you to a third party without your knowledge – with the result that you might be (unknowingly) affording them the same level of trust that you do with the people you *do know* in relation to information you share. It makes for a rather unsettling thought.

You might also think that those unscrupulous individuals who are intent on hacking systems and gaining access to information, may decide that it is an easier proposition to hack into the systems held by such outsourced agencies, on the grounds that running on considerably lower budgets, necessarily means that they would not be as tough a nut to crack as the client organisations.

But putting the obvious question marks over the IT infrastructures to one side, what about the actual data security expertise that exists within BPOs? How do they address the question of adherence to the *Data Protection Act*? Well, in a nutshell the policies are generally what one might class as peripheral. When you consider the complexities of the *DPA/GDPR*, and how this act should be interpreted and operationalised, it is a matter for highly skilled and qualified professionals to be engaged and employed in order to ensure that there are workable practices in place and that any issues are addressed with proper advice and support.

In brief, the individuals who fulfil the role of *Data Protection Officer (DPO)* or information security officer should really be legally qualified either as a *Chartered Legal Executive*, or *Solicitor*, or *Barrister*. Indeed, in many organisations such a person would be the *Corporate Legal Counsel* or somebody within corporate legal affairs.

In BPOs however, it would simply not be economically viable to have such a person undertaking this role. In fact, in many of these BPOs, there isn't even a *Corporate Legal Counsel* in position. Often the legal roles are undertaken in the first instance by somebody within the company secretariat or more than likely an HR Manager. That may seem a little odd – and indeed it is – but *HR Managers* tend to be the individuals within an organisation who have the most day-to-day involvement with legal professionals, albeit mainly employment lawyers.

Data protection policy however is within outsourced contact centre organisations often not actually viewed as a legal issue. The individuals most commonly entrusted with responsibilities for data protection matters will be IT professionals as they are the ones who have the most knowledge in relation to the IT infrastructure that is in place to keep servers secure. Therefore, when it comes down to the most common situations where personal sensitive data will be handled and processed, there will be very little oversight in place that regulates this on a day-to-day basis. More than likely, there will be a data protection fact sheet which details the responsibilities of individuals in everyday situations. This might include, for example, a directive that individuals should never write down names and bank details on pieces of paper. This should always be done digitally on an individual system, for example using *Notepad* or *Microsoft Word so that* all notes are perishable.

Unfortunately, in the last 30 years or so, I have never worked in a BPO where bank details were not copied down on paper and I've never worked for a BPO where there was not at some stage, serious issues with fraud being perpetrated using client customer data that had been incorrectly handled within the operational teams.

In some instances, individuals join the company specifically to gain access to information that they can then pass outside the business to other people who can then use this to criminal ends. The most common scam involved the provision of credit card details that would then be used or more specifically sold on to people providing international telephone services. So, somebody giving their card details for a refund on their retail order may find a month later that they have racked up a £2,000 bill for telephone calls to Pakistan.

This is a problem that has never ever been fully addressed, often because it is simply not acknowledged. The customer may have an idea that their card details may have been compromised through their dealing with a blue-chip company, then often they will look for alternative sources for the issue as on the face of it, they would be dealing with a reputable business which ostensibly has secure systems in place for the protection of personal and sensitive data.

What they do not realise, of course, is that their information was not handled by organisation x with a stellar reputation but by organisation y – the murky old shoestring BPO – which had very few effective protection measures in place.

In the perception of the public, the matter only becomes truly visible within the context of *offshore* services. This is because it is then evident that *'Kevin'* or *'Martin'* with whom they have been dealing with their service issue, is clearly based in New Delhi or Bangalore where the level of trust between customer and organisation evaporates rather rapidly. And this is the good reason. Fraud in *offshored* contact centre services is so rampant that it would be incredible to view it simply as an incidental risk. Customer details can be routinely farmed out en masse to organised crime elements who run dedicated contact centres processing fraudulent activities using the data they have collected. Whereas in the UK the criminal activity is propagated by individuals and clusters of criminals, in *offshored* locations it is a whole industry.

It could even be described as a form of outsourcing in itself.

§

BPOs do however make some attempts to meet the requirements of the legislation, however, this is often with ridiculously inept results. I can remember one case where a data *Subject Access Request (SAR)* was made and still not actioned after 300 days. The reason? The *DPO*, who was the Head of IT (quelle surprise), had sent an email to the Finance Department to enquire about different methods of the data subject making their £10 payment. The Finance Department had not replied. The IT manager did not chase the enquiry, so the *SAR* was not fulfilled.

And that is not an isolated incident.

On another occasion, we were considering what exemptions needed to be considered in relation to a *SAR*. These were, I think, other pieces of confidential data contained in documents that were potentially going to be disclosed which we needed to be redacted. When I suggested that we should contact the *ICO* in relation to these exemptions to make them aware of our rationale for doing this, I was informed by the *DPO* that we were safe to make the exemptions without reference to the *ICO* because they fell within our company definition of what should or should not be disclosed!

Absolutely incredible that our own data protection expert believed that his own personal interpretation of regulations would suffice in meeting our legal and regulatory requirements.

I thought at the time that you couldn't make this sort of thing up, and it was at this point after speaking to a senior colleague, it was reaffirmed that our *DPO* had neither training nor qualification to make any decisions in relation to policies and procedures for the handling of data. He was simply an IT expert who could answer questions on the physical steps that were in place for the digital storing of information. Incredibly as part of the same conversation, the view of our *DPO* was that only emails sent to an individual or sent by an individual needed to be disclosed where that individual was the data subject.

Bonkers.

As a result, when that person was mentioned in correspondence or in documentation, there was no disclosure. Unsurprisingly, things started to unravel with a later disclosure issue where a complaint had gone to our client, and there was a subsequent conference call with the client's *DPO* present, who was a qualified Solicitor. I was fortunate enough to be present on that call when our company was mercilessly shredded and left in no doubt that our exposure in that matter was surpassed only by our gross incompetence.

I still wince at the unrelenting shoeing that our *DPO* received on that day to which his only defence was: *'but I was following our policy'.* Every time he articulated that position the level of aggression and tempo of the vitriol ratcheted up several notches until the point where he had no further response and did not dare to offer such a fundamentally insane justification for his stupidity and ignorance. Interestingly – and this may be even more telling – that individual remained in his position as *DPO*, no action was taken internally, nor was there any additional training or support offered, and the BPO concerned no longer services that client.

It was the largest and most profitable account that the company had.

§

Of course, there are some measures that are taken to protect the processing of data which are well-meaning but again in practice are fundamentally flawed because the individual is tasked with the implementation of policies in practice are either the wrong people or even worse are the wrong people who are also unfortunately incompetent. The exchange of data between BPOs and their clients is a key area where breaches may occur. This is because thousands and thousands of spreadsheets and reports with customer information are exchanged on a daily basis, and the way to do this securely costs money that BPOs are unable to make available. The most frequent mode of communication of data sheets is of course email which involves passworded *Word, Excel* or *Access* files being pinged from server to server where the level of security protecting the transmission of such messages can range from secure to inadequate or to simply unknown.

For lots of BPOs, the passwording of the document concerned is deemed to be sufficient without an appreciation that any password-protected *Microsoft* document can be accessed in about 30 seconds by a layman with the right program. Fortunately, a large number of contact centre organisations with whom I have had dealings have now cottoned on to the fact that such a flaccid approach to data security is flagrantly unacceptable and have made a moderate investment in file transfer protocol *(FTP)* capabilities which allow files to be uploaded to secure locations within the BPO's own network and the provision of passcodes to external organisations that enable them to access the data.

There does however seem to be a fundamental flaw in the way that BPOs approach the use of such technology. Owing to the sheer number of files that need to be transferred between multiple stakeholders in multiple client organisations, there is typically an approach that companies take in order to simplify this approach across all client accounts and to make the process more user-friendly.

Firstly, this will involve everybody within the organisation using standard passwords for their *Excel*, *Word*, and *Access* files. What they then do is ensure that all of their clients have the standard link and that they have bookmarked that in their Internet browser. Therefore, when creating an *FTP* passcode after uploading a new file, it is simply that piece of information that needs to be sent to their client organisation when they exchange the data. The client clicks on the standard URL, enters the new passcode, and then uses the standard file password in order to access the data.

I have encountered around five or six BPOs who use this kind of approach. They are therefore organisations who have realised the obvious, i.e. that email is not secure and have elected to use *FTP* in order to communicate their data. Have a cigar, Einsteins.

However, in making this process more user-friendly in a multi-stakeholder and multi-client environment, they have exposed themselves to a further fundamentally basic flaw. Quite simply it means that any file that is sent to the *wrong* organisation can be accessed by anybody in that wrong organisation who is aware of the common password (which is likely to be a common word associated with the BPO, possibly even the name of the company itself!) The absurdity of the solution is that there is protection of the data only against people who might be able to hack into the email system of either the BPO and or their client but no protection where the access code is simply sent to a different organisation with whom the BPO may be performing business.

In the first scenario, anybody who has the technical skills to hack into email communications between two parties is probably going to be able to hack into a *Microsoft Excel* file. After all, this can be done using programs that are readily available on the Internet if you know where to look. However, this is probably unlikely as people with that level of hacking skills to intercept emails are probably not going to be interested in information which may or may not have value from a mobile phone or online retail customer.

In the second situation, there is no protection at all and yet this scenario is probably more likely where the *FTP* passcode is sent by email and to the wrong address after somebody, for example, has used auto-populate in the email address field. In this scenario, a data protection breach would occur in an instant – personal and sensitive data would have gone to an unauthorised source whose only connection with the data subjects would be that they were also clients of the same company that serviced the data subjects themselves.

Aside from the flagrantly criminal breaches that are commonplace within BPO environments, the majority of the last 20 or so serious data breaches I encountered within BPO environments followed this mode.

Confidential customer data transmitted to the wrong client organisation was easily accessible, owing to the use of standard passwords. In such cases, the recipient of the data would not even have to form any intent to access a file to which they were not entitled to have access as they would simply use the password that they use for accessing every other file from that same BPO.

What is even more bizarre, and I am not exaggerating this in the slightest, is one company that set up their FTP facility to generate an embedded password as part of an access link. This meant that their clients did not need to save a standard link and wait for a bespoke password that could be used for every file that was uploaded, they simply needed to click on a link that would take them straight to the file concerned. Fantastic for the equally cataclysmically dense client, who did not need to employ any mental faculties in order to access their data but catastrophic in further weakening the already questionable integrity of a process that so fundamentally failed to protect customer information in accordance with the statute.

§

In summary, data protection policies within BPOs are yet another example of the many facades that are created in order to create the illusion of service or allow the commentary of justification to outsource that BPOs can present to their customers or shareholders. It is a subject that I've touched on in other areas of this book, namely that the assumption that BPOs are these deviously clever organisations who pull the wool over their clients' eyes is itself a myth. Naturally, there are examples when of course they do deceive, particularly on the occasions when they overcharge or charge for work that has never been completed.

However, clients are in on much of the illusion. In outsourcing the services in which they do not wish to invest, in the knowledge that a premium service could not possibly be provided at the rates that they pay to the outsourcers, they are compromising the integrity of their services and underselling their customers.

On the subject of data protection, however, they are compromising on legal responsibilities as they are fully aware that BPOs run threadbare organisations that have neither the expertise nor the resources to ensure that a piece of legislation with the complexity of the *DPA/GDPR*.

Therefore, when they are handling extensive amounts of customer data, often of a sensitive and personal nature, this is frequently done to the detriment of customers. As if this was not bad enough, the customers themselves are no longer able to have an informed choice as the involvement of the third-party outsourcers is largely unknown to them. To the BPOs themselves, the implications of the *Data Protection Act* are largely immaterial. It is a piece of legislation that moves up the agenda within BPOs only after a serious breach has occurred and has become known externally. The priority for action then becomes one of damage limitation.

Over and above the laxness displayed by many BPOs, the risks are exacerbated by the increased demands by stakeholders for greater connectivity. Allow me to share a brief case study with you that exemplifies this.

'The BPO has enabled email access through a web interface. Email can therefore be accessed from any third-party unit, over any internet connection. Once an email is opened, any attachment can be opened, and it will be automatically downloaded to the hard drive or downloads folder of the unit used. As this is an automatic part of the operating process, the movement of data is not flagged, nor questioned. At this point the information within the file – whatever it is – is no longer controlled.

Outlook Anywhere is enabled as a default. To access email, it is not necessary to be connected to a VPN. Therefore, any file sent via email is accessible and can be copied without control. Also, email is susceptible to interception over insecure wireless networks.

While file activity is monitored over the network, the ease with which individual files can be 'leaked' to C drives is a concern. As a matter of course, employees download data from the different CRM systems and from the network and work off their desktops. Many leave files (i.e.) on the hard drives which are vulnerable to loss or open to offline and unsanctioned communication.

The flow of data from the CRM system is also a risk, as ad hoc reports are configured so that when run, are downloaded automatically to the C drive of the user. At this location, the movement of the data can be monitored only if transmitted via the company network. If the laptop is lost or connected to an alternative internet connection, the information is at risk of loss.

Employees can copy and work on any files (that they are authorised to access) containing sensitive data and leave these on hard drives/desktops. It is recognised that the insertion of portable media can be traced via endpoint security measures, so the workaround is that when offline or outside the Company Network, files can be dragged and dropped to cloud storage undetected.

Similar 'leakage' can occur when files are moved to desktops. In individual file movements, this would not arouse suspicion, though just one file might contain business-critical information. Of course, these files are within the network and are able to be monitored.

The free use of smartphones in the contact centre which are equipped with cameras allows for screens to be photographed and images saved to personal (non-organisation) cloud devices instantaneously.

Further to this, iPhones issued to managers are allowed to be connected to personal iClouds rather than company-controlled space. Again, this facilitates the transfer of data which goes under the radar of existing checks.

Access to Webmail and cloud services is not restricted for managers and allows for data to be freely moved to outside the company network. This can of course be done offline – if notebooks are removed from the premises – or via a personal hotspot if set up on a smartphone.

Free portability of notebooks and local storage of files allows for the portability of leaked data that sit on them.

While Sophos monitors files whole destination is a usb storage device, it cannot monitor usb connections to a media device.

In summary, the company data is at risk of loss through the following:

1. The ease at which sensitive data can be moved outside the network without detection. This is because the monitoring process does not detect the step stages that the data moves which cumulatively add up to data loss.

2. The underestimation of insider risk.

3. The conflation of 'unquestioned authority to read and use' with 'unquestioned authority to move and store'.

An interesting case study was taken from a report put together by a BPO employee and submitted to the *DPO* and Head of IT.

No action was ever taken in respect of any of the points made.

Now confident should we all feel about organisations we do business with holding our personal and sensitive data?

We all need to do our research before we buy.

As a director of a BPO once told me:

'If there was no penalty for crime everyone would be doing it'.

When you take that comment within the context of what you would actually have to be proven to have been done in order for the *ICO* to take action, you can understand why in terms of risk management, BPOs put so little into the adherence to the *DPA/GDPR*. How many major fines have been handed out by the *ICO* in accordance with their enforcement programme? Not many?

For many of the breaches, it will be impossible for victims to trace the source back to BPOs. For all but the most voluminous and high-profile cases, there will be no penalty.

The only ones who lose out are the victims – *customers like you and me.*

30 – Blowing the Gaffes

After having covered a number of the major themes, it is probably worth touching on some of the individual anomalies and quirks that I've encountered in the course of my career working within some of these less-than-salubrious organisations. Pride of place probably should go to the unmitigated disasters that occurred that were often comical though at the same time painful to experience.

I remember one Christmas when a BPO was delivering a donation line service to a major charity, which understandably would have been there busiest time of the year. The task fell to somebody to program the opening and closing of the lines which needed to close at just before midnight on Christmas Day.

Unfortunately, the occupant of the decision-making chair closed the line at 0000hrs on Christmas Eve rather than at 2359hrs – essentially 24 hours early. In practice, this meant that for the 24 hours on the busiest donation period of the year, our lines were closed. Typically, none of the call centre managers noticed this, and so it was estimated that they lost several hundred thousand pounds worth of donations. Needless to say, that account was not retained in the following year.

A true catastrofuck.

These types of situations were however not unique, and I can recall another time again at Christmas when the lines failed to open on a major customer information service team and the team sat there on Boxing Day (all on triple time – yes please) and did not answer one single call. Yet again the managers in place failed to recognise that any of their team were not doing anything and did not take any action. Yet again, this was another account that did not last for much longer after that incident.

Issues with opening lines were however not just restricted to operational ineffectiveness. A client who was the provider of holiday and leisure services had failed to pay their invoice over a number of months. After a considerable degree of chasing, the Account Manager in charge of that particular client's business sent them an email stating that were invoices not settled by a specified date, he would simply cut the lines. The invoices were not subsequently paid, so he cut the line just prior to Easter at the start of a major advertising campaign. This predictably had catastrophic results in that area of their business and the account was withdrawn from our company. Unfortunately for us – or them depending on your perspective – they subsequently sued us for breach of contract.

The BPO naturally counterclaimed for unpaid invoices that were still unsettled. The matter ended up in court where a number of colleagues needed to attend a preliminary hearing before ultimately the matter was settled out of court after the accrual of many thousands of pounds worth of legal fees on either side. Whilst not a truly sensational anecdote, it does highlight the fact that highly impactful decisions could often be taken by managers under their own steam. Again, this is not the type of decision-making process that you would expect in a mainstream organisation, and I have to say, I have not encountered such approaches in any business where I have subsequently worked outside of the BPO arena. I admired the manager concerned though. One of the very few who had real balls. Memorable from the day in court though, was a rather savvy judge who appeared very au fait with *SLAs* and abandonment levels and the rationale behind them. He talked more sense than came from either deposition on that day in court.

§

A few employees came back as clients, which was always a tantalising prospect but in most cases the reasons why they had been bombed from our payroll soon became abundantly clear in their vendor management performance, which usually meant they didn't last long. Often they were so bent on revenge, they went route 1 and catastrophically spotlighted their own delusional motives. Thank you and goodnight.

Some of these ex-colleagues were hired by clients as vendor managers – bad because they represented knowledge (about contact centre manoeuvring and worse still, us) applied with purpose (a client's interest). These were interactions that had to be managed with care. The most appropriate tactic was to insert them into your own intrigue by *bigging them up* in front of the actual client so that they had an equally good reason to value you as much as their contract. A nice piece of encouragement for them to see your support as a facilitator for their ongoing engagement with the client. Only too pleased to oblige!

§

One of the things that struck me most when I first went to work in a BPO, is that under one roof there could be 20 or 30 teams of people dealing with customer service queries for a whole range of companies. Now from the customer perspective when they call in, they think they are speaking to the actual companies themselves. But with branded responses, it may sometimes be very difficult to ascertain exactly to whom you are speaking when you make contact. And with a highly competent and well executed quality service, it arguably shouldn't really matter.

This close proximity did however cause a number of issues on different occasions, particularly with the handling of data and personal information. In one place where I worked, it was already known to a number of clients, particularly those in the automotive industry that we were providing services for competitors, so they often made the request that these accounts were situated at the very least on different floors and in some cases, on different sites. But for others, they were completely in the dark – until an incident might occur when the balloon would really and truly go up.

One such incident occurred in the years after the deregulation of the gas industry where a company I worked for had accounts for several different organisations. At the time, we were processing applications from customers who were leaving *British Gas* and were seeking services from those who had entered the market, for whom we were providing customer support. This was of course the era when online forms had yet to be introduced and even email was something of a novelty. We therefore heavily publicised telephone and fax numbers, and it was via fax that these applications were received and then subsequently redirected to the parent organisation.

However, we had only one fax machine in operation and the same individual would load up the facts with piles of documents and then send them in bulk in one transmission through to the relevant company. Given our rudimentary processes in relation to quality control, on one occasion he mistakenly faxed customer details of over 300 customers over to the wrong place. As you can imagine, the recipient of the faxes was amused as to why or indeed how such data could have come from us when it clearly pertained to one of their rivals. But one of the things I learned very quickly in the BPO world is that adherence to the *DPA* and any subsequent actions or safeguards that need to be taken in the event of a breach are routinely discarded – unless it becomes clear that what has happened might be evidenced by reference to an independent third party. In other words, if nobody is in danger of finding it out, under the carpet it shall be swept. Extraordinarily for both of those august bodies, we continued to work for an extended amount of time.

§

Possibly the most nerve-wracking moment I think though, came a number of years ago when one BPO ran a very small service for an American-based company that at the time had imploded in a monstrous scandal involving huge federal investigations. A phone call came through simply with the instruction to close down the account with immediate effect and shred and destroy all documentation. It was so secret that, at the time it occurred, the individual in charge of the operation did not disclose that fact to any other person with responsibility. It was only a number of years later, in the course of a chance discussion, that everybody learned of how a worldwide scandal had fleetingly collided with their world.

Of course, these examples are some of the more striking ones I have encountered in the course of my connection within this eye-opening pseudo-industry, but let us not forget the run-of-the-mill business as usual tactics that are often employed.

Backlog of emails? Not a problem, simply delete them. After all, how many organisations continue to employ BPOs who simply use Outlook where there is no audit trail or means of measuring emails that come in and then emails give a response? For those who use a CRM platform that does measure the arrival and answering of emails, one of the common tricks in relation to the management of an email service level is to ensure that emails that fall just outside the *SLA* during a period are pushed to the back of the queue so that the organisation has an opportunity to answer freshly arrived emails within the service level so that the overall figures are pushed up. Now this may be argued to be perfectly legitimate as there is no manipulation of data involved.

However, it is a striking example of exploiting a loophole and the naivety of clients in order to produce a number that ticks the boxes i.e. the *SLA* percentage figure while producing a service for other clients that is actually poor.

It is all part of the doublespeak of outsourced contact centre terminologies and deliverables. No one blinks twice at providing a poor service as long as the numbers tell a different story on the face of it.

§

The cut-throat nature of these businesses was never too far from the process. On more than one occasion the scoring matrix for redundancy processes was amended after those in the pool at risk of redundancy had been assessed when the results did not give the company the 'right result'. After the amendments were made, it then enabled the BPO to draw the line in the right place and exit the problem employees via redundancy. This will frequently happen if illness or lateness have too high a weighting which can then be downgraded so that the more subjective criteria, for example, adherence to company values, can be brought into play and leveraged to downgrade the persons concerned.

In some of the companies, it would simply be a process of reducing headcount and the site leader would select names and have them exited. This would typically be in low headcount roles, such as Facilities, which could avoid the need for dispute and whose tasks might largely be fulfilled at a regional level. On one less than memorable occasion, a member of staff was earmarked for redundancy and the company allowed him to go through the relocation process – giving notice on his flat and moving 100 miles in the knowledge that his new role was no longer going to be there and that he would be dismissed within 2 weeks. Why they didn't just tell him up front and pay him then, is anybody's guess. Just rank incompetence, I guess.

Not one eyelid was batted in the making of that particular horror story.

§

Operations was not the only location of characters who might add a smile to the day or perplex you to the point of total exasperation.

Facilities was one such department that was often featured. Once, when a roof was leaking and there was crackling coming from what was thought to be the wiring on the top floor, a call was put through to the Facilities Helpdesk explaining what was happening and confirming that the said water was being captured in a rapidly-filling bucket. Expecting a series of instructions that might have helped to safeguard employees, such as confirmation that the power might have needed to be shut down and an indication of what desks the affected staff might have needed to move to, there was one question:

'What colour bucket are you using?'

More inconceivable tales involved the car-parking facilities, particularly when one of our disabled employees requested an adjustment to be made, namely the provision of a car park space close to the office. The space was duly identified and, as with all other spaces, a sign was erected with the employee's name. Unfortunately, in brackets after his name was the word *'Disabled'.* Nice and subtle and one might add, promptly removed and replaced.

The levels of insanity reached new depths though when one employee requested a change to their carpark space, owing to the size of their car and the issues with manoeuvrability. This is a common issue with car parks that are frequently not purpose-built and where the markings are closer to theoretical in relation to standard space sizes rather than practical and taking into account variability of vehicle type. As with all spaces, they were marked with a laminated piece of A4 with the employee's name printed. After some discussion, the change was agreed with employee moving into the spare space right next to the one they had, and the spare space being allocated to what was the incumbent's space. A straight swap.

The next day, it became clear that a new name sign for the employee had been printed and assigned to the new space – all good. However, the original space had the original sign still in place but with a piece of blank paper stuck over it. A rather transparent piece of paper so that the employee's name now clearly presided over both spaces. When it was pointed out that the original name sign simply needed to be moved from one space to the other, the revelation was met with genuine and heartfelt thanks with an accompanying congratulatory sentiment on the ingenuity of the person making the suggestion. Not even a hint of embarrassment. Confined to a bubble and oblivious to everyday thought processes – the hallmark of BPO life-sentence staff.

§

Other classic one-off gaffes that stood out as memorable. On one occasion a BPO was hosting a *thought leadership* event in cooperation with a major consulting organisation and had in the region of 30 attendees from a variety of blue-chip businesses. Now some bright spark decided that it would be a good idea to wedge open the front door of the building to facilitate access for people bringing in bags and display stands. Sadly, the building was located in the middle of an inner-city area of questionable repute and some passing scoundrels entered and removed about 10 laptops belonging to the various guests. All while the security guard was breaking out the sandwich platters in the boardroom, instead or, erm, attending to security.

On a different occasion, a fire alarm was set off which disabled the electromagnetic locks on the doors between floors. As everyone evacuated, unscrupulous fiends facilitated the further evacuation of laptops and other electronic equipment. *Ker-ching!*

§

Another involved a senior manager who had a particular penchant for the politically incorrect, and sometimes the absolute extreme. On being informed that a maker of a popular brand of chocolate would be visiting the contact centre, he approached a member of the team (Ugandan I believe she may have been) and observed that she must have been happy, what with (*x* organisation) visiting.

Huge fallout – not from HR, mind, who were the epitome of gutlessness and fence-sitting – with one of the culprit's own team stepping up to the plate and demanding that apologies be made.

Mindbendingly, the apology delivered went along the lines of a mumbled,

'Sorry to have called you chocolate but you are'.

Even more mind-blowingly, nothing came of it. It is hard to believe how someone would avoid losing their job, possibly an unblemished record, were it to happen today.

Revenge was served though, coldly, and precisely. The chap concerned was something of a fiery individual who used to have quite challenging telephone conversations with his wife or another such concubine. In those days, with a shortage of offices, some of the senior managers would sit in fenced-off cubicles. When the guy would be on the phone sounding off to his wife, some of the team members would tape him and review the rants for their own entertainment.

When the said client did indeed visit, they requested that some sales calls be put onto a tape for them so they could be played at an internal sales conference. The calls were duly added on to a tape which also included some of the managerial wife-rants.

Unfortunately, the client decided to listen to the tape in the car en route to the airport, so the tape was not played through to the full conference. The client did however gain a rather interesting insight into the demeanour of the manager concerned and, as I understand it, took the opportunity to make their observations at a more senior level. In due course, while this may not have been directly related to this particular incident, changes were duly put in place.

§

While there are more grandiose degrees of resistance reflected in the various incidents of sabotage, employees also like to indulge in more subtle coping strategies. One of these will be the collation of so-called 'blackmail files' which will be filled with any loose printout found (the prevalent use of network printers has greatly contributed to this as people are often unaware of what printer their document will arrive on) and can include various personal emails that are sent, and for which are for some inexplicable reason frequently printed out. Why people insist on printing out what are in effect suicide notes, nobody is really sure. Perhaps it is like the book reader in the age of the e-book who has to have the physical experience of feeling the printed page. These stray white rabbits, along with the documented evidence of any skulduggery are often kept in reserve by the downtrodden staff who can them pull them from the proverbial hat when the chips are down. Just to possess them will make the holder feel just a little less vulnerable as the days pass. Another one for the blackmail file.

Such classics entitled: *'Roses are red, violets are twisted'* and *'I want you; I need you'* were swiftly swept up and filed. No sense in delving into the main body text of these messages, but the titles were all that could be printed by a family newspaper.

Another classic was the dynamic duo of managers who would raid the boardroom before senior client meetings and proceed to lick the bottoms of the biscuits that were freshly piled and with fresh tea and coffee awaiting the company's guests. Always fresh, tasty, and moist, those biscuits.

Or the team of Advisors who, during a break on an evening shift, discovered an office door unlocked and proceeded to hold an impromptu tea party, sampling all manner of her rather delectable tea bags, carefully placing the used sachets back in the wooden *Twining's* presentation box. The story itself is rather pedestrian, but the reaction the following morning bordered on the comical. The victim of the theft actually screamed with a pitch so high, only the neighbourhood dogs truly appreciated the impact of the previous day's scurrilous events.

§

One freak worked voluntarily on the switchboard when his temporary contract came to an end. Happily, though, his CV went on to reflect that he was an *Account Director* during this time. Nice work if you can get it.

§

As a piss-take of his Team Leader who had been pushing hard on lateness, a guy strolled into the call centre – yawning and still wearing his pyjamas and dressing gown.

§

I have mentioned the tendency of BPOs to omit to add contingency planning into their operations with the concept of series methodologies – a chain of dependencies with one fault leading to all the lights going out.

Never is this truer than in the case of IT teams who typically chain together their networks, particularly following mergers, and acquisitions. Now there have been a fair amount of these in the past 30 years and the various satellite sites tend to be bolted on and networked to the home site where the main servers are housed. This was after all the most preferred option of those running their businesses on the cheap as opposed to paying for Cloud subscription services.

Sadly, the Achilles Heel in this case has nothing to do with IT Infrastructure but everything to do with air conditioning which, as anybody will tell you in BPOs, is the least reliable – even less so than the staff themselves – attribute of the business.

Most are housed in large open-plan buildings that are not purpose-built, so the aircon units are overworked, poorly synced, and generally messed about constantly throughout any given working week. Given the regularity that they break down (evidenced by the fact that the aircon maintenance men will typically have their own parking space), it is again bewildering that the prospect of them breaking down out-of-hours is not properly planned for. And when they do, and this affects the aircon in the IT systems room, it's system down – on all sites. And that is a huge amount of reputation, billing and compensation wrapped up in that one small area of poor planning and even worse management. I have known it in one company to happen, not only once but twice in a three-week period where the servers overheated and caused irreparable damage to motherboards. Cue meltdowns throughout the business, in terms of both service delivery and personal sanity.

Sometimes, almost freak incidents occurred which really did underscore the fragility of the half-baked approach to customer delivery.

A duty manager, looking to demonstrate how the emergency message would be applied to the call centre as a development point for one of their team – which of course closes down the lines – and then bring them back up was unfortunately out of the loop on one key fact. This was that the IT team were in the process of re-coding the emergency process and owing to a last-minute emergency on the Friday in question, they had not completed the build for the second part of the process.

Accordingly, when the manager actioned the closing of the lines, it worked perfectly. They then listened to the line message – which again played perfectly. And he then executed the command to re-open the lines – which, er, did not work at all.

The net result was a trainee supervisor who had received a demonstration of two-thirds of the process and who now as a bonus – and this was likely to be a once in a lifetime experience – was witnessing a fully staffed contact centre with no capability to handle any customer enquiries.

What made it even more challenging, was that the BPO was running on an obsolete platform for which there was no longer any supplier support. Buy cheap, buy twice was the mantra of the day as the head honcho had to be called out of hours to authorise an out-of-warranty repair, of course at distress rates.

At least on this occasion common sense prevailed. The manager concerned, who had at least been acting with the right motives to develop his staff, was totally beside himself and whatever the circumstances, the impact on him was punishment enough. The IT team did not escape unscathed as in any event, the correct functionality should have been in place at all times when the centre was operational. The real lesson for all though was around the need to ensure that operational services were supported by adequate infrastructures and that cutting corners really can come back to bite you, often as the result of unpredictable and random circumstances. It was of course never heeded and once the issue was resolved, the company once again reverted to the combination of wing and prayer as the basis for its operational delivery.

§

But there were some tragic times and some sad folk.

One guy who went up like a rocket and down like a stick had a dark complexion and rather thick eyebrows that he would shave horizontally to make them look much thinner with the result that he had thin black eyebrows with thicker white stripes directly above them. Sort of Dick Dastardly moustache eyebrows with these white stripes that might have been rolled on by a bloke painting white lines in the road. I mean, dudes like that just don't survive in the pseudo-prison environment of BPOs. The teams smell fresh meat, and they tear them apart.

I think his replacement was another guy who had some sort of orange hair going on and they just tore strips off him. In the end a supervisor convened a meeting where they all had to have some sort of 'truth and reconciliation' session. That just sent him beyond the point of salvation, and I think it did for her too – deservedly so.

Another oddball went away with the team on a course for a telephony upgrade and instead of the evening team social, went to some play or the opera. Unusual, but each to their own. That evening, by subterfuge, the team got access to his room and lifted the contents of the mini bar off the pressure pads, which led to a not inconsiderable 'bill' being racked up. What merriment there was when he went to settle his bill the next morning.

>A £5 mini-Toblerone? Yes, please – two.

§

Another guy later fell to his death from a derelict building just up the road from his former office, ostensibly the result of trying to fly under the influence of drugs. A sad end to what should have been a productive life.

§

Another chap walked back into the call centre from the toilet and a couple of mini-turdballs rolled out from the bottom of his trousers into the middle of the open-plan floor. Anybody got a toothpick?

§

The lonely guy who created the imaginary relationship with an advisor client-side, who was then thrown into disarray when the client announced that she would be on a later client visit. The poor chap went into meltdown as he frantically had to get agreement from practically everyone on-site to not mention the relationship owing to the current sensitivities of the problems they were working through together. To the credit of his colleagues, they played along and the whole relationship story was allowed to die gracefully.

Others slid further into personal chaos as their tenure with BPO companies continued. One poor chap would constantly sidle up to people, engaging them in conversation and dropping in comments like:

'It's all kicking off at the moment...'

and:

'Somethings going on, mark my words'.

and when pressed for further information he would disappear enigmatically with a,

'I'll catch up with you later'.

or something equally non-committal. In over 5 years he never divulged anything of interest. Who knows what strain of paranoia was driving him? Now there would almost certainly be plenty of intrigue in whatever BPO you would be situated – however, he would have been a million miles away from anything remotely titillating. But in his head, he was front and centre of the action.

Also, the clean-cut lad who joined the organization, a fresh-faced and diligent temp, only to return 18-months later as a whacked-out, drug-addled psycho who was so permanently off his face that he bought an "invisible friend' as his representative to a disciplinary hearing. When the hearing manager sought advice from his boss on how to proceed, he was simply informed that he should continue and take in an additional glass of water for the 'friend'.

Absolutely true as I live and breathe.

The last anyone heard, the guy in question was serving 3 years for holding up buses with a syringe. Now that was not some kind of impressive *Derren Brown*-style magic trick – he was holding them up, as in robbing them. A veritable clucking junkie as they say in the hood.

And of course, in most BPOs you will have at least one person Siamese-twinned with all matters *'char-i-dee'* who will in time be unmasked as the least charitable of them all. While they remain on the one hand ostensibly determined in their quest for an MBE, they are simultaneously creaming it straight off the top (as well as the bottom and the middle).

I know of one whose downfall came when a lady went to the jewellers to get the battery changed in her watch, a leaving gift that had been purchased by the charity cheerleader. Turned out that the battery could not actually be replaced because the watch was disposable. Not worth a squirt. Evidently the bulk of the colleague collection had been trousered and a little cheapy slotted in there for the dear departing colleague. Caused a stink and the powers that be decided on a closer look at the charity queen. After a surreptitious audit, the culprit exited the business after being caught pilfering vouchers (what else?) and computer equipment – all caught on pinhole cameras. It was never clear how much equipment or monies had been liberated from the organization by that particular robber, but the 007-style moves employed to snare her suggest that it was probably not just the odd *High St shopping voucher* going astray. No charges were ever brought which was just as well as the cops would still likely be filling out all the paperwork 25-odd years later.

§

Of course, in businesses with large numbers of younger people who did not know any better and quite frankly did not care (!) relationships abounded, often with quite bizarre outcomes with managers enlisting the help of dungaree-clad young chaps to assist with the weekend gardening (direction unknown) to aggrieved rent boys kicking off in Reception. On one occasion, the father of a spurned young lady turned up in the reception to have it out with one of the managers, who was something of a *John Major* figure himself charisma-wise, and angry pop exposed said manager for initiating extra-curricular *Ugandan discussions* with a girl young enough to be his own daughter.

Others, rumbled after less than discreet evenings out, were picked up by their spouses and in one instance, the ensuing argument while the car was in motion, led to an unfortunate by-passer going over the bonnet and through the windscreen.

After one interesting liaison, another, minus a contact lens, drove home through a maze of narrow streets with cars parked on either side and awoke the next morning to find his company car rather crumpled – and minus a door.

On one occasion, a chap who was experiencing domestic upheaval, just moved into the office and thanks to some sort of deal with the Namibian security guard, slept under his desk for more than a month. When confronted, he raised the question of his organised crime link and serious people 'who would take it personally', were he dismissed.

Twenty-five years later, we are still checking underneath our cars in the morning.

Add to this the manager who faked mental illness to get several hours off work each week, who was then subsequently cuckolded by a colleague while off skiving who knows where, only to be left with bringing up someone else's child for 17 years and counting and you can see that there is no end to the madness that prevails.

Not to mention the girl who without fail would be carted off by paramedics at every turn from work, socials – even a glimpse of her was caught on the local news being ferried away on a stretcher at a local festival. Never anything wrong with her – she just loved being at the centre of it all.

Other desperately sorry tales involved the tremendously sad story of the Team Leader's mother and her terminal illness and the support that the management team gave during the difficult time and also the subsequent bereavement. How pleased they were to hear that of the later recovery that would have embarrassed

Lazarus when, long after said Team Leader had left, she was seen in Sainsbury's with Mum looking sprightly, chipper, and fully resurrected.

We were also later sad to hear of a former colleague who – only after he had left – had been exposed as having served a 15-month sentence for dealing Class As and who had become rather agitated when on a night out, someone had seen his current account balance of £36k. Though perhaps he had been a consultant at some stage in his career?!

§

Pride of place must however go to a young lady who excelled herself in the folklore of her organisation one morning when her team noticed an unpleasant and pungent smell emanating from their work area. They checked shoes and the immediate environs but nothing. Not even the slightest slither of a stray turd or partial turd. After a while, this young lady (we will call her *X* – not her real name) asked for a discreet word with the Team Leader.

X had, apparently been out the previous night, and after drinks and curry, had inadvertently 'pushed one out', so to speak upon arrival in the office. She was however stoic and absolutely matter of fact about it. No qualms or embarrassment.

The Team Leader gave her permission to return home and change an off she went.

Later that morning, time passed and after a few hours, no sign of *X*.

Team Leader phoned *X*, who answered clearly upset and sobbing. Actually distraught.

It transpired that *X* had indeed gone home, cleaned up and changed. Then returned to the office. However, at the front of the office – a mock Georgian terrace – were a small flight of steps. She had given it a quick hop, skip and jump up the stairs, at which point...

...she blew another one back into her pants, warp speed ten.

At this point, she was broken. But she had carved out her place in history in contact centre legend. Forever known as 'Two-times (*X*)'.

As we have noted already, crazy times and on occasion, crazy people. But most of all, crazy places.

Endnote

It is an easy thing to get caught up in the slipstream of a rogue organisation like a BPO contact centre. For many – the vulnerable, the displaced, the directionless, these businesses represent a facilitated way into the mainstream with their limited barriers to entry. They are a magnet to those on the social and mental peripheries.

Flypaper for freaks.

For everybody though, once you are in employment, you have the means to start living your life. Car, house, holidays, mod cons, family. All of which require commitment, in terms of time and money.

And the money part means that you are committed not only to what you are purchasing but also to the source of those funds. And that is when those organisations turn the screw and make more demands on your time.

And then the repetition, the pointlessness, the stress – layer upon layer, day after day, month after month. It all adds up, and all the while you are ever more aware of your helplessness.

Little wonder that serious mental health issues abound. And for those afflicted at the point of hire – they spiral, sometimes irrevocably.

For those BPOs with 70% or 80% turnover, well, I applaud those who leave. They have had the courage to bail out and start anew on firm foundations. While those who are the most downtrodden are those seemingly at advisor level, it is certainly the case that the bigger you are, the harder you can fall. As BPO staff move up the ranks, they take on more commitment. Yet they frequently become cocooned in terms of their exposure to progress, honing only the subversive skills of value within a BPO. Consequently, their skillsets can be restricted which in turn may have limited transferability. They then find themselves, in their forties and fifties, rug pulled beneath them, fully committed, in a world that has passed them by.

'*There's nothing available at my level*', they will complain. Wrong. There is plenty at their level but not at the level of pay and status they were used to.

The author Octavia E. Butler wrote[xiii]:

'Sometimes, one must become a master to avoid being a slave'.

which is an intuitively valid point to make. But never suppose that becoming a master in a BPO gets you freed from your shackles. In BPOs, you also have to avoid becoming a master or at least any master who is below the very, very highest level. If you don't, you forget who you really are, and in your quest to be that someone else you start unwittingly putting in place shackle after shackle. This in turn slices off layer after layer of your personal freedom, leaving you more and more at the mercy of whims of the BPO charlatan army.

When you throw in your lot on a false premise, do not expect the interest payments to last forever. Working for BPOs means that you are in the short-to-medium term carrying the bags. Only the shareholders take home the big prizes.

But people just don't see it until it is too late.

While the underlying scam in BPOs is largely recognised by the mid-senior management players, that will still not stop the greasy-pole merchants from racing around at breakneck speed doing the bidding of those in control.

Unfortunately, this can and does lead to lifestyle choices that are not conducive to a high standard of personal health and there are countless examples of premature demises, doubtless exacerbated by long hours, little exercise, a poor diet and excessive consumption of alcohol, cigarettes and anything that gets them through the day.

And for what? A sports tournament or an annual award in your name where if you are really lucky, they may even spell your name correctly on the trophy.

There are *Sexy Sadies* at every turn, seducing those who are either too vulnerable, desperate, or incapable of recognizing how the mechanics of these businesses work. The people come and go, burning out all those around them and staying just long enough to springboard into the next enterprise.

The BPOs themselves rebrand and refresh, just shedding their skins to allow them to move onto the next vipers nest of their making.

Think about what kind of environment can create a whole world where people so effortlessly fall into doing routine tasks that they do not understand. And when they do understand them, they know them to be wrong. Where the aims and essence of the organisations are based on not actually achieving stated goals but on creating a series of impressions. Where whole careers can be built on creating an illusion which in turn evaporate into the ether as quickly as the bubble itself when it bursts.

Is it any wonder that those who join these BPOs – normal, sane rational adults, end up losing the plot theatrically and spectacularly? It's like dark version of reality television, except that it is reality itself.

Sadly, it is those who enter this world who are already vulnerable who will provide the greatest spectacle before they crash.

Change is however not impossible. Much lies with customers making changes about the products and services they consume and challenging those who compromise quality and security. It is about client businesses, the huge blue-chip names, stepping away from the precipice and re-thinking more moral and ultimately more efficient, effective, and yes, profitable commercial strategies.

Invest in the implementation of more effective contact and information structures and they would not need to make use of the backstreet business abortionists.

For potential employees, think twice. Or go in with your eyes wide open. Take the money and keep planning – you might be selling your time, but do not sell your soul. Remember – real eyes realize real lies.

For employees of BPOs, get onto the front foot and start to plan your exit – regain your ability to make choices. Yes, it takes time and cannot be done overnight. But even having your exit planned out will make a world of difference to how you feel about yourself and life.

But whatever you do, make sure you enable yourself to walk away.

Because when it suits them, they will walk away from you, and they will not give it a second thought.

Irrespective of what you decide to do, let us hope that this has given you not just some insight but a range of insights. Take on board what you will and make changes.

For some, we will not need to ask for whom the bell tolls – for others, it is merely a chime.

But change on the part of individuals is essential if real change is to be achieved. For unless you take action, the blue chips, the BPOs and all the other charlatans clinging on to the sorry BPO bandwagons will not be disappearing any time soon.

But act you must.

Once you have made up your mind to jump, start preparing the groundwork. It may take many months, but this is the time to sort out your finances and start to familiarize yourself with the current jobs market and its processes. Just by starting your plan, you will have begun the process of taking back control (this time for a planned and effective exit ;-)

This might take weeks or months – sometimes longer. You will however immediately feel the burden starting to lift. You will be taking the first steps in calling the shots. Start working for yourself, not for them. You have a responsibility for yourself forever.

It doesn't cut both ways. Those who profess to be leaders in BPOs, do not lead – they exert pressure and authority. Effective leaders make sacrifices and, when the time comes, their teams make sacrifices for them.

How many times do you truly see this in the BPOs where you have worked? It would be a rarity, that's for sure.

However, do not ever regret that you entered this BPO space because simply by looking around you, you will have become sensitized to factors that you will from now on recognise and manage effectively as your own personal journey continues.

They say that knowledge is power though arguably anybody can open their minds in order to *know*. The real power comes from an ability to *understand* and then *to act*.

If these malfeasants intend to continue with their BPO charades, then so be it. Along the way, a small number of them will get rich on the back of it. Never be disheartened by that because there will always be a section of the population who make a fat dollar from immorality. You will see it in all avenues of life.

Make sure that you have carved out an alternative route because the BPO rollercoaster will one day hit the buffers. Look at the cycles of change that have occurred in the last 25 years – ultimately that will continue and the BPO organisations that we see today will cease to exist as we know them.

You will see only a small number of monoliths that will be forced to operate in accordance with high standards of compliance and possibly regulation, most likely as an arm of the major professional services/consulting firms.

When this happens, very few of those who think they have these great careers in BPO will still be in the game because their personal collateral will, in this very different context, start to look very light indeed.

Planning your alternative route now will mean that you have a chair to sit down on when the music stops.

And that is what I did myself. Though along the way, I coasted for an inordinately long while. In fact, almost to a complete halt while I worked my obligatory notice period.

Naturally, during this period of leisurely downhill skiing, the accounts I was working on also somewhat lost momentum and effectively ground to a halt. Not that anybody noticed, mind you. That is because during that time I was effectively ostracized which meant that nobody asked me for progress updates on my work, and I did not provide any.

They never learn, do they? Best months of my career to date.

Most gratifying of all though, the time coasting and at equastandstill did allow me to write this book. In its entirety.

As a result, I will be eternally grateful to the ineptitude and slipshod chaos-mongery of the BPO world that allowed me – fully funded – to slide effortlessly, finger raised in singular magnificence, into the world of authorship.

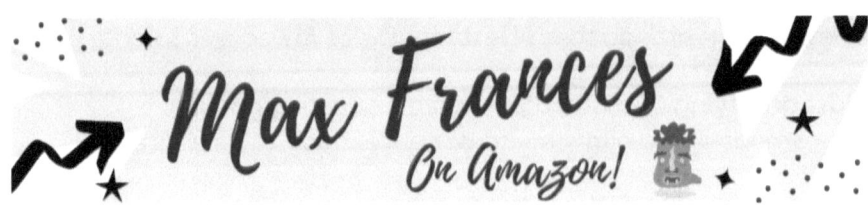

Notes

[i] Foucault, Michel. *Dits et Ecrits vol I*. Paris: Gallimard, 1994.

[ii] Foucault, M. Préface de Michel Foucault à la traduction américaine du livre de Gilles Deleuze et Felix Guattari, L'Anti-Oedipe : capitalisme et schizophrénie (1972) (Trans 1977)

[iii] Vonnegut, K., *Cat's Cradle*, Holt, Rinehart & Winston, New York (1963)

[iv] https://www.virgin.com/richard-branson/say-yes-instead-no 24 January 2018

[v] Nietzsche, F. , DIE FRÖHLICHE WISSENSCHAFT (*The Gay Science)* (1882, 1887) para. 125; Walter Kaufmann ed. (New York: Vintage, 1974), pp.181-82.]

[vi] https://www.icaew.com/-/media/corporate/files/about-icaew/who-we-are/icaew-governance/chief-executive.ashx

[vii] Steve Jobs: His Own Words and Wisdom, Jobs, S. Cupertino Silicon Valley Press (2011)

[viii] https://www.virgin.com/richard-branson/celebrating-stars 23 November 2015

[ix] Bakhtin, M., *Discourse in the Novel* (1935). Emerson, C. and Holquist, M., trans., in *The Dialogic Imagination* (1981), pp. 293-294

[x] Lennon-McCartney, *Sexy Sadie*, *The White Album* (1968)

[xi] Chomsky, N., *The Common Good* (1998)

[xii] Woodcock, J., *Working the Phones - Control and Resistance in Call Centres*, Pluto Press (2016)

[xiii] Butler E., O., *Wild Seed*, Chapter 1, p11 in *Seed to Harvest*, Grand Central Publishing (1980)

www.ingramcontent.com/pod-product-compliance
Lightning Source LLC
Chambersburg PA
CBHW021810170526
45157CB00007B/2523